WRITTEN BY MARTIN MELHUISH

The SUPERTRAMP Book

WRITTEN BY MARTIN MELHUISH

The SUPERTRAMP Book

FEATURED PHOTOGRAPHERS:
KANDICE ABBOTT AND REED HUTCHINSON

Sound and Vision

Omnibus Press

Exclusive Distributors:
Book Sales Limited
78 Newman Street, London W1P 3LA, England.
Omnibus Press
GPO Box 3304, Sydney NSW 2001, Australia.

Produced, conceived and packaged by CM Books,
a division of Norris Whitney Communications Inc., Toronto, Canada.

Published in Canada by
Sound and Vision, 84 Bleecker Street, Toronto ON M4X 1L8, Canada.

© Copyright 1986 Omnibus Press, a division of Book Sales Limited
ISBN (Canada) 0.9691272.2.7
ISBN (UK) 0.7119.0787.0
Order No. OP 43637

All rights reserved. No part of this publication may be reproduced or transmitted in any form or by any means, electronic or mechanical, including photocopying, recording or any information storage and retrieval system without permission in writing from the publisher.

EDITOR: Kathy Whitney
ART DIRECTOR: Janet Christie

PHOTOGRAPHS:
Kandice Abbott – pages 176, 177, 179, 186, 187, 190, 191.
A&M Records of Canada Ltd. – pages 30, 33, 40, 55, 66, 67, 68, 96, 119, 126, 127, 128, 132, 163, 174.
Decca Record Co. Ltd. – page 14.
Dezo Hoffmann Ltd. – page 12.
Michael Fackelmann – page 19.
Scott Gorham – pages 180, 181, 185, 188.
Ulrich Handl – page 19.
Reed Hutchinson – pages 16, 23, 24, 27, 29, 40, 44, 45, 46, 47, 48, 49, 50, 52, 53, 54, 56, 64, 65, 69, 72, 80, 82, 83, 84, 87, 89, 90, 91, 92, 93, 94, 95, 97, 98, 99, 100, 101, 102, 103, 104, 105, 106, 107, 108, 112, 115, 116, 117, 120, 122, 125, 131, 134, 135, 138, 139, 140, 141, 142, 144, 145, 148, 149, 150, 151, 152, 153, 154, 155, 156, 157, 159, 160, 161, 165, 166, 168, 169, 170, 171, 172, 180, 182, 184, 190, 192.
Henry J. Kahanek – page 90.
Dee Lippingwell – page 29.
Stanley A. Miesegaes – pages 17, 18, 20, 21, 23, 25, 31, 33, 34, 147, 160.
MCM Records – page 14.
Polydor Records – page 15.
John Rowlands – page 42.

ARTICLES:
Courtesy of *London Evening News* – page 31.
Courtesy of *Oxford University Press* – page 13.
Courtesy of *Ritchie York* – pages 12, 13, 14, 15.
Courtesy of *The People,* Aug. 22, 1971 – page 38.
Courtesy of *Liverpool Echo,* July 3, 1971 – pages 36, 37.
Courtesy of *Melody Maker,* July 10, 1971 – page 39.
Courtesy of *Melody Maker,* Jan 4, 1975 – page 74.
Courtesy of *Melody Maker,* Jan. 18, 1975 – page 78.
Courtesy of *Record Week,* July 25, 1977 – page 137.
Courtesy of *Rolling Stone Magazine,* July 12, 1979
  No. 295 – pages 146, 147.
Courtesy of *Music Scene,* December 1979 – page 138.
Courtesy of *Rock & Folk,* December 1979 – page 158.
Courtesy of *Star Magazine,* December 1979 – page 158.
Courtesy of *Illustre,* July 27, 1983 – pages 182, 183.
Courtesy of *Basler Zeitung,* July 1983 – page 183.
Courtesy of *Le Suisse,* Aug. 18, 1983 – page 189.

ALBUM COVERS:
Supertramp © 1970 A&M Records, Inc. – page 35.
Indelibly Stamped © 1971 A&M Records, Inc. – page 35.
Crime Of the Century © 1974 A&M Records, Inc. – pages 71, 73.
Crisis? What Crisis? © 1975 A&M Records, Inc. – page 86.
Even In the Quietest Moments © 1977 A&M Records, Inc. – page 118.
Breakfast In America © 1979 A&M Records, Inc. – page 143.
Paris © 1980 A&M Records, Inc. – page 162.
Famous Last Words © 1982 A&M Records, Inc. – page 173.
Brother Where You Bound © 1985 A&M Records, Inc. – page 190.

Used by permission. All rights reserved.

Production by Whitney Graphics, Toronto.

Printed in the UK by Scotprint Limited, Musselburgh, Scotland.

CONTENTS

9	INTRODUCTION	
12	CHAPTER ONE	Background on the British Pop music scene of the mid '60s.
16	CHAPTER TWO	Rick Davies' history through several bands until the inception of what would soon become Supertramp.
24	CHAPTER THREE	Roger Hodgson answers an ad in *Melody Maker* magazine titled "Genuine Opportunity." His biography up until that point is covered.
30	CHAPTER FOUR	Rick and Roger, at the musical helm, experience growing pains and personnel refinement. During this period, two albums are released – *Supertramp* and *Indelibly Stamped*.
42	CHAPTER FIVE	In search of a bass player, Supertramp audition and accept one Dougie Thomson, into the bosom of the Supertramp family.
46	CHAPTER SIX	A number of chance encounters bring American-born Bob Siebenberg (known until "...*famous last words*..." as Bob C. Benberg) into Supertramp.
56	CHAPTER SEVEN	John Anthony Helliwell's illustrious musical background and influences are discovered.
66	CHAPTER EIGHT	The *Crime Of the Century* experience develops with great enthusiasm into Supertramp's first American visit.
86	CHAPTER NINE	Supertramp asks the musical question *Crisis? What Crisis?*
94	CHAPTER TEN	The British and European *Crisis* tour and the move to America.
118	CHAPTER ELEVEN	Chapter Eleven proves that *Even In the Quietest Moments* there can be much clamour.
138	CHAPTER TWELVE	Supertramp finds that *Breakfast In America* can be the best meal of the day.
162	CHAPTER THIRTEEN	A stay in *Paris* provides Supertramp with the basis for a live album that suits their perfectionist leanings.
166	CHAPTER FOURTEEN	"...*famous last words*..." are spoken and Supertramp contemplates the future.
176	CHAPTER FIFTEEN	The World Tour '83 concludes the history of the current version of Supertramp with the departure of Roger Hodgson. The remainder of the group looks to the challenge of the new Supertramp era.
193	ACKNOWLEDGEMENTS	

INTRODUCTION

When did I first hear the name Supertramp? No matter really, I doubt if I could put a date on it if I tried. As a writer in the music field in Toronto in the early seventies, albums and press releases would come in and be dealt with in remarkable numbers in those days. I do recall though, that the first Supertramp album and the follow-up *Indelibly Stamped*, held a rather unprominent position in my record collection for a few years lodged without fear of disturbance between Stravinsky and The Best Of the Swinging Blue Jeans.

In 1975, married and settled in the rather trendy Beaches area of Toronto, our social life was almost exclusively centred around radio and record people. Our closest friend at the time was one Charly Prevost who held the position of director of national press and publicity for A&M Records Canada. Few nights would go by without Charly dropping by with the latest 'hot' discs from A&M that served as the musical background for a lively discussion on the state of the music business.

Charly was a "music man" in the truest sense of the word. He honestly loved most of the music he promoted and his enthusiasm was infectious. He had been through many jobs in the music business at this point, from radio announcing to record retailing, but it was obvious that his current position with A&M Records, whose credibility with the media has been established over the years by their personal approach to the marketing of music in Canada, had given him a new perspective and enthusiasm for the record business.

One memorable night during this period, Charly phoned up and was bubbling over with excitement about a new record entitled *Crime Of the Century* by a British band called Supertramp that had just come in. "No kidding," says I, flashing for a moment on the tattooed tits that had illustrated the cover of Supertramp's second LP *Indelibly Stamped*, unwisely letting my first impressions get the better of me. "I'm on my way over," says Charly. I put the kettle on for coffee.

About half an hour later, Charly arrived and soon after Supertramp's *Crime Of the Century* was on the turntable at a volume that might have convinced the neighbours that the band was giving a personal concert in our living room. I don't think that a word was spoken through the first listen. The overall sound was awesome. On second listen, the songs began to come into focus. *Crime Of the Century* did not leave the turntable for weeks afterward.

It was shortly thereafter that Supertramp

made their first visit to North America and made a quick visit to Toronto to do a little promotion before their tour. One rainy Sunday afternoon, over a cup of tea at the A&M promotion office then located in downtown Toronto, I had my first meeting with the members of the band. As it turned out, it was not to be our last.

Shortly after this Toronto visit, the group, obviously impressed with Charly's love of the music and engaging personality, offered him a position with their organization initially as road manager and then as an indispensable part of their management company Mismanagement Inc., headed up by Dave Margereson.

Charly toured the world with the group in their Crisis? What Crisis? period, and after a personal crisis of his own, he took a break from the band and came to Montreal to spend a few months at my house while he handled local promotion for Arista and Chrysalis Records. It was during that period, prompted by some of Charly's many road stories and my increasing respect for Supertramp's perfectionist leanings in their music, that I decided to start work on a book that would, in the future, document what I felt would be the group's imminent rise to prominence in the rock world.

Charly finally went back to Los Angeles to rejoin Supertramp before the 1977 Even In the Quietest Moments tour and I opened a research file that over the years would be embellished by personal interviews with various members of the band, relevant press clippings and various pieces of Supertramp memorabilia.

By March of 1983, the file was bulging and just prior to the group's North American and European tour of that summer, I spent a couple of months in California with various members of the band who offered their help in the compilation of some of the personal material found in this book and put aside time for some long conversations over dinner, by the pool, on a yacht, in a studio, in the hills and in one case, in a motor home speeding along the Ventura Freeway.

This was a period of turmoil within the group. It became obvious that Roger Hodgson's decision to leave the band to embark on a solo career was irrevocable and yet a world tour loomed before them in the wake of the release of their *Famous Last Words* album. The tour was a great success but at its completion, Supertramp's creative future fell squarely on the shoulders of Rick Davies with the departure of Hodgson.

As I write this, Supertramp's latest LP, *Brother Where You Bound?* has just been released and Roger Hodgson, with his first solo LP, *Eye of the Storm*, under his belt, is back in the studio working on the follow-up. As it was in the beginning, both Supertramp and Hodgson as a solo artist, find themselves in the position of having to prove themselves once again. It is a challenge that I would have to believe is a source of renewed enthusiasm and commitment for both entities.

This, then, is the Supertramp story to date and perhaps there has never been a better time for its telling.

For the music, the memories and the hospitality over the years I am deeply grateful.

Famous last words, indeed! ☐

Martin Melhuish
Montreal, June, 1985

The Beatles

Manfred Mann

Chuck Berry

CHAPTER ONE

Undoubtedly, the Old Historian would have thought Supertramp to be a $300-a-night hooker.

However, I respectfully submit the following on the origins of Pop music and the scenario into which five diversely talented musicians of ambition and dreams stepped during the magical musical days of the sixties, to emerge in the seventies as one of the world's most respected rock entities.

"Johnny B. Goode," urged Chuck Berry and Lennon was.

There's Pop music history in a thimble.

It was 1963 and the musical rumblings from the north of England were becoming more pronounced. There was a whole lotta shakin' goin' on and as the seismograph began to register, to many people's amazement the epicentre was identified as Liverpool where the Rock 'n' Roll of four likely lads named John, Paul, George and Ringo was sending increasingly violent shock waves to the rest of the country.

The Merseybeat they called it, a musical movement that would put the port of Liverpool on the world map. And given the time, place and circumstances, perhaps there is nowhere else in the world that could have proven such a fertile ground for the mating of American Rock 'n' Roll with the popular British sounds of the day that included traditional jazz, skiffle, big bands and balladeering.

Since the cotton trade boom of the last century, Liverpool had been one of the most important ports in the North Atlantic; a doorway through which American cotton passed on its way to the mills of Lancashire and, in darker days, a hub of the thriving African slave trade.

In the sixties, more than cotton was being carried by the "Cunard Yanks" to the port of Liverpool. They brought with them many of the trappings of the American culture such as blue jeans, Cokes, cigarettes, comics, sneakers and records by acts like Chuck Berry, Little Richard, The Coasters, Carl Perkins, The Shirelles and The Miracles. Many of these artists became major influences on the musicians who were playing nightly in the quickly burgeoning club scene in that area.

In the early sixties, the Liverpool sound expanded its borders when local impresario Alan Williams established links with clubs in Germany like the Blue Angel and the Star Club in Hamburg. Over the years, many British acts would make the trek to Germany to polish their sound on the gruelling club circuit there.

As the Beatles emerged to international prominence, the Liverpool sound exploded paving the way for the conquest of the charts by other Scousers like Gerry and the Pacemakers, The Searchers, the Fourmost, Cilla Black, Billy J. Kramer and the Dakotas, the Swinging Blue Jeans and the Merseybeats.

"When the Beatles happened," Richard Neville, the publisher of the notorious OZ Magazine insightfully suggests in his controversial book *Playpower* (published in 1971), "the man on the beach who was forever having sand thrown in his face by the muscular bully became a star. John Wayne mounted his mare (not without effort) and cantered off into the sunset. From then on, the pigeon-chested weaklings always got to fuck the best girls. The pop symbols mounted their guitars and rocked to the centre of the stage. To account for the tough poignant cynicism of their early music, critics have observed that the Beatles grew up in the shadow of the Bomb. To account for the manners of the sixties generation, it should be remembered that we all grew up in the shadow of the Beatles ... the Rolling Stones, Animals, Manfred Mann, Kinks, The Who and a score of other now forgotten sounds which finally buried those panic attempts to revive skiffle, jazz, the big band, white sports coats, pink carnations and community singalongs.

"Even today, people who should know better believe that 'pop and thought do not go together' (to quote a BBC producer). The Beatles proved patently that they did."

But the Beatles weren't the only story on the British music scene in those days. In London, Rhythm and Blues music was booming in clubs like the Marquee and the Flamingo, with acts like Alexis Korner's Blues Inc., the Graham Bond Organization, John Mayall and the Spencer Davis Group becoming the musical school of hard knocks for many of the top artists of the late sixties.

The Alexis Korner group was a rather flexible musical unit and over the years people like Charlie Watts, Ginger Baker, Jack Bruce and others would pass through the band. Mick Jagger was often a featured guest vocalist singing his favourite song of the day, Chuck Berry's "Delilah." So popular had R&B become in London that on July 12, 1962, the Alexis Korner group was offered a live spot on the BBC radio show *Jazz Club*. A dispute ensued between the BBC and Alexis Korner because they wouldn't pay Mick Jagger as vocalist in the group because they had only contracted for six musicians and

The Rolling Stones

Eric Burdon and The Animals

Jagger made seven. In the end, Jagger suggested that, rather than sing with the band that night, he would put together his own group and go down and play the Marquee Club in place of Korner for that evening. The line-up of that pick-up band included Keith Richards, Elmo Lewis (alias Brian Jones), Ian Stewart and Dick Taylor. The Rolling Stones - who would spearhead a major R&B boom the following year that saw the emergence of bands like the Yardbirds and The Who (Maximum R&B) - were born.

In 1966, the underground culture took hold in London initially along the lines of the scenes that were happening in New York's Greenwich Village and San Francisco's Haight-Ashbury. In London clubs like UFO, Middle Earth and the Roundhouse, a number of so-called "progressive" groups like Pink Floyd, Kevin Ayer's Soft Machine and Procol Harum, stretched Pop music's borders and experimented with sounds and visual ideas never before seen in the rock world. Mabel Greer's Toyshop that appeared briefly at Middle Earth during this period included Jon Anderson and Chris Squire, who, along with Steve Howe (performing with his band Tomorrow over at UFO on Tottenham Court Road) would go on to form Yes in the late sixties.

The blues tradition was continued by artists like John Mayall, Long John Baldry, Cream, Jimi Hendrix, Fleetwood Mac, Free, Jethro Tull and the Jeff Beck Group featuring singer Rod Stewart.

The music scene in Britain, and London specifically, had never been more active and suddenly the record business started to take notice of some of these progressive groups. Chris Blackwell's Island Records, among the first to recognize the potential of this new Rock movement, signed Traffic - a group put together by Stevie Winwood, the former creative light behind the Spencer Davis Group. Fairport Convention, Jethro Tull, Spooky Tooth and Free, joined the Island roster shortly after.

A number of independent labels from the U.S., including A&M and United Artists, were also fast to explore this new specialized, predominantly album-oriented, progressive market as were American corporate labels like RCA and Warner Brothers. At the same time, a new touring circuit of colleges and universities opened across the country. As the sixties came to a close, the British Rock scene was in full nova. □

Traffic

The Cream

Spencer Davis Group

CHAPTER TWO

Rick Davies
1968.

It was to this flourishing music scene that one Richard Davies returned after spending close to two years in Europe on the club circuit riding the roller coaster of good times and bad times in the music and film world. Arriving in England, Davies was amazed at the diversity of music that was proliferating throughout the country. Though dubious at first, at much of its artistic merit, he found that bands like Traffic and Spooky Tooth were actually thriving, playing the type of music that he had always dreamed of creating himself. It was a revelation and catalyst in his determination to put together a band that would put form to some of the musical ideas that had been percolating in his head over the last few years.

Davies, an ambivalent fellow of serious countenance that belies his propensity for unexpected comedic outbursts, was born of a working-class family at Eastcott Hill in the small town of Swindon, Wiltshire on July 22, 1944. Swindon is the highest point on the railway line that runs from London to Bristol on England's west coast and its economy has been dominated by the railways since the day that Daniel Gooch, then the superintendent of the Great Western Railway, chose Swindon as the site for a massive railway works. Picnicking by the railway line one day with his chief engineer, Gooch casually picked up a stone and threw it, announcing that where the stone fell, he would build what was to be the Swindon Railway Works. It eventually covered 323 acres and was the focal point of labour in that area.

As a young boy growing up in Swindon, it became obvious early in his childhood that music was going to play a large part in his life. Unfortunately enough for those who lived within earshot, including his parents Dick and Betty Davies, percussion had become Rick's all-encompassing passion. If it had a surface and some resonance to it, you could bet the young lad would be beating the living tar out of it with anything that was handy.

When it became obvious, despite numerous subtle persuasions to the contrary, that young Richard was bound and determined to become the Little Drummer Boy incarnate, he was packed off, sticks and snare drum to take professional lessons. It was a transient relief for the family and there must have been some consolation in the thought of their young lad trundling off to a local hall to regale some poor stiff, on 50p an hour and cotton stuffed in his ears, with his pot-bashing and paradiddles.

"When Rick was a little boy, a friend of my

husband made him his first drum out of a biscuit tin," recalled Rick's mother. "In those days we had a shop opposite the Town Hall and there was an open square where the library is now. Visiting bands used to play there and Rick used to rush downstairs to listen. At Sanford Street School, music was the only thing he was any good at but they advised him against being a musician because it was too precarious. Our household was a rather noisy one as Richard grew up. At one stage, someone from the noise abatement department came to try and put a stop to it."

When Rick was 12, he was brought to his first organized band as a snare drummer with the British Railways Staff Association Brass and Silver Jubilee Band in Swindon, a spot he occupied until the age of 15, when suddenly he discovered Rock 'n' Roll.

It was not long after that Davies joined his first amateur group known as Vince and the Vigilantes featuring Ginger Frantic on vocals. "He couldn't sing but he sure could move around," is about the only positive thing that Rick remembers about that particular period of his musical career.

It was during his stint at the Swindon Art College that Davies became more and more convinced that music was to be his calling and had by this time started to teach himself piano. His mother would often accompany him on piano for his drum practice. His aunt, Lilian Gregory, who lived in nearby Horsell Street around the corner from his mother's hairdressing shop in Regent Circus, had a piano that she kept tuned especially for Rick. Many afternoons were spent at his aunt's place over endless cups of tea tinkering with the boogie-woogie style of pianists like Meade Lux Lewis and Fats Domino, who for a novice, were the easiest to copy.

It started out as a bit of a lark really but he soon saw the possibilities in keyboards for expanding his musical horizons.

"I really liked to play the drums, but I just couldn't get into the type of music as a drummer that I wanted to play. In the end it was like you had to do it yourself, so I eventually felt strong enough on the keyboard to start up a little Rhythm and Blues group while I was in college. I had an old Hohner electric piano, which was the cheapest that you could find, mainly because it was the *only* electric piano around at that time."

At Swindon Art College, Rick put his newly-acquired piano to use in a band he called Rick's Blues, which at one point included Raymond O'Sullivan. Irish-born O'Sullivan, who also attended Swindon Art College, would later change his name to Gilbert O'Sullivan and have a highly-successful solo recording career in the early seventies in the wake of a number of hit singles that included "Nothing Rhymed," "We Will," "Alone Again (Naturally)" and "Claire." When Rick later married, O'Sullivan flew over to Long Island, New York to be Rick's best man.

O'Sullivan would recall that period during an interview with Pamela Holman of New Musical Express in March of 1972. Before meeting Rick, Gilbert had been in a band called the Prefects.

"By that time I'd started studying at Swindon Art School," recalled O'Sullivan. "The Prefects used to play at places like approved schools, borstals and mental institutions for kids with rare diseases. There you'd always get fantastic receptions. It was good experience and I was gradually writing more.

"I left them to join Rick's Blues, which had Rick Davies in it. He now plays in Supertramp. Rick had originally taught me how to play the drums and piano - in fact, he taught me everything about music. He was a brilliant drummer, but plays piano now.

"Most of our material was blues, which was a bit ridiculous because I didn't understand it. All I loved was the Beatles. Rick couldn't understand this; he was playing records by people like Fats Domino all the time. You know, when I used to rush out and buy the latest Beatles' records and dash round to Rick's place to play it to him, he'd slip Jimmy Reed back on the turntable.

"Still playing drums, I joined that group and Rick was playing electric piano. We had a sax player and a great singer and we used to do all the blues stuff. We were very popular in Swindon and I think we would have turned professional but for the fact that our lead guitarist was on an apprenticeship and didn't want to quit that."

While still at school, Rick's father became ill, and in a rather selfless decision, Rick left the Art College, disbanded Rick's Blues and went to work as a welder at Square D.

"He loathed it," remembers his mother. "When he came home in the evenings I used to say: 'What sort of a day have you had?' and he'd answer: 'Don't talk to me about it!'"

In September of 1966, Rick got an offer to join a professional group known as the Lonely Ones that were based in Folkestone, a port town on the east coast of England. The group, which was basically a soul band, had originally been formed by Noel Redding, the bass player who

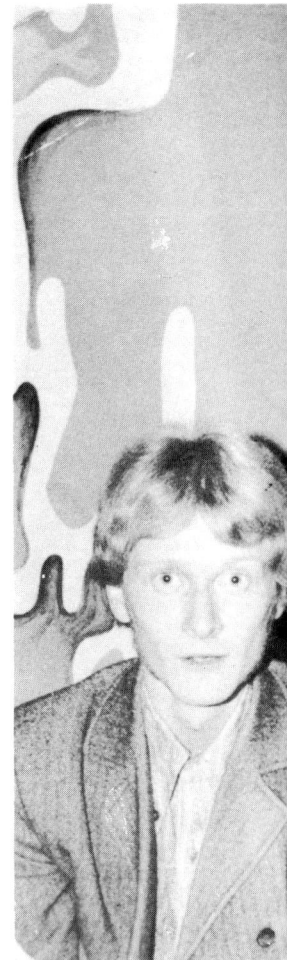

The Lonely Ones – early '67 - (l - r) Keith Bailey, Trevor Williams, John Andrews, Martin Vinson and Rick Davies.

David Llywelyn and George Moorse.

would later become known for his work as part of the Jimi Hendrix Experience.

The original member of the Lonely Ones had been John Andrews, a bass guitarist and vocalist that everyone knew as just Andy. He had started out as an apprentice motor mechanic but at the age of 16, he met Noel Redding and they formed a group known as the Strangers which eighteen months later, in 1961, became the first version of The Lonely Ones, lasting two years. Noel and Andy split up because Andy wanted to get on with his apprenticeship as a mechanic and Noel wanted to go professional as a musician. Andy formed a part-time band called the Travellers that lasted about thirteen months but in September of 1964, Noel and Andy got together to reform the Lonely Ones. After a year Noel took his leave again but the Lonely Ones continued on with guitarist/vocalist Trevor Williams and drummer Keith Bailey joining in March of 1966 and Rick hooking up with them later that same year.

In October of 1966, the Lonely Ones headed out on the normal circuit of ballroom clubs in England before making their first trip to Europe to play at the Griffin's Club in Geneva and a date in Dijon. They returned to England for three-weeks before heading for Rome on May 1, 1967. It was only supposed to be a two-week engagement but when it was over they decided to stay in Europe for a while and headed for Geneva, Switzerland. In July of 1967, the band changed its name to The Joint.

It was in Geneva that The Joint was offered a contract to handle the music for a film entitled *What's Happening*. It was not, needless to say, an Academy Award nominee but it was here, during the shooting of that particular film, that they met David Llywelyn who was to become the catalyst for a number of rather bizarre turns of fortune that would, in the years ahead, pave the way for the eventual chain of events that would see the formation of the first configuration of Supertramp.

Having played an engagement at the Etonnoir in Geneva, Llywelyn took The Joint to Munich where they began work on the music for a second film entitled *Der Griller*. (Here, George Moorse, the director of the film enters the picture.) Apparently, Moorse and Llywelyn had some musical aspirations of their own (Moorse was a lyricist and Llywelyn a composer) and they saw The Joint as a practical vehicle for their own musical compositions.

Through the early months of 1968, The Joint played a number of clubs in Munich and made a few forays into Switzerland to places like Zurich,

St. Gallen and Winterthur while working on the music for a further two films - *Jet Generation* and *Lieber und so weiter*. In June of 1968, The Joint became a five-piece group with the addition of Steve Brass of Swindon, who had been a former bandmate of Keith Bailey in a group called the Black Souls.

On the face of it, it might have seemed that The Joint was in a rather stable position - with the film work and a regular engagement at the P.N. Club in Munich - but the finances were in a dismal state and in reality they were actually stranded in Munich. The picturesque gateway to the Bavarian and Austrian Alps, Munich is a city of theatres, museums, art galleries, parks and the landmark cathedral Frauenkirche, of the famous Cuvillies Theatre and the Deutsche Museum and the Tierpark Hellabrun, one of Europe's largest zoos. A fine city if you have the money to enjoy it but the group was battling to keep destitution away from their door at the P.N. Club where they were living on a diet of the *soup du jour*.

At this point, David Llywelyn had been rabitting on for days about knowing a friend of independent means who lived in Switzerland and who just might be interested in helping out. That was all well and good, but for The Joint it was hard to take a side glance at that kind of fantasy when reality was staring them square in the face.

"We thought, 'Sure, pull the other one!' but then again it was worth a try," remembers Rick. "We were living on soup at the P.N. Club. We'd play at the weekends and that would give us enough money to last us through until Thursday when we had to pilfer until Saturday."

One particular Saturday, the band awoke to find Llywelyn missing with a note left for them saying that he had gone to Switzerland. A month passed, then two, and just at about the time that the band had given up hope of seeing him again, Llywelyn called.

"He's interested in seeing you," said the excited voice on the other end of the phone. "He wants to talk about putting money behind you."

The group was incredulous. Perhaps this was it, the big break they had been waiting for. Plane tickets were arranged for and they headed for Geneva to meet this mysterious philanthropist, Stanley August Miesegaes, affectionately nicknamed Sam.

They had been to Geneva before but coming into this idyllically set city that lies at the junction of the Rhone River and Lac Leman in the shadow of the Alps' highest peak Mt. Blanc, the whole world seemed to sparkle with promise and expectation.

And there was Sam. He was a refined gentleman of the old English school, of genteel manner and a soft spot for the arts. He was actually Dutch but his parents were divorced before the war and while his mother decided to stay in Holland, his father, an invalid, took Sam to England and put him through school at such exclusive establishments as Harrow and Launceton in Cornwall. While Sam was at Harrow, his father died and shortly after Sam moved to Neuchatel in Switzerland where he got his diploma in languages (French) and business. He met his wife Liliane there and they ended up eloping to Versoix just outside of Geneva where they set up housekeeping at a villa they named Aganippe. (Aganippe was in Greek mythology, a place particularly revered by the Muses, the nine goddesses who were regarded as the source of artistic inspiration.) A catalyst by any other name could not have been as eccentric and lovable a character as Sam.

From the moment that they met, Sam was bubbling over with ideas about the band persuing some of David Llywelyn and George Moorse's ideas of taking Classical themes and marrying them with Pop music. For the first few weeks at Aganippe, The Joint set up their creative base in the large music room and they dreamed a lot, they schemed a lot, and played ping pong.

In July of 1968, Sam wrote a letter to Bill Downs, who headed up a management and publishing company in New York, regarding a possible business relationship and his enthusiasm was obvious.

He wrote: "I am convinced that the trio David Llywelyn, George Moorse and The Joint have something terrific to offer. Unfortunately neither David nor the Joint have had the possibility and the opportunity to work relaxed. So far they have done music for films, of which I have seen two - *Jet Generation* and *What's Happening*. The only good thing about these mediocre films is the music, and this seems to be the general consensus everywhere, especially for *What's Happening*. Furthermore, I have the feeling that David and The Joint have been limited so far in their possibilities when they do film music since this requires a certain adherence to the scenario.

"Having met, David and The Joint decided to remain together. However, because of money problems, and because artists in general have difficulty in managing themselves, I took it upon myself to give them this possibility they so rightly deserve. I am fortunate enough to be able

The Lonely Ones – Munich, early '67.

to lodge The Joint (five members now) and to offer them a music room where they can, for the first time in their lives, really get down to preparing a hit. David will be coming down next week with new material, this time not for film, and George at the end of June, full of lyrics."

During this period, Sam completely re-equipped the band as they began preparations for a planned record of Llywelyn and Moorse's music. Berton Cantor, a friend of Sam's who also lived in Geneva, with some rather heavy musical connections, actually approached one of the world's top managers of the day Albert Grossman regarding a possible business relationship with The Joint. Cantor, after some correspondence and dinner one night in New York with Grossman and Janis Joplin, got only lukewarm response and the matter was dropped.

It was an example of the activity that was going on around the group at the time. By January of 1969, The Joint had recorded a demo of five songs in Munich before returning to England to await some news of interest from record companies and management firms that the tapes had been sent to.

At this point, the band was beginning to have second thoughts about being used as a vehicle for Llywelyn and Moorse's music and it was pretty well decided that they would begin to work on their own compositions.

Early in 1969, The Joint signed to the Robert Stigwood Organization in London, a deal that had been set up by Sam's company Pulsar Promotions Establishment. A number of bookings were set up for the group in England through March and April of 1969 while talks were going on between David Llywelyn and Billy Gaff regarding a planned recording session for the group at the Marquee Studios in London, while the group took up residence at the National Hotel on Bedford Way in London. Gaff had worked with Small Faces and would later go on to manage Rod Stewart.

The Joint made a trip to Switzerland on May 13, 1969 for an appearance on Swiss television in Geneva, then returned home to London the next day to continue their club dates.

Sam did not come to London that often to see the group but he stayed in touch on a regular basis from Switzerland. The only problem with that was that Sam had this annoying habit of phoning up at all hours of the morning from Geneva, completely pissed and talking a load of codswollop for hours on end.

Early one morning Sam phoned Rick who was living in Finchley at the time, waking him out of a deep slumber.

"Hello boys," came the voice from the other end of the phone. "Look outside your window!"

Rick, half asleep and turning the air blue with some mumbling about the nature and quality of Sam's parentage, trudged over to the window and looked out. There was nothing in the street but an old, decrepit coach. "Shit!" hissed Rick, a bit annoyed at himself for falling for what he thought was some practical joke by Sam. Picking up the phone receiver, Rick was about to let Sam have it.

"There's nothing out there but an old coach, Sam. Do you realize...."

"It's all yours boys," interjected Sam before Rick could utter another word.

Rick's initial annoyance turned to excitement and having hung up with Sam, he woke the rest of the band and one by one, they congregated in front of Rick's place to inspect the latest of Sam's gifts. The coach, as it turned out, was not in the finest of shape, but what it lacked in appearance it made up for in practical application - transporting the band to gigs. Andy, The Joint's singer, hopped into the driver seat, started it up and drove around Finchley while Rick and the rest of an extremely delighted group whooped it up and played football in the back.

But, alas, the elation was not to last. Suddenly, one day, without any prior warning, Sam took the bus away from them and Rick who was quite miffed at this abrupt action, flew over to Geneva to see what was wrong. Sam explained that the band wasn't living up to his expectations and that he wanted out. It was quite a blow and it turned out to be the final back-breaker for The Joint which broke up shortly after.

"I knew the band wasn't that good," Rick would remember later. "But everyone was heartbroken when we had to split. We were so close."

Apparently Sam's displeasure with The Joint had been growing over those last few months but it all came to a head when he saw the band perform at the Marquee Club in London in June of 1969, as he explained in a letter to his lawyer Michael Rabin at the time.

"When Liliane and I saw The Joint the week before last at the Marquee, I suddenly felt bitterly disappointed," he wrote. "Disappointed at having had such faith in a group with such little faith in themselves. Disappointed at having weathered such an occurrence at Aganippe and at having sacrificed so much because of my faith in them. Disappointed at having been so naive. The week before last they were just a second-rate

Sam's Villa Aganippe, Versoix, Switzerland.

amateur group with no enthusiasm, playing negligently, out of tune, with memory lapses, with the same old faults coming out, with equipment that has taken quite unrespectful and wanton bashing, and with one new number representing the work of their three month's sojourn in England on RSO's payroll, and last but not least, playing without a road manager who had had enough of the whole situation. It dawned upon me that I was in fact, by developing our relations and contracts with RSO, giving RSO a sinking ship. The boil had to burst. Its bursting has shed a new light on the scene, bearing in mind that, apart from a few numbers for the most part composed by David Llywelyn, John Andrews and Rick Davies, RSO was not exactly raving about the group, no more than most of the record companies whom I approached.

"Richard Davies is undeniably the most gifted musician in the group. By being perhaps just that, he had been bogged down and had resigned himself to circumstance. We have decided therefore, and he agrees, to form a new group around him but with a different name, in which he will be the king-pin. We have budgeted and planned this venture. John Andrews and Phil Ingham (the road manager) are game to help Pulsar organize this with efficiency and without salary. At the end of the year we will still have a record out."

Sam did take Rick under his wing and finally persuaded him to return to Aganippe to work on his new musical project.

"I went over to Sam's to try and write my own music so I could get enough confidence to start something off my own back and I stayed there just writing," recalls Rick. "Of course, all sorts of crazy ideas popped up from Sam, like Rick Around the World In Eighty Tunes where we'd hire a few landrovers and go around the world. We'd sit in an Afghanistan village and be influenced by the music and then go onto somewhere else. It sounded fantastic, but it wasn't real at all and we abandoned the idea."

By the summer of 1969, Rick felt particularly happy with some of the material that he had written and it was decided that he should return to England to start work on putting together musicians for his next musical project. In August of 1969, Sam rented Rick a place called Botolph's Bridge House on Burmarsh Road in West Hythe, Kent as a base of operations.

During this period, Sam wrote letters to both Dave Llywelyn and George Moorse explaining once again where he felt things had gone wrong with The Joint and their musical aspirations.

To George Moorse, with whom Rick had written his first song entitled "The Other Side," Sam wrote: "Rick, now he is assimilating his hurdle of conscience, has come out with some bloody good material - neither dopey nor vicious nor naive and sugary, just rhythmical music full of humour with lyrics meaningful to ordinary Toms, Dicks and Harrys. No great Turnstylian revolution is involved, at least for the moment."

To David Llywelyn he wrote: "I think you are a bit hard on Rick. In the light of what he has done during the last three weeks, I think he is far more commercial than you or I ever rightly imagined before, and I look forward to playing you the tapes we did yesterday. And you know as well as I do that every good musician fully assumes and fully rejects music before coming into his own. You have, so why shouldn't Rick?! Really Dave, I believe that Rick, having fully assumed jazz, and not any type of jazz, but that of Duke, of a Getz or of a Kenton, this together with the extraordinary sense of rhythm he undeniably has, and this again complimented by his great sense of humour that can make kids and adults laugh instead of making them look glazed, all this makes me feel that Rick really does have something to offer, now that he can fully express himself."

To find musicians for Rick's new band, it was decided that auditions would be held after placing an advertisement for recruits in the classified pages of *Melody Maker*, Britain's long-standing newspaper on the music scene, read religiously each week by people in the music business and fans alike.

The ad was headlined "Genuine Opportunity" and it was this particular announcement that caught the eye of an aspiring young musician in Oxford by the name of Charles Roger Pomfret Hodgson (Roger Hodgson) as he was flipping through the pages of the paper over breakfast one morning. □

Rick at the piano during a Joint rehearsal.

CHAPTER THREE

Roger Hodgson in the early '70s.

Folding back the paper to frame the advertisement, Roger Hodgson read the copy a couple of times. "Genuine Opportunity." Well, there certainly hadn't been many of those knocking at his door lately, and though the ad intrigued him, and those ambitious thoughts of making it big in the Rock world still played in his head, he had to face facts; he was quite terrified at the whole prospect as well.

Hodgson was born on March 21, 1950 in Portsmouth, Hampshire, one of Britain's oldest seaports located on the south coast, an area steeped like fine aromatic Darjeeling in its own history. It was the port "from which England's fleets have sailed to victory and to which they have never returned in defeat." As a reminder of those past glories, Nelson's ship Victory that fought in the Battle Of Trafalgar stands on permanent display in the oldest dry dock in the world. In the Portsdown Hills at Portsmouth stands Porchester Castle, one of the most spectacular structures left behind by the Romans in Britain fifteen centuries ago when Roman galleys used the port and the Roman engineers built the castle to protect the British shore against the Saxon hordes. There was Old Portsmouth, with its narrow streets and old houses; the Hard, where they brought ashore the lifeless body of General Wolfe after his victory on the Plains Of Abraham in Quebec; the inns that were so well know to Nelson and his men; the venerable churches. And up beyond the dockyard in Commercial Road, a modest, two-storey house with attic in which the greatest of British writers, Charles Dickens, was born in 1812.

Hodgson's early childhood was spent here in a very sheltered existence that revolved around family and school, outside of which he really didn't get to know many people.

Then there came a move to the countryside just outside of Oxford, the birthplace of Richard the Lionheart and the native heath of the hallowed halls of Oxford University with its ancient traditions and scholarly atmosphere. It was here, again in historical surroundings, that in Hodgson's pre-teen years, music really started to blossom for him.

"Music got me through childhood," remembers Roger. "A psychiatrist who was helping me once told me that."

He started playing guitar at the age of 12 when, with his parents recently divorced, his mother Gill managed to put her hands on his father's guitar and turn it over to Roger. Shortly after, he was sent off to Stowe School, a private boys' school in Buckingham.

"The whole idea of becoming a musician

when I left school sustained me through the trials of being a teenager at a boarding school of 600 boys and having to fulfil my duty of an education to my family," recollects Roger with a slight grimace. "I just accepted going to school. I wasn't particularly a rebel. I considered it something that I had to do to please my parents and I knew, that when the day came and I was through with it, I would leave that part of my life behind. I just didn't get off very much on what I was being taught and besides that, I didn't find it very relevant."

*"I can see you in the morning when you go to school,
Don't forget your books, you know you've got to learn the golden rule.
Teacher tells you to stop your play and get on with your work
And be like Johnnie - too-good, well don't you know he never shirks
- he's coming along!*

*After School is over you're playing in the park
Don't be out too late, don't let it get too dark.
They tell you not to hang around and learn what life's about
And grow up just like them - won't let you work it out
- and you're full of doubt.*

*Don't do this and don't do that
What are they trying to do?
- Make a good boy of you
Do they know where it's at?
Don't criticize, they're old and wise
Do as they tell you to
Don't want the devil to
Come and put out your eyes.*

*Maybe I'm mistaken expecting you to fight
Or maybe I'm just crazy, I don't know wrong from right
But while I am still living, I've just got this to say
It's always up to you if you want to be that
want to see that
want to see it that way
- you're coming along!"*

Roger Hodgson and Rick Davies
© Copyright 1974 Rondor Music (London) Ltd. and Delicate Music Ltd.

So the guitar became Roger's solace from the realities of organized education. He'd tried piano lessons at school but really it did more to put him off the keyboards than to endear them to him. The regimented routine of scales and rudiments made it sheer drudgery. It was not until Roger left school that he would return to the piano and find the potential in it for further expression, putting form to some of the musical ideas that had lived with him over the years. It was one of the examples of his undoing some of the damage that had been done in his particular school experience.

Though introverted in many ways, Roger had started writing music almost from the day that he received his first guitar and actually gave his first concert of all original songs a year later in the Oxford area. He was shy and had a real fear of crowds that he admits still persists to this day in differing degrees, but he loved performing and that overcame any phobias that he might have had.

"When I look back on it," says Roger with a grin, "much of it was just the normal shyness of youth that I think everyone goes through. I was very shy of women and I think that goes back to my boarding school days. It affected the way that I thought about females and it was very damaging to me. Quite honestly, if I hadn't left school and joined a Rock and Roll band, I might still be a virgin today. Music was my way of attracting attention to girls because I was a little too timid to do it any other way. I was too awkward and felt very shy so Rock and Roll became my way of impressing girls. Thank God it worked sometimes!"

Roger left school at the age of eighteen having accomplished two reasonable grades on his A Levels and never went back.

Almost immediately upon leaving school, Roger formed a group called People Like Us with friends George Bowser (bass), Chris Tookey (piano) and Mark Henshall (drums). Roger played guitar.

Along the way, they actually reached the point where they recorded a single at the Decca Studios entitled "Duck Pond," backed by "Send Me No Flowers." It saw the light of day on May 30, 1968 and at best estimation it dropped from sight that night.

The press release announcing the single, gave more insight into the band's humour than details on its members.

"The idea of People Like Us originated in a dingy igloo in the Kalahari Desert, where the four members were trying to grow fish," the bio began. "Forty days and forty nights they laboured in the wild, composing a multitude of songs, three score and ten in all, until one day they begat Duck Pond, a lilting mallardy.

"George, our bass guitarist, was born at an early age, since when he has achieved considerable height, but irregular proportions. He

A reminder of the past on a sign outside the A&M Records offices in London.

Roger performing "Asylum" in London.

and Chris write most of the group's songs, and George himself has managed to write Nowhere Man no less than four times.

"Chris picked up the piano at the age of eleven but exchanged it for a recorder because it was too heavy for him. He now plays piano and organ in the true tradition of Christian charity - his left hand never knows what his right is doing.

"Roger is assumed to have been born sometime, but will not disclose his particulars. He says he is leaving them to science. He plays guitar and writes a lot of songs about fairies, which is a bit worrying.

"Mark was found under a bush: An experience which had an unsettling effect on him, since he was seventeen at the time. He plays the drums in a world of his own and prides himself on being enigmatic."

Later Chris Tookey would get into musical theatre writing the music for such projects as *Rock Panto* and the rock musical *Hard Times*. George Bowser eventually moved to Montreal in the seventies and became well known for his club work there as a solo act and as part of the duo Bowser and Blue.

As Roger's passion for music, and a showcase for it, grew, he came up with all sorts of wild ideas as to how to accomplish the goals he had set for himself.

He had heard stories of the Duke of Bedford, an eccentric and wealthy man who lived nearby, and the thought crossed Roger's mind that he might just be eccentric enough to want to back an aspiring Rock musician. He let the thought simmer in his mind for a while and, at about the same time that he had determined to go and knock on his door and lay out his plans to the Duke, he got to know a few of the members of Traffic who were just rising to international prominence from the British progressive music scene. Actually, it was Traffic's road manager, Albert, that took an interest and promised Roger all sorts of things.

Albert was going to take his tapes to Island Records, Traffic's record label, which at that point was revolutionizing the British record industry with its novel approach to the new music and the artists that were creating it. It was a label that gave artists some freedom to create and for Roger, that was the company that he dreamed of being involved with. Shyness notwithstanding in those days, Roger tempered any diffidence or naivete that he had with a large helping of drive and ambition.

As it turns out, Island Records, or should I say Lionel Conway of their song-publishing arm,

Blue Mountain Music, took the bite, and Roger found himself in a studio with Elton John on piano, Nigel Olsson on drums and Caleb Quaye on guitar, under the group name Argosy. They recorded a single entitled "Mr. Boyd" for Dick James Music that was released subsequently on DJM Records. It was a flop but apparently there was some consolation in the fact that legendary BBC disc jockey Tony Blackburn had liked it and there was talk of it reaching number 28 on the charts in Kansas City.

It was around this time that Roger's eye caught the ad headlined "Genuine Opportunity" in *Melody Maker*. The initial brush with the record business had made Roger even more bound and determined to get involved with a group that had similar aspirations to his own and there was something about this particular call to audition that held Roger's attention. His mother had noticed his interest in that section of the paper and reading the ad she urged him to go down to London and give it a whack.

Though he was a little hesitant at first, he decided to go down and see what it was all about.

When he arrived at the audition being held at the Cabin in Shepherd's Bush, a multi-faceted music operation run by Tony and Pat Novissimo, he found the usual chaos associated with this type of selection process in full clamour. As his turn came, he went to the middle of the room, slipped on his guitar and sang his version of Traffic's "Dear Mr. Fantasy" in the same high-pitched voice that would later become an integral part of the Supertramp sound.

But we jump ahead of ourselves here. Rick Davies, who had called the audition was not in earshot because at this point the road manager was holding the audition. So Roger packed up and headed for Oxford not altogether optimistic about the impression he had made.

As it turns out, a second day of auditions was being held, and once again Roger's mother pushed him up to London figuring that if he showed some enthusiasm for the project it might make a further impression.

Once more he arrived at the audition to find few things changed - wall-to-wall musicians and the hall looking like a full-line music store at inventory time. At one point in the proceedings, one of the guys who seemed to be in charge, went over to Rick. "That pushy snob from Oxford has come back," he confided to Rick.

Oh, this was brilliant! First, the doubt about Rick even hearing him sing the day before and now some class-conscious twit prejudicing his case before the judge. It was looking grim and it entered Roger's mind to go for a quick Bacon, Lettuce and Tomato and head back to Oxford.

As it turned out, just about the time Roger was set to hit the road, the audition had to stop for a few hours and Rick invited him out to the local pub for a chat. They got tanked up, told jokes for a few hours and just generally commiserated about the difficulties of getting a musical project off the ground. It had become evident to Roger that Rick had no idea what was going on with the audition and was lost in the barrage of music that had been paraded before him in the rawest of forms over the last day and a half. He was thoroughly enjoying this period of light relief and conversation outside the rehearsal hall and Roger listened in fascination as Rick told him about Sam and his adventures in Europe.

During the conversation, both musicians had recognized a lot of similarities in their approach to the music world and it was becoming obvious that something was going to come of this chance encounter.

"I was all primed up to impress him," Roger now recalls. "I think I actually told Rick that it was me playing the guitar on my single when actually it was Caleb Quaye. I think the reason he thought I'd be good in the group was because of my high voice. He realized the commercial potential of that right away. That's what he told me later anyway."

Having auditioned on guitar, Rick asked Roger to switch to bass, another instrument that he had mastered over the previous few years. One of the stumbling blocks to a new group is usually financing, but in this case, Sam - who had paid for the auditions though he hadn't made an appearance - was standing by with the hard cash.

With Rick and Roger at the core of the new group and the money in the bank, representing freedom to create, how could something wonderful not come from this project? The answer was soon to come. □

Roger at his Malibu house.

Crisis What Crisis tour, Canadian leg.

Supertramp II
Sept. '71
(l - r) Roger, David Winthrop, Kevin Currie, Frank Farrell, Rick.

CHAPTER FOUR

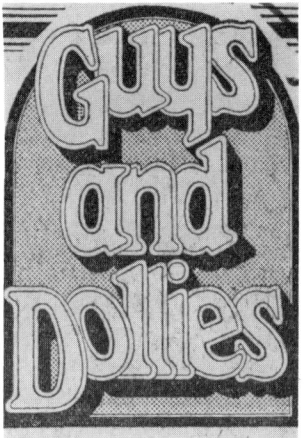

SUPERTRAMP SAM WON'T TALK MONEY

YOU'VE heard of Supertramp. But you probably won't have heard of Sam. He's the guy who made them.

Stanley August Miesegaes is 38, a former charter pilot and a pianist who never quite made the concert platform.

He's rich, doesn't ever talk about money, he says, and lives in Geneva. He bombs over to London to hear Supertramp.

New group

A year ago Sam lifted drummer Rick from a failing group called The Joint—"they just weren't musical enough" — and formed a group called Daddy.

The name changed—"which was just as well" and Supertramp started playing gigs at the P.N. club in Munich.

"Supertramp," says Sam, "is the sublimation of his musical soul..."

6F EVENING NEWS, Tuesday, October 13, 1970

Sam and Roger

The band, which Rick initially named Daddy, began to take shape over the next few weeks with Rick bringing in guitarist Richard Palmer, a tall, imposing and rather pompous fellow who had previously written some lyrics with King Crimson. A succession of drummers followed that included a one-day stint by Nigel Olsson who hardly endeared himself to the other band members by asking for a personal car as a prerequisite to his joining, and a longer term by Keith Baker who had previously been with The Joint.

The fact that Rick had played drums himself surely had something to do with the rigorous selection process that they went through on settling on the right percussionist. One day at an audition, the final consensus fell to Bob Millar, who was told rather loftily by Richard Palmer on his acceptance, "In short Bob, you've struck gold!"

The group was complete, but whether this particular quartet had the Midas Touch was still to be seen.

In particular, Rick was quite satisfied with the musicians he had surrounded himself with. "There was a huge change happening at the time I was away in Europe," Rick recalls. "That change was like Traffic, Jethro Tull, Spooky Tooth, sort of nice up-and-coming bands which I wasn't aware of until I went down to see Rory Gallagher and Taste at the Lyceum. Only then did I reckon on the possibilities that something could happen because I didn't rate myself as a big Pop star and I thought to get anywhere I was going to have to be like that. But with the new bands coming up, there was a new standard to live up to and that's what we were aiming for.

"Roger, Richard and Bob were all aware of these groups so having them in the band was sort of an education for me. It was great because Richard Palmer was going on about Traffic and the Band, getting into their lyrics and I had never thought about their lyrics before."

Sam had rented Rick a house in the countryside at West Hythe, Kent and had provided some very expensive, custom-made musical equipment which was temperamental and, without a qualified sound engineer to work it, the overall sound quality was nothing short of tainted. But compared to what other struggling bands in their formative stages were going through, this was the lap of luxury.

Though Sam didn't appear too often, he continued to inject money into the project from Switzerland.

"He would wire the money up to us when we needed it," remembers Roger, "but it wasn't that abundant. For every cheque that arrived, we had to have a fight with Sam and persuade him that we really needed it. It sometimes wasn't all that easy and usually we ended up surviving on about nine pounds a week, which in those days wasn't really too bad seeing that the country house was being paid for and the equipment was pretty decent. For the first few months we were all stuck in this house outside Surrey and we drove each other nuts."

During that first year, the band rarely mixed socially and even ate in shifts to avoid each other. It got to the point that they had few friends because when they came to the house, the vibe was so bad that few returned.

One person that visited the band during that period in January of 1970 recollects that, "Rick was drunk at the time and telling very long and very disgusting jokes to anyone who would lend an ear and the rest of the band was half-heartedly trying to get a rehearsal jam started, with only partial success."

As Rick had spent some time in Germany with his band The Joint playing the P.N. Club in Munich, some old contacts were renewed and shortly after, armed with only four rather lengthy songs, they headed for Europe.

Recalls Roger: "There was a seven-minute version of "All Along The Watchtower," the epic "Season Of the Witch," which on a good night could well surpass the ten-minute mark, and a couple of originals. We arrived at the P.N. Club to find that we had to play five half-hour sets. That knocked us into shape really quickly and we ended up rehearsing during the day to build up a repertoire and playing at night for five weeks. Speaking for myself, it turned out to be one of the most enjoyable experiences of my life. The band had sort of a love affair with Munich and we knew a lot of people there.

"The club itself provided a flat to live in with everybody in two rooms. There were women coming in and out and never any clean sheets. I can still picture Rick's bed. It was a mess. The sheets always ended up in a roll on top of it instead of spread out. The club owner consistently complained that we didn't keep the flat clean so he never used to pay us. He was a very stingy guy."

While Daddy was in Munich playing at the P.N. Club, Haro Senft Filmproduktion made a short documentary film on the group entitled *Daddy: Portrait 1970* that included the band's performance of "All Along the Watchtower" and a composition by David Llywelyn entitled "Turnstyle."

During that period, Sam stayed in touch from Geneva, flying in once and a while to see what progress was being made.

"Sam doesn't live in a particularly real world," laughs Roger. "I think he inherited his money and to this day, he's very wealthy. Though he's quite eccentric, he has a great heart. Half the time he makes sense and then he'll make one totally outrageous statement and you'll wonder what he's talking about. When he gets some drink inside him, he's impossible. He's got a lovely wife though and she manages to keep him together most of the time."

When the five week club date was completed in Munich, they went off to stay with Sam in Geneva and worked in a local demo studio putting together material for what they hoped would be their first album.

At this point, because a number of bands (including Daddy Long Legs) had emerged with names that were similar to Daddy, they decided that a name change was in order. As far as anyone can remember, it was Richard Palmer who came up with the name Supertramp from the book *The Autobiography Of A Supertramp* written by R.H. Davies in 1910 about the adventures of a wealthy Englishman who takes to the road as a hobo in America.

Returning to England, a few more songs were laid down at former Yes-keyboardist Patrick Moraz' basement studio. Sam represented the band for a while when it came time to approach the record companies but he was new to the game and, in the end, they got involved with Harold Shampan who took their tapes around.

Sam had never really considered himself a manager in the true sense of the word but, rather, liked to be regarded as a father-figure in the project. Though he was instrumental in putting together most of the deals that the group made with companies like Dick James Music, Chrysalis and A&M Records, he realized the need to associate himself with people that had had more practical experience in the music business.

In Geneva, Sam had met Bill Wills, who was Peter Sellers' manager and had also had played a bit-part in the Beatles' saga. Through Wills, he met Theo Cowan, who was based in London and was, amongst other things, Peter Sellers' press agent. Cowan in turn introduced Sam to Harold Shampan, who had worked with the Rank Organization and Dick James Music before opening his own company. Shampan became Sam's London-based associate and was later instrumental in getting Supertramp their first recording contract.

It was A&M Records in London that first

Supertramp I

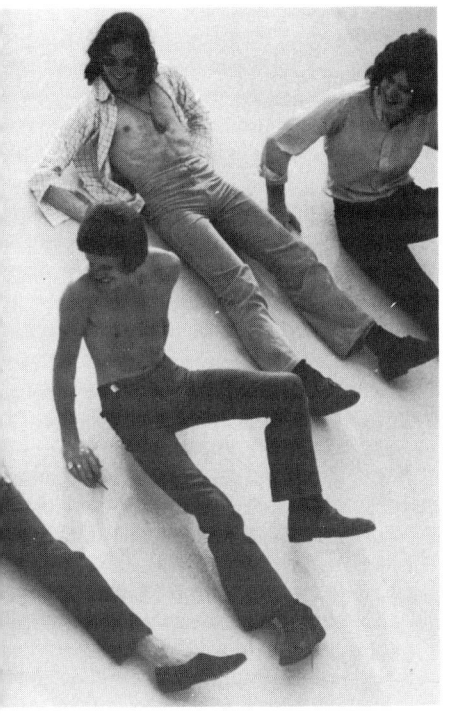

heard something in Supertramp's music that warranted further exploration and shortly thereafter the group found themselves working at the Morgan Sound Studios in London, recording what was to be their first album for A&M.

Now, because of some preconceived notions about the way that recording worked, it's just possible that the band put themselves through some unnecessary hardship in laying down the tracks for this first LP. Roger laughs to recall it now: "Actually, the first album we decided to record in overnight sessions. You see, we had heard that it was the groovy thing to do night sessions so the first LP we recorded from midnight to six every night on purpose. We'd heard that all these groovy bands like Spooky Tooth and Traffic stayed up all night to record so we figured we'd do the same. Maybe there was some magic in it.

"It was an hour from the house in Surrey to the studio in London so we'd set off at eleven o'clock and arrive at midnight. We recorded for about six hours and then drive back between six and eight in the morning. I was the mug who had to drive and we were all sprawled out in this Mini that was the car we used to get to gigs. There were five of us in that car and it could get rather uncomfortable during that one hour drive. There was no reason in the world to record during those hours except we thought it was the cool thing. Invariably our engineer, Robin Black, would fall asleep on us in the middle of the sessions, which were pretty intense as it was, because we fought a lot with Richard Palmer."

"We were very green then," notes Rick. "There was this thing about not having a producer. Bands weren't using producers then and we decided 'Yeah, we're not going to have a producer. Paul McCartney's not using a producer, why should we use one?'"

The writing process for the first LP had involved Rick, Roger and Richard. Rick would come up with an interesting chord progression, Roger would put a melody on top of the chords and Richard would put lyrics to the melody. That, with variations, was the general mode of creation in those days.

Shortly after signing their contract with A&M Records, Supertramp returned to Munich once again to work on the soundtrack of a film entitled *Fegefeuer* (Purgatory). Their original music, along with that of David Llywelyn's which included excerpts from an epic piece that he had written entitled "Apocalypse," was eventually incorporated into the film.

The first Supertramp album, released August 14, 1970, was quite an eclectic affair to say the least with Rick playing organ, piano, electric piano, harmonica and vocals; Roger on bass guitar, flageolet (a modern, straight flute not normally used in orchestral work), acoustic guitar, cello and vocals; Richard on electric and acoustic guitars, balalaika and vocals, and Bob Millar on percussion and harmonica. But the record had its moments like the twelve-minute-plus "Try Again" and the first side's feature, "Maybe I'm A Beggar." This was no small indication of where Supertramp, with minor detours, were headed musically in the future.

Described in the liner notes of *Indelibly Stamped*, which was to be Supertramp's second recording effort, as an album with a "melancholy mood," the first LP flopped commercially yet was well received by many critics. To this day, Roger still has a soft spot for that record. "It was very naive," claims Roger, "but it has a good mood to it."

Judith Simons of England's *Daily Express* reviewed the LP and commented: "This debut record album by a group of promising musician-poets is rather more melodic than most discs which pass under the label 'progressive pop.' Side one, which includes several short pieces, conveys a wan atmosphere - voices are childishly husky and there is much wailing harmonica. Side two gets off to a really swinging start. The mood is upbeat and positive with some fine organ playing."

A real morale booster for the group during this period came in the form of a photostat of an article from the American publication *Zygote* which had been sent over to them from Larry Yaskiel at A&M in London. It was a review of their first album by writer Allan Richards and was very complimentary.

"Not yet known in America, Supertramp, the

Supertramp I records at Trident, London, early '70   (l - r) Rick, Bob Millar, Roger, Richard Palmer

> c/o 43 Eastcott Hill
> SWINDON.
> Received
> 27 10 72
>
> Dear Sam,
> what can I say? What can anyone say.
>
> Your letter arrived at a peak moment of tension within the group. We had the material, the players, the history, but it seemed we would flounder amid managerial quarrels. For myself it will take time to realize what has happened, being clueless as to what was going on in your far away head. I could only hope for the best. It has been only two months since we have finally (please God) our bass playing member. We've been building from there, so there's a long way to go. Whatever it's to be (sink or swim) your contribution to Supertramp was of course
>
> essential and if we actually get to make any money from this (game!) then I am sure nothing would please me more than to repay you. I'm sure the same goes for Dave and Rog.
> I know I've said very little in this letter. I hope to say more anothertime
> love
> Rick

group and the album, promises to be one of the next big attractions from our British cousins. Rarely is a new group described in superlatives, but this one earns every adjective, as they are an incredibly learned and aware ensemble. This is but their first recorded album (done totally on their own), yet it flows with the experience and wisdom of a group which has recorded several LPs.

"The musicianship is indeed at a very high level. Richard Davies, Roger Hodgson, Richard Palmer and Robert Miller, not only utilize many instruments but also play them all with expertise. Supertramp brings to mind the Incredible String Band and King Crimson because of their diversification and free-formed compositions. But Supertramp never treads upon anyone else's domain. They are meticulously, sensitively, delicately original. They are Renaissance men from the fourteenth, sculpting a musical phrase, carving a lingering riff, inventing a melodic design, painting a tender portrait of what music should be.

"Listening to their song Try Again, one understands how expressive this group can be. The arrangements are unformulated, reaching intricately for spontaneity. This song can't be perceived just as a musical feat; one has to view it as a pastoral painting. There is so much to feel. So much sensitivity has been drained from each note to create an idea. They will play a few measures of whispered words, and then prance off into a willowy organ and flute-toned instrumentation.

"Their music is tinged with English-Scottish tones, bluesy effects and orientally flavoured harmonies. They can't be categorized musically, and I wonder if they can indeed be called musicians. I get the impression that these men are really artists who are using their instruments as a canvas to create moods and paint pictures.

"One of the outstanding songs is Surely, a beautifully melodic ballad arranged for softened emotions and a quiet-stay-at-home-evening for two lovers. Nothing To Show is a driving blues-like tune which, like Try Again, becomes involved in intricate instrumentations. It's A Long Road is an oriental-style tune featuring a guitar riff played in eastern harmonies. A jazz-blues piano and a harmonica most remembered from the Mersey sound entwine into a very weird yet exquisite effect. I can't believe that a group who has recorded only one album together can be this superb.

"Supertramp has a unique consciousness for music. They approach their work as carpenters or painters do theirs, and actually do paint their feelings. A musical phrase is not used to fill in a lead; a solo is not given or taken because it seems 'right'; and an accompaniment is not selected because there should be 'this' or 'that.' They have an incredibly sharp and coherent sense of what to play.

"If they can reproduce live what they do on record, I have a feeling that Supertramp is going to be another one of those Procol Harum, Ten Years After, Jethro Tull British supergroups. Keep your ears open. Remember their name, Supertramp."

If the debut album did nothing else, it enabled them to go out on the road to play live and that first year, playing before a large number of people, the record sales were substantially boosted. Audiences, not ready for a whole set of original music, were often treated to a couple of old standby numbers like "All Along the Watchtower" and "Season Of the Witch" from their Munich days, to keep them from getting too restless. Regular stints on *Top Gear* were keeping them alive financially. And then there was a memorable gig at the Croydon Greyhound just outside of London that drew the largest crowd of their career to that point. Optimism reigned, but shortly after Bob Millar quit the group and things came to a grinding halt.

There was also a feeling of restlessness in the band at the time - the notion that it was not meeting its full potential. This manifested itself in a number of changes that took place during that period.

Richard Palmer had really never gotten along with either Rick or Roger and it was obvious that something had to give. Sam realized it too and during this period, he flew into London to ponder the decision of whether to send either Richard Palmer or Roger packing from the group. After a long telephone conversation from the Mayflower Hotel, where he was staying in London, to his associate Harold Shampan, it was decided that Roger should stay and Richard should go.

Roger had been working with Supertramp while still under contract to Blue Mountain Music for which he had recorded a single with the group Argosy entitled "Mr Boyd." The next day, Sam bought out the contract for 500 pounds and Richard Palmer was informed of the decision.

Palmer's reply to Sam came in the form of a rather poetic note quoting Frank Loesser's "Guys and Dolls," received on July 23, 1970, that read simply: "And the devil he said 'Sit down! Sit down, you're rocking the boat!' Okay

I'll sit down. Apologies and love, Richard."

His note to the group read simply: "Fuck you!"

Roger moved over to guitar and keyboards at this point and when the musical chairs had stopped, they had brought in Kevin Currie on drums, Frank Farrell on bass and augmented their sound with the addition of Dave Winthrop on saxophone.

It was with this line-up that Supertramp entered the studio once more to do what Roger refers to as "the survival album to put ourselves back in the good books of our manager. There was no theme worked out for the album and we were floundering."

It was during this unstable period that drummer Kevin Currie, who had been in backup groups for such singers as John Walker and Billie Davis and used to be with Orange Bicycle, held the group together. "Unless he'd come in," Rick would later comment to *New Musical Express* writer Tony Stewart, "we'd probably have folded again. We needed someone to...believe in what the band was doing. He really got us believing in ourselves again."

In an article that he personally wrote for the British music paper *Record Mirror* in May of 1971, Kevin explained his involvement with the group and talked about the first album.

"I joined Supertramp about two months before we started work on the new album," Currie wrote. "I had to do three auditions and the band saw 87 drummers and 93 guitarists. They didn't find a guitarist and eventaully, Roger, the bass player, played guitar, so Frank joined on bass just after we finished the album.

"We'll be rehearsing now for a few weeks, then we go to the P.N. Club, Munich for a few weeks to break the band in to coincide with the release of the album.

"What can I say about the album...it's right where we all are at the moment. We're not out to impress all and sundry with our musical prowess, virtuosity, etc. We like to think that people who buy the album will listen with their heads, not their ears, but we don't mind.

"If they get something out of it that we didn't consciously put on it, then good for them. We think it is quite a varied album. Most of our live gigs are colleges which means we're only exposed to people who want to know anyway. We hope the album will find its way into the possession of people who wouldn't normally associate themselves with 'groovy' college bands.

"The fact that Supertramp are still together is a minor miracle in itself. When the first album was being made, the personnel scenes were really bad. Vans and cars breaking down one after another.

"Eventually the guitarist and drummer left the band. That was it. As far as people in the business were concerned, we're now slowly convincing them they were wrong.

"We had a gas doing the album. We were in the studios all over Easter and we wrote and produced it ourselves. People don't realize it but the studios and studio engineers all affect the way the album comes together.

"It was recorded at Olympic Studios in Barnes, which is a really nice studio. And the engineer Bob knew exactly what we were trying to do without anyone having to say anything."

Kevin joined the band in February of 1971 and that same month on February 28, Supertramp played a concert at Stowe with Genesis.

In April, Roger made the switch from bass to lead guitar and Frank Farrell, who had previously been with the Ray King Soul Band, Joe Jammer and Johnny Johnson, joined the group.

In May of 1971, there had been much conjecture that Roger and Rick might leave Supertramp to join Paul Kossoff and Simon Kirke of the recently-disbanded British band Free, in another musical enterprise. Paul Kossoff had rung up Roger to explore the possibility but that was about as far as it went.

By this time the band's sound had changed to thickly-layered rock a la Traffic, but they just weren't making any inroads. They weren't falling back and they weren't moving forward either.

Rick recalls their stage show at that time: "It was all Rock and Roll really. We used to get people up on the bloody stage and it was just chaos, hopping away doing about three encores, but there was meat and potatoes behind it. No more or less people would come to the next gig."

Indelibly Stamped was released by A&M, this time not only in Britain, but in the U.S. and Canada as well. "God knows why we called the album *Indelibly Stamped* or why we put the tattooed lady in the nude on the cover," grins Roger. "A friend of Rick's had this idea to go and photograph this lady with tattoos all over her and we said, 'Sure. Why not?'"

The cover did manage to cause a little controversy as the British newspaper *The People* reported:

"The roses rambling across Marian Hollier's bosom were not really meant for public exhibition.

"Until some imaginative character decided

A & M.

DURRANT'S

LIVERPOOL ECHO
LIVERPOOL,
LANCASHIRE
ISSUE DATED

Kevin joins Supertramp

JOINING Supertramp early this year was no shoe-in for Liverpudlian drummer Kevin Currie.

Recalls Kevin: "I had to do three auditions—short lists and things—and the band saw 87 drummers and 93 guitarists."

Currie, who played with semi-pro. groups on Merseyside before going to London and taking up music full time, got his chance when Supertramp split apart after the successful release of their first album last year.

The reconstructed group spent a total of 100 hours in the recording studio producing their second LP, INDELIBLY STAMPED (A. & M.), a considerably lighter and more varied offering than the original group's rather melancholy debut album.

that her tattoos would go nicely on the jacket of a long-playing record.

"Marion, 26, was photographed - topless - and she now appears rather prominently on the sleeve of a record called Indelibly Stamped by the Supertramp pop group.

"Down in Picton Street, Bristol, Mrs. Grace Barance, a counter assistant in a record shop, was shocked.

"'The sleeve is immoral,' she said. 'In the shop, we usually hang sleeves up, but we couldn't possibly have a thing like this on display.'

"Now the shop won't even stock the record let alone display it. 'It just isn't nice,' said Mrs. Barance, a widow with a grown-up daughter.

"The shop manager, Mr. Ray Pugh said: 'Mrs. Barance thought customers might be offended, so I agreed not to stock it.'

"It's not a total ban though. 'We'll order it for anyone who asks for it,' said Mr. Pugh.

"Marian of Clevedon, Somerset was paid 45 pounds for posing for the record cover.

"'I wasn't too happy about posing bare-breasted, but the 45 pounds decided me,' she said."

Shortly after the album was released the group talked to *Record Mirror* writer James Craig about some future plans for Supertramp.

"Over the period of an hour, they drifted, one by one into Stan Webb territory - the Coach and Horses in the west end.

"Rick Davies and Kevin Currie hiding behind their beards, Roger Hodgson in contrast with his clean-shaven face. Three of the members of Supertramp, a five-piece band whose reputation is growing due to their live appearances and two albums.

"Rick is the quiet one, sitting fingering his beard and mooting over each question. Kevin is the ebullient one, with the typical Liverpudlian chat bursting with strong adjectives. Roger is a combination of the two, sometimes sitting in silence for a long time, sometimes interjecting with a string of comments.

"One of the topics is their latest album Indelibly Stamped. Released a few weeks ago, it has received a good response, is selling well, and has aroused some controversy due to the tattooed nude on the sleeve.

"'We were thinking of the possibility of re-recording a track off the LP as a single,' says Rick. 'Of the ten tracks, eight have been suggested as singles by different people from A&M Records to our managers, even ourselves. We'll be recording again soon and intend to cut a single. Whether it will be an album track or a new number, we don't know yet, songs don't grow on trees. Still, we're going to record several numbers, so we'll pick the best.'

"One point their two albums have proved is that Supertramp are strong songwriters who give great attention to melody. A hit single is bound to spring from their fertile minds and they don't think it will split their audiences. Up to now they have played mainly at colleges and universities and, due to releasing only albums, have been put into the 'progressive' bag. But the group don't like being pigeon-holed. Categories, they feel, can damage an artist. There is simply good music and bad music and labels tend to confuse the issue.

"'We want to record something that sells, that appeals to people. We want to write music that is lasting,' says Rick. 'That is why Supertramp is taking its time, not rushing to get into the limelight. When I formed the group, I always intended that all the members swing together, not only in their music, but in the way they think musically and in the way they get on together. That is why there have been changes in the past. You could have good, original material, but it can be ruined if the people in the group don't feel it.'

"'The only group we relate ourselves to is The Beatles,' says Kevin, while Rick groans and Roger hisses at him. 'No, seriously, The Beatles inasmuch as they just encompass everything that's tasteful in music. There is so much variety in their songs that you can't put a brand on their music.'

"'Taste' is a word that crops up frequently in their conversation and that is how they would like to describe what they're trying to achieve in music."

The rest of September for Supertramp was taken up by a tour of England with Ten Years After and Keith Christmas that opened in Bristol on September 14 and closed in Birmingham on October 4. The press was kind to the band and Sean Sowry writing in *New Musical Express* reported that the band had complete command of the audience in London during the two-night stand at the Coliseum.

"Excellent musicians with a good line in spiel, a strong melodic content to their composition and a driving rock beat, they proved that they're soon to emerge as a topline outfit," Sowry continued.

Chris Charlesworth of *Melody Maker* who also attended one of the shows commented: "Supertramp, in support, hadn't enough time to get things moving, but they were a more than adequate support act who should blossom forth during the next 12 months."

At the Liverpool gig on September 15, Dave Winthrop arrived at the Philharmonic Hall, where Supertramp was to play that night, only to find that none of the gear had arrived and their set had to be cancelled. To allay some of the frustration he felt, he went outside the hall, took out his sax, and gave an impromptu one-man concert. A crowd gathered and he picked up 30 pence before a couple of coppers showed up to ask him to move along. He was apparently disturbing the patients of a nearby hospital.

Ray Townley, writing in *Rolling Stone* magazine, once referred to *Indelibly Stamped* as "...an unsatisfactory blend of jazz and heavy metal." It was as charitable a description as any, so there we will leave it.

This was to be an apocalyptic, yet maturing time for Supertramp. The events that transpired during the time of *Indelibly Stamped* would have far-reaching consequences for the group that would leave their mark, in a positive and a negative sense, right up to the present day.

Sam, having come to the end of a very long rope, finally severed his ties with the band, something that Roger commented on later in the group's career. Agreeing that Sam's financial assistance had certainly made the lot of a struggling Rock band much easier, he pondered the long-term benefits of any creative entity having the way made too easy for them and concluded, "spending Sam's money wasn't a good thing for us."

Shortly after his departure, Sam would send a very touching letter to the band indicating that he had never been in it for the money. He was involved, he said, because his heart was in the music. He didn't care about the contracts and the other legal details. He forgave them their debt to him, which was estimated at about $150,000 and he closed by wishing the group the best of luck for the future.

In a letter written to Rick on October 6, 1972, Sam made the final break with the group.

"We are sorry it has come to this. You see, we liked music. We still do. But it's hard isn't it with all those interferences or absences.

"We invite you presently and formally to forget us. Everything.

"We want however to insist on one point:

"We want you to keep your Hug organ, your Wurlitzer, and be responsible for the p.a. system and the drums, plus all the other bits and pieces. We want Dave to keep his wind instruments. We should like Richard Palmer to receive the acoustical guitar. We should like to give Andy what he took.

"Godbless."

Roger replied to Sam's decision to let the group go about a month later. He wrote:

"Dear Sam and Liliane,

"For the last few months, I have been trying to write to you, each time stopping because I wasn't writing what I felt.

"Thank you for what you did. I am truly sorry it had to come to that, but very happy in the knowledge that you put friendship and music before so-called 'pride' and money.

"It is very hard to know what to write. A lot has happened in a year, it is difficult to know where to begin. The group has become such an intense thing, I sometimes wonder whether I can handle it. When you're up, you're up and when you're down, you'd just like to forget everything.

"In July, I took LSD for the first time, which was the happiest day of my life. I could write pages trying to explain it and it would be impossible. The reason I tell you is because I believe we are searching for the same thing - the true meanings of life outside the one man has created for himself - money!

"Rick has not taken it and is too frightened to and I must keep quiet until he changes his mind because you have got to want to take it, although I weep when I think of what he is missing and what Lennon, Dylan, Zappa, The Band - all of them discovered.

"I am getting carried away but it is so easy to.

"Whatever the future may bring, the next time we meet is going to be a gas!

"I have not said half of what I wanted to say but hope that what I have said makes sense.

"Much love, Rog."

Sam's reply in part was enthusiastic as usual:

"For Gawd's sake, let's keep in touch. I know Rick - he writes when Jupiter kicks an eclipse - once every, perhaps, million years or so. And tell that bastard of a Dave to write me! And keep fucking going! And get good management to 'handle' you. 'What goes up, must come down.' Chaos! Newton or the Band, or was it BST?"

Rick did write in length to Sam shortly after:

"Thanks for the letter. It's nice to know you're still enthusiastic toward the group though I guessed you would be.

"I have already included the idea of 'game' in a lyric to a piece called Asylum and it should be on the next LP. I think it will be a very intense album with the pick of pieces written over an

Supertramp II
(l - r) Rick, Roger,
Kevin Currie, David
Winthrop, Frank
Farrell

Ban bare breasts

I AM AS broad-minded as the next man, but I was surprised to see bare breasts on the cover of Supertramp's "Indelibly Stamped" album. I was also astounded to see contraceptives on the cover of Birth Control's album.

Are album covers going to get more obscene? If so, something should be done to stop it. Because it is mainly the 'younger generation' who buy these records. — C. ANCELL, 8 Robertson House, Tooting Grove, London, S.W.17.

Melody Maker, July 10, 1971

eighteen month period. We have just visited Chrysalis following a very well received set on John Peel's Sound Of the 70s radio programme and asked them to let us do less gigs for more money. We really have worked exceedingly hard in the last few months doing lots of dates but for little reward. They thankfully see our point of view, so we should be able to start thinking about recording. Our minds have become fuzzy with the amount of gigs not to mention various colds and flu bugs which have effected practically everyone.

"We are slowly eliminating the old stage material. Gone are Long Road, Nothing To Show, Potter and Poppa Don't Mind. They are replaced by five others you don't yet know.

"Our stage performance is our biggest concern for worry at present though we still get encores, we lack an amount of sparkle and continuity. It's been depressing lately working with a band called Roxy Music (4 gigs) who are nothing but sparkle and continuity but with positively minute compositional and musical ability. They have become huge overnight.

"The whole business is depressing at present with so few good bands, non-stop rubbish on Radio One and the trade press succumbing to the money people. Our publicity since Indelibly Stamped has been four spots on Sounds Of the 70s (John Peel still holds out hope). Amazing we've had any gigs at all.

"There's talk (as there has been for years) of us bringing out a single very soon. Should be exciting.

"Russel, our ever loyal servant, has become without doubt to my mind, the top roadie in the land, sad to say he may soon be leaving. He's thought of some incredible scheme to make himself untold millions. He disappears on off days to study 'the plans.' All I know is he's going to ask Coca Cola for 25,000 pounds. There's always the hope he'll be turned down. I'm writing this down in 'Coulings' huddled around the parafin stove about to boil two kettles for my five hot water bottles, plucking up courage to go upstairs to my allotted (supposedly) haunted room where I shall shiver myself to sleep counting the different shapes of mist that emerge everytime I breathe out and trying not to be strangled by cobwebs everytime I breathe in. I'm thinking of putting my nose in a glass of hot water overnight and training the cat to sleep on my feet.

"Love to you, Liliane and the kids.

"P.S. Heard new mammoth production of Tommy the other day. You may like it."

The group later phoned Sam while they were in Europe on tour. "Unfortunately Sam was drunk when we phoned him," recalls Roger. "He spent the whole hour we were on the phone trying to dissuade Rick from his upcoming marriage. 'Two more years boys. Two more albums. Immortality! Fuck marriage! Fuck marriage!'"

Sam was an incredible character, no mistaking, and Rick and Roger would put a close to this particular chapter in their career with a short but heartfelt tribute to their early mentor on the *Crime Of the Century* album. "To Sam." was the simple dedication that spoke volumes of their love and respect for the man who had paved the way for their music to be heard around the world.

Another major blow floored the group during this period. Someone had mentioned that it might be a good idea to go up to Scandinavia where the people were apparently just mad over the type of Rock being played by Supertramp. It wasn't a bad idea they figured. After all, who knows what new horizons might be viewed from this new northern perspective.

They went by bus, touring mostly in Norway, and realized very quickly that their optimistic view of Scandinavian Rock tastes had been slightly overblown. They ended up stranded there and were bailed out to the tune of 500 pounds by their displeased record company.

They arrived in England broke, without a manager and Samless.

Though not obvious at the time, the appearance on the scene of Russel Pope was to shape the future of Supertramp in a practical way as well as act as a catalyst for a long-term change in the relationship between the two creative forces in the band, Rick and Roger.

Pope, who was soon to become the behind-the-scenes sixth member of Supertramp, is a

Russel Pope

native of Johannesburg, South Africa. Meeting Roger and coming to work for the group as their sound engineer, he worked with Steeleye Span in a similar capacity. In even earlier days, he had been a musician in a band with Toney Shepherd, who would join Supertramp as light technician at about the same time.

Pope is a technical genius who, as well as loving the music, always listens to things for how well they sound both in concert and on record and how well it is played. His dedication to audio excellence was obvious from the first and when not physically working at a sound board it was not unusual to see him off in a corner, quietly studying books on audio engineering and pondering endless sheets of graphs.

Quiet spoken and introverted in many ways, Russel is normally given a wide berth when he is at work. Perfection is not his goal but his preoccupation, and when the pieces aren't falling into place to his satisfaction, he can be as ornery as a cornered rattlesnake. Over the years, the concert sound quality that he has brought to the band borders on legendary.

That was Russel's practical contribution to the make-up of Supertramp. However, to understand his subtle influence over the creative make-up of the group, one has to explore the effect his relationship with Roger bore on his subsequent association with his songwriting partner in Supertramp - Rick Davies.

"Around the time of the first two albums, I was just a subject of my conditioning," Roger reveals quite candidly. "Up until that point, I had led a very sheltered life. It was very unreal. I never had to work and I'd come from a family that was pretty well off. Going to private school, which was an unreal existence in itself, I was isolated pretty much from what you could refer to as 'the street life' and my value system was very bigoted along public school lines. I had a pretty moral outlook on the world but nothing of real substance or foundation.

"When I first met Russel, he had looked into all sorts of alternative thinking, taken acid and been exposed to those things that were very much a part of the cultural revolution that took place in the sixties.

"I used to have these huge philosophical arguments with Russel and he used to win all of them. I used to realize that he was right and begrudgingly accept the fact. I remember that he always used to end up by saying simply, 'Take acid! You'll see.' He could see how conditioned I was by my upbringing and that I really needed a way to break out of it. I wanted to break out, but I wasn't convinced that acid would do it because I didn't know what the hell it was."

But finally, Roger did try LSD and for him it made all the difference. "It showed me a whole other reality," he recalls. "I just started reprogramming myself. I would never recommend it, but I needed to break out of the conditioning that had a hold on me. I can see now that there are other ways of doing it, but acid was there at the time. What it did was to open up part of my mind that normally, in a conscious state, I was not aware of. Now, the danger is, if you are imbalanced in any way or not comfortable, it'll freak you out. I came close a couple of times. I did it for a period of three or four years, every four or five months as a refresher or reminder. I was pretty much afraid of it and approached it with a lot of respect and as a learning experience.

"Once, during that period, I dropped some very early one morning. I started playing my guitar and it was the first time that I understood how the musical flow should be. I wasn't playing the instrument; the music was just flowing. It was as if the instrument and I were one. I think that showed me that the music is there and, now, I just have to quiet my mind down or lose myself in it and the music starts coming through."

It had always been a class difference and their diametrically opposed family backgrounds - Rick from the working class and the years spent on the road with various bands and Roger straight from a private school into the Rock world - that had always put a certain amount of strain on their relationship. Now, with Roger exploring areas of his own world into which Rick had no desire to follow or investigate, the only mutual channel left for communication was through their songwriting.

In entering the music business, Roger, besides the need to create music, has said that in those early days it was a way of breaking away from the stifling atmosphere of his regimented upbringing and schooling. Rick, on the other hand, was, beyond any musical considerations, motivated by fear. "Fear of being slung back into the factory," as he was once quoted as saying.

If it is true that opposites attract, the period that followed the recording of *Indelibly Stamped* was going to put that credo to the test. Roger, the seeker and philsosopher, stood at one pole and Rick, the cynic and realist, stood at the other. How they formed their own particular musical world between them would depend entirely on how they related to each other on their one common ground - music. □

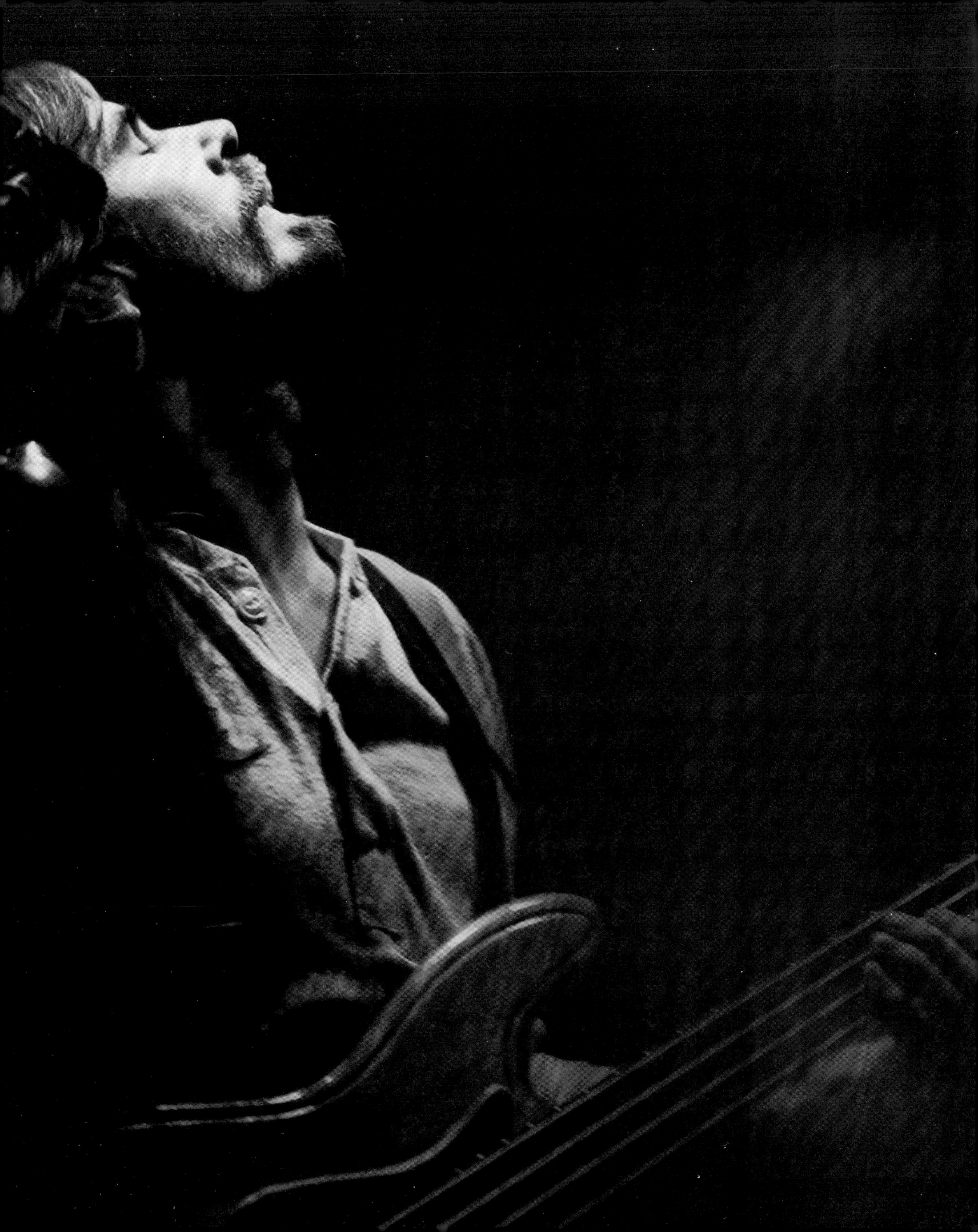

CHAPTER FIVE

In January of 1973, Roger, Frank Farrell and Kevin Currie did a little moonlighting as Chuck Berry's backup band on part of his English tour that included a date at the Rainbow in London.

Writer Neil Lyndon of the magazine *Honey & Vanity Fair* was backstage in London and described this scenario:

"'Who am I playing with tonight?' Chuck asked. 'The same people as last night,' the promoter said, as if asking for approval. Chuck raised a quizzical and mockingly surprised eyebrow. The Roy Young Band had been backing him throughout the tour until they had quit, two nights earlier, apparently claiming Chuck kept trying to teach them how to play their instruments while they were on stage. Chuck had met his new backing band, Supertramp, in Manchester the previous night, only 20 minutes before they took the stage. He seemed amused that they had survived the encounter to a second round.

"Oblivious to the restlessness of the fans, Chuck was tuning up in the wings with Supertramp's lead guitarist (Roger), pecking lightly at his beautiful Gibson and putting his ear close to its as yet unamplified strings. All this time shaking his limbs loosely like a wet Labrador, his brown suede jerkin and vivid blouse shivering against his thin body the while. Then in a flurry, to the call of 'Ladies and Gentlemen, the King Of Rock 'N' Roll,' he was on and leaning indolently into Roll Over Beethoven with Supertramp chugging efficiently behind him."

By February of 1973, bass player Frank Farrell had left the group to pursue his own career which would eventually lead him to a stint with Leo Sayer's band. Again, the classified section of *Melody Maker* was put to good use and the call to audition went out again.

This time, the remnants of Supertramp held court at the Pied Bull Pub in Islington, a suburb of London. One of the hopefuls to show up was a young Scotsman by the name of Dougie Thomson. His brother Kenny (who now manages Chris de Burgh, but would be involved in the Supertramp organization later in their career) had introduced Dougie to Supertramp's music after he had seen them previously at the Marquee Club in London and bought their first record. When Dougie saw the ad in *Melody Maker*, it clicked in his head and he decided to go along and see what was happening.

The scene that greeted him when he arrived at the Pied Bull almost made him turn on his heels and head back to London.

"It was obvious that they were seeing how ludicrous auditions were and had had enough," recalls Thomson. "Dave Winthrop, the sax player, had gone off to play pinball, Rick was slouched at the piano with a sleeping bag over his shoulders and a crash helmet on his head, and Roger and the drummer Kevin Currie were trying to get the audition organized. I played for a few minutes and left there thinking, 'Those poor bastards have got a job ahead of them!'"

Dougie returned to London with little optimism about getting a call but a few days later Roger did phone. He told Dougie that he was the only one that the band could remember from the auditions and invited him to come over to the house that they were living in at the time, stay for a while and see what developed.

"When I first went over to the house, Roger played me tapes that included the songs "Rudy," "Bloody Well Right," "Breakfast In America," "If Everyone Was Listening," "Another Man's Woman" (though it wasn't called that at the time), and one or two others," says Dougie. "Those songs were all in the pot in those days and even in their raw form you could hear their potential. I decided to stay and it just went from there."

Dougie Thomson, was born in the rough and tumble industrial city of Glasgow, the Gateway to the Highlands, on March 24, 1951. He's enthusiasm personified. His ebullient personality and practicality in all matters was to serve Supertramp well in the years to come. Known affectionately to some as the "Glasgow Gourmet" because of his outspoken opinions on the merits of the finer eating establishments around the world, Dougie sort of drifted into music in the early sixties when he was in school and the Beatles were just emerging.

"Glasgow is a tough city," says Dougie in his thick Scottish brogue, "and I grew up there attending a Protestant grammar school. That's how life is segregated in Glasgow, along religious lines. You're either Protestant or Catholic and that's the end of it. It was drummed into me from a very early age by my parents to aim for a secure career and a good education, which I did, until the age of 18. I was a fair student and worked really hard to get my grades, but when it came time to make the transition from grammar school to university, I just couldn't see furthering my education. I needed to get out and do something and coincidentally, during that period, I had started playing music and getting into school bands. I had been accepted for the University of London to study to be an architect or an engineer but I had also applied to be a navigator in the Royal Navy a few times, so there were a few options open but music won out in the end."

Dougie's first taste of performing came in school when he joined an amateur folk group. A couple of his mates had guitars so they got together once in a while for a bit of a sing-song. Later, when it came time to select an instrument, the bass was his immediate choice.

"My father was a navigator who was very keen on my scholastic abilities," says Dougie. "He really didn't encourage the music side of me until the time that he realized it was a viable profession. I have two brothers, Ali and Kenny, and they both got involved in the music and I got blamed for that."

Later, Dougie's dad would take an avid interest in the business and Dougie suggests that he would probably have loved to be involved himself in one way or another. "He's a frustrated promotion man," laughs Dougie. "If they had offered him the job of promotional representative for A&M Records in Glasgow, he would have taken it in a minute."

Dougie would play in a number of groups in Glasgow during the early days of his musical career, but in 1969 he joined a band that had aspirations beyond the borders of Scotland. They decided to strike out and explore the German club scene and for a while they played a number of bar gigs in and around Frankfurt.

"I had putzed around Glasgow for a few years," says Dougie. "There was a lot of competition but there was also a lot of work as well and we normally worked for six nights a week. But you can only do that so much before you burn yourself out. London and the big magical future was far away. Germany represented a chance to get away from the local scene you'd grown up in as well as make some money. It wasn't a lot, mind you, but it was beer money, money to get by on.

"There were so many Americans in Germany because of the military bases and that became one of the biggest parts of the music circuit. We played a lot of the bases and clubs that the Americans would come to and that's when I first discovered Iron Butterfly and music of that sort." Dougie is quick to add that "In-A-Gadda-Da-Vida" did not become part of their repertoire.

Though the work was gruelling, Dougie had no complaints and looks back on that carefree period of his musical career as a lot of fun, almost completely devoid of the pressures and responsibilities that come when a successful music career dominates your every waking hour.

After the German experience, Dougie moved back to Scotland and found the music scene there to be kind of flat. A number of other Scottish groups like Frankie Miller, The Average White Band and Stone The|Crows, were migrating south to London; Dougie figured that it was time that he explored the possibilities there. He packed up all his bits and pieces and moved down to London to seek fame and fortune.

"It was quite a big move at the time because I didn't have any money or a place to stay. I ended up staying with friends and most days I would get out the *Melody Maker*, plough through the want ads and go off to auditions. It was just soul-destroying and finally I had to sell all my equipment because I didn't have any money. That's how I existed. I just sold everything I had and soon I decided it was getting out of hand so I got a job."

Perhaps it was just Dougie's practical side at work but at this point he had a wife, Christine, and a child on the way. He got a number of jobs during that period including a stint in a shipyard fitting exhaust systems into small boats.

"After selling my gear, I moved in with some other friends of mine in London," recalls Dougie. "I got to know a Scottish guy by the name of Gordon Neville who at that time was the singer in the Alan Bown Group. The guy I lived with was a guitar player and he'd just picked up a gig with Alan Bown so I saw them a number of times and at that point met the band's sax player John Helliwell."

As luck would have it, depending on which side of the fence you were, Andy Bown, the bass player for the group, got sick and they held auditions for a replacement. Dougie was urged to come along.

"I whipped the albums out the night before, learned the songs and went off to audition the next day," says Dougie. "They gave me the job there and then, in what was to be the last version of the Alan Bown Group."

Dougie spent about six months with the band before they finally split up and he and John Helliwell, who had become close friends, along with a few other members of the Alan Bown Group, put their own band together.

It was really quite a dead end situation. They didn't particularly want to play live and went through the usual machinations of trying to get a record deal. When the money started to get tight, John Helliwell and Dougie left to do whatever jobs they could each drum up as musicians.

"We worked at the same thing," remembers Dougie, referring to his and Helliwell's situation at that time. "Sometimes we worked in bands together and sometimes as individuals, playing strip clubs and other club gigs just to put some money in the bank. You could earn 50 pounds a week playing these clubs. That was a fortune then. I'd never seen that type of money in my life. You had to work from nine at night until three in the morning, six nights a week so it wasn't an easy quid. But it was something and that's the point I had reached when I went down to audition for Supertramp."

After the audition and the initial meeting with Supertramp, there must have been some doubt in Dougie's head as to just where he fit into the scheme of things. He learned some of the songs and went to the gigs, but he never played with them.

Of course, things in the band weren't exactly what you'd call ticketyboo. As a matter of fact, they were downright chaotic. Dave Winthrop, the sax player, was quickly losing interest in the whole thing and drummer Kevin Currie had a habit of not showing up on certain nights.

"We did one gig in Swansea when Kevin didn't turn up," remembers Rick. "Me and Rog split the drumming duties between us because we needed the bread, otherwise we'd starve. It actually didn't go down too badly."

But what of Dougie? "I used to say, 'Well, what's happening guys?' and I finally started to realize if it was left to get a decision, nothing would have happened. So I figured I'd better start making some decisions here. I finally started playing regularly with the band which at that point still consisted of me, Rick, Roger, Kevin and Dave. I gigged around with them quite a bit and boy, things were tough. We even had to borrow money from Roger's mother for enough petrol to get to a gig."

Soon Kevin Currie, an excellent musician, who had never really fit into the band because of his rather dominant personality, left and things were beginning to look a bit grim.

Before Currie had departed the scene, Supertramp had done a number of concert dates with Frankie Miller, who at that time was being backed by the British pub band Bees Make Honey. The drummer for the Bees was a transplated Californian by the name of Bob C. Benberg who would later recall that he had been impressed with Supertramp from the first time he had seen them. Little did he know then that fate was about to take a rather practical turn for all concerned. ☐

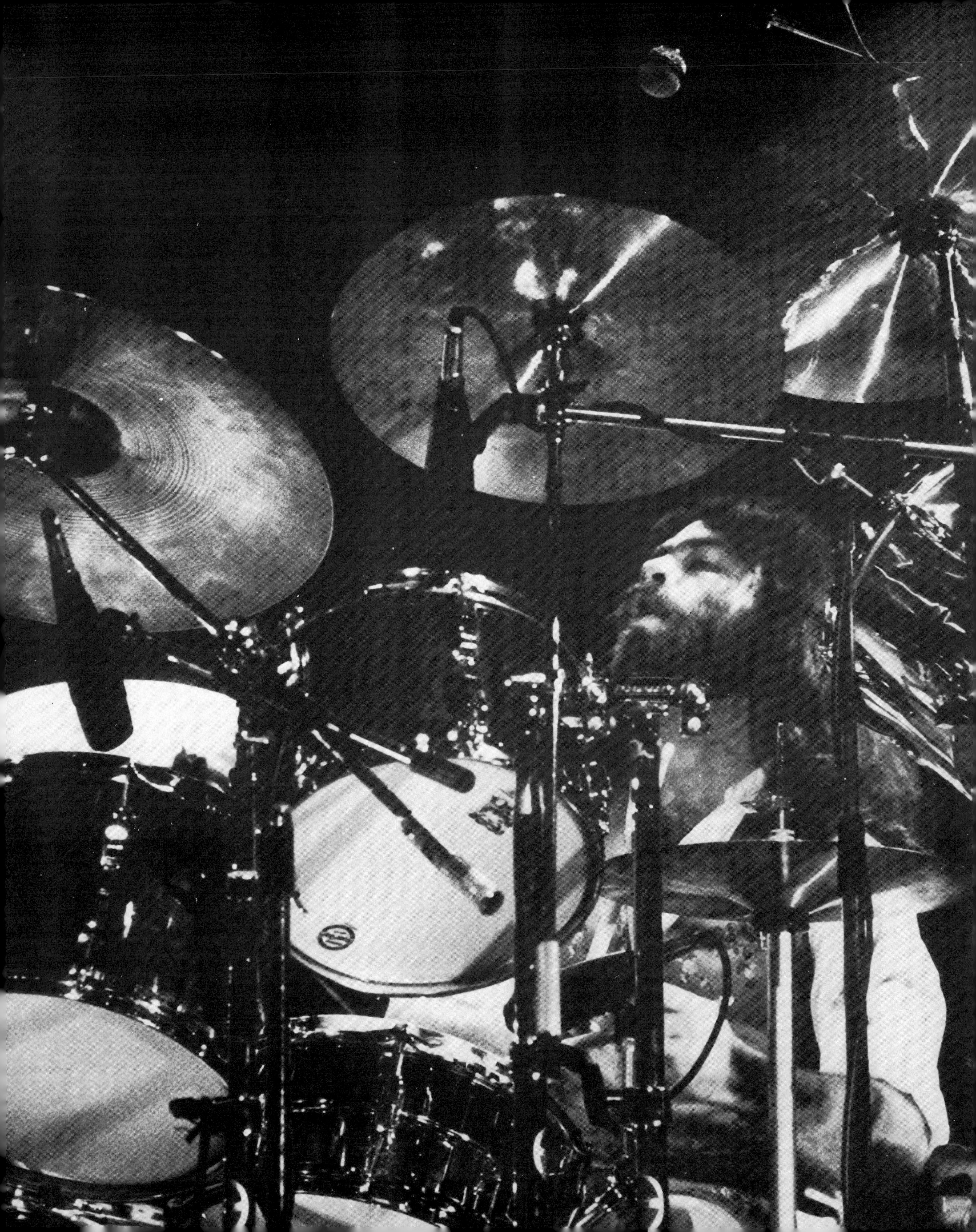

CHAPTER SIX

Note: Bob Siebenberg changed his name to Bob C. Benberg early in Supertramp's career and back to Bob Siebenberg on the *Famous Last Words* album.

Bob Siebenberg, 1967

In the early seventies, though the British music scene was booming on an international level, a very insular music scene labelled by the music press as "Pub Rock" sprung up in a number of drinking establishments in and around London.

True, it was not a new manifestation as there had been a number of London pubs like Klooks Kleek, the Crawdaddy and the RickyTick Club that also provided live entertainment for their quaffing clientele. Still, in its new form, the pub owner acting as promoter would present live Rock acts right in the bar rather than in some back room. There was usually no charge for admission but drinks were a little more expensive. Though the bands had to work long hours for short wages, the apparent benefit was that they could expand their repertoire and tighten up their act in front of a live audience without having to leave London and go on the road with its accompanying expenses.

A number of bands during that period, including Eggs Over Easy, Brinsley Schwarz, Ducks Deluxe (managed by former David Bowie publicist Dai Davies) and Bees Make Honey, followed each other in holding down residencies at pubs like the Tally Ho in Kentish Town and the Kensington Pub in Russell Gardens.

Now as it turns out, the Kensington Pub was right behind the Olympia and across the road, and over a wall from where Rick, Roger, Dougie, Russel Pope, Tony Shepherd, various girlfriends and visitors shared a house in Holland Villas Road, London W14.

Thirty-five Holland Villas Road was a regular hive of activity. Four people were on the lease but in actuality, twelve people were living there.

On the ground floor, there was a dining room with a large table; a living room with a grand piano and a leather-bound sofa; and a kitchen. On the first floor, Roger's sister Caroline and Maggie, Roger's girlfriend, had two of the three rooms. In the other were some Australian friends, the Bolos, Nigel and Nicky. Halfway up the stairs was a shower that served as Rick's living quarters - an art studio in the day and a bedroom at night. In the attic, accessible by a retractable staircase, lived Ken Allardyce and his girlfriend Barb; Russel Pope and his girlfriend Sue and Tony Shepherd and whoever he was with at the time. A whole lot of tapestry divided it into little rooms.

Ken and Tony recall the day the whole scam almost came crashing down around their ears when without prior warning, the landlady showed up at the door with some appraisers to have a look at the house.

"Maggie, who I think was on her way to a modelling job at the time, answered the door," remembered Ken. "She said, 'Yes can I help you?' When the landlady said she wanted to see the house, her mind went into overdrive. She showed her around the ground floor and as she was looking around, Maggie was trying to think of how to keep her out of the attic. As they came up the stairs past Rick's digs in the shower, he locked the door, waited until they passed, and headed out to wander around Shepherd's Bush."

Adds Tony: "We were all up in the attic with our heart's pounding and we can hear Maggie on the landing below us doing this number. She was making excuses about rats in the attic and anything else she could think of to keep the landlady from going up to have a look around and when it looked like that wasn't going to work, Maggie said, 'Nobody's going into the attic because I have an invention up there that hasn't been patented yet!' The landlady gave her a few minutes to clear it up and she headed down to the basement."

Continued Ken: "While she was in the basement apartment, that was rented by some other people, Maggie came up to the attic and in five minutes we had everything rolled up in a carpet in the corner of the room. We dismantled Tony's brass bed and pulled down all of the tapestries and pictures on the wall and then in various states of undress we all scampered down to the parts of the house that she had already checked. I still remember Russell sitting on the bed, reading the newspaper saying over and over again, 'It won't work. It won't work.'

"The landlady came back finally and took a quick look around and satisfied that everything was in better order than she had expected, left with the appraisers while everybody breathed a long sigh of relief."

"That was really bizarre when we had that house, the big house in Holland Villas," remembers Rick. "This big house. Joe Cocker was in there at one point and there was only supposed to be four people to pay the rent, which was astronomical, and there were twelve of us in the end. There were people in the roof and all over the place. I was living in the shower.

"You should have seen the scene when the landlady came round to collect the rent. I've never seen anything like it. She came around about ten in the morning and it was like panicsville. The alarm went off, I got up, walked straight out the door with me pullover on. It was pouring with rain and I just walked around Shepherd's Bush. I didn't have money for breakfast or anything. I ended up bumming a quid off someone. I expected everyone to be out in the street when I got back. I was surprised. Everyone was still there. It was like a farce. People stark naked rushing from room to room as they were showing the landlady around. There were people hiding in the cupboards. They were going to check the attic and of course, there were tents in there."

So this Supertramp seventies commune was thriving around the corner from the Kensington Pub where, one particular week, Bees Make Honey with drummer Bob C. Benberg were playing. It was here that Supertramp would tender Benberg an offer to join the group and where Benberg, common sense aside, would accept.

But to trace the long line of events that would bring Bob C. Benberg, a California native, to this crossroads in his career, we have to go back to Glendale, California where Bob was born on October 31, 1949.

Glendale, a suburb of Los Angeles, is middle class and very white and Bob remembers that during the Watts riots, they literally blockaded every entrance to the area with shotguns. It was here that Bob grew up with his father, stepmother (through whom he inherited two stepbrothers and a step-sister Patti) and his brother Bill, who's now a physical education teacher and varsity football coach in Utah.

"Bill was a Triple A baseball player in the Los Angeles Dodger organization," recollects Bob. We were a real baseball family. When I was too little to play, I became the bat boy and would show up to all the practices. I used to get really angry because I wasn't old enough to actually play in the game and by the time I was eight, which was the Little League age, they instituted the Tee Ball League. In that league you didn't have a pitcher. You just hit the ball off a tee. That would encompass players of the ages of eight and nine and then you would progress to the Little League from the age of ten to twelve. I had been unofficially playing Little League since I was six or seven so I was just shattered that by the time I was ready to go into the Little League, they turned it into a Tee League which was pretty wimpy."

Outside of sports, Bob's musical instincts were piqued at an early age by his father who had been a fan of a number of Dixieland bands like the Dukes Of Dixieland and The Firehouse Five Plus Two. Spike Jones records were always on the family turntable and Lawrence Welk was watched faithfully on the

Bob Siebenberg, 1967

TV back in the days when he had players like clarinetist Pete Fountain on the show.

"I used to always watch the drummer Johnny Kline in the band and bash along on pots and pans," says Bob. "There was just something about percussion that fascinated me. My brother Bill, who's older than me, would bring home Bill Haley records and some of the other artists that were big during the fifties, so that became another musical influence and I remember many a night going to sleep with my radio on next to me."

The musical inclination got its first practical application when he was in the fourth grade.

"The Unified School District would send around a conductor who would oversee all of the school bands. At one of the school assemblies, I remember him saying, 'If you want to be in the school orchestra, come up and see me afterward.' I didn't need a second invitation. I went up there and headed straight for the snare drum. I didn't know what it was called then. I just said, 'I'd like to play this.' And he said, 'Okay!' It wasn't a drum kit then. There was another guy playing the bass drum, but that was the beginning for me."

Shortly after joining the school orchestra, Bob went down to a local music store to rent a snare drum and working there at the time was Spencer Dryden, who was to become the drummer for the Jefferson Airplane from its inception in 1965 until 1974. He was working as a drum teacher.

"He was really a fascinating character - a real beatnik," recalls Bob. "I think he was the first guy I ever saw smoking dope. This was in 1963 or 1964 and I was only 13. I didn't know what marijuana was back then except that it was a no-no. It was a pretty Bohemian music scene back then and I played in a few groups that came out of that."

But, the surf music scene was about to explode in California with the Beach Boys, the Big Kahuna and Beach Party Bingo. Stewart Kessler, a Southern Californian music journalist, encapsulated the feeling of that era in a piece that appeared in the book *Rock and Roll Will Stand*, edited by Greil Marcus.

"With surfboards, peroxide, and my first truancies, came the first sounds I could really identify with - surf music," wrote Kessler. "Coming in the midst of the great early sixties wasteland of rock 'n' roll, the era of Frankie Avalon and Annette Funicello, surf music not only gave us our songs, it rode on the crest of our self-created religion. We could identify with surf music because it provided optimistic solutions to our fifteen-year-old problems, gave us an

The Expressions
Blues Band, 1967
(l - r) Ron Reeves,
Bill Iberti, Bob
Siebenberg, Bob
Clark, Ken Glaster

instant identity, and represented our specific interests - songs even mentioned our beaches. As opposed to the sexless Paul Anka muzak of the time, surf music introduced a kind of pimply pornography into lyrics, like "Take It Off" by Dick Dale and the DelTones. Following the success of "Surfing Safari," the Beach Boys' first really big one, we were deluged by literally scores of surf songs and surf bands, and these bands created a movement. The musical myth of the surf god was accepted and projected by thousands of adolescent kids as we walked on the beaches in our surf club jackets and tee-shirts. By accepting the banal myths of sixteen-year-old high school musicians, we in effect brought those myths to partial actuality. The surf bands preached redemption through surfing; we bought boards, Woodies, zinc oxide, created a beach cottage industry, and felt ourselves to be part of the International Beach Conspiracy, a revolution in mores and values."

Bob also remembers the effect that that era and its music had on him.

"In the eighth or ninth grade, Dick Dale and the DelTones were the hit in Southern California and people were starting to get into surfing. He was the big deal in those days. He had just gone from the Rendezvous Ballroom in Balboa down in Newport Beach to play in a place called Harmony Park in Anaheim, which is a real tough place. I used to stand on my tip-toes to hand in my $1.50 because you weren't supposed to be in there unless you were sixteen, so I tried to be as tall as I could.

"Dick Dale was the guy that really made me want to be in a band. I'd go down with some friends and see him all the time. Dale was kind of a tough nut and pretty greasy, even though he was a surfer. Somebody would come up to him and hassle him because the chicks would be digging him or something and he'd finally reach the point where he'd had enough. He'd take off his guitar while the band was still playing and take the guy who was giving him trouble out into the parking lot and they'd thump on each other. Nine out of ten times, Dick would get the best of it, come in all scruffy having taken the assholes out of his hair, slap his guitar back on and get right back into it. I remember he used to drive this black Corvette. He was quite a character."

Bob's brother Bill was a senior in high school at the time and a number of his friends were musicians. A rehearsal area was set up in the garage and from their initial jam sessions, they formed a group called the Expressions that initially played surf music, but with the advent of the Beatles and the Rolling Stones, they added more and more of their material to the set list.

"We also used to play a lot of blues and early John Hammond stuff like "Baby Please Don't Go," so we were purists in that way. We didn't really play the Pop stuff coming off the radio - Herman's Hermits or Paul Revere and the Raiders. We never really sunk to that level. We were always a bit more groovy than that."

Across town, there was another band called The Jesters that included a young bass player by the name of Scott Gorham, who was later to become one of Bob's closest friends, though their initial feelings for each other were far from what you might call "brotherly."

"Scott was about two years younger than me and while I was going to Glendale High, he was going to Hoover High, our cross town rivals. He was in the hip band on that side of town and I was in the hip band on this side and we used to throw knives back and forth. We didn't like them and they didn't like us. The girlfriend that I had at that time used to be Scott's, and word had it that Scott was spreading some nasty rumours about her. Now, I only knew this guy from seeing him around town but I didn't like him. So, one day, after hearing one of these rumours, I went over to his school after class to have a showdown with him. I caught up to him in the schoolyard but he denied that he had ever said anything about my girlfriend, so we just stood around arguing. I was scared. I'd hardly ever been in a fight in my life. We kept stalking each other and suddenly this girl comes up and just starts screaming at me. 'How dare you pick on my big brother? Who do you think you are? Just get out of here!'"

The planned bloodletting sort of fizzled out after that and peace reigned, though the crosstown rivalry continued.

The Expressions came to a grinding halt shortly after when the singer was drafted into the army and the bass player got the call from the navy. Bob then moved on to a group called the Ilford Subway, named after the guitar player in the group who was from Ilford, England. "He was the only English guy anybody knew, and in those days, it was very hip to be English in California," says Bob.

It wasn't long after the group started that Scott Gorham would cross Bob's path again. The band needed a bass player and this particular afternoon, the group was trying out some likely candidates to fill the vacant spot.

"I drove into this little place that we were rehearsing and I see Scott walking down the street with his bass in his hand and I thought to myself, 'What the fuck is he doing down in this area?' Then it suddenly dawned on me that we were auditioning a couple of bass players, and he was one of them. I figured, 'There's no way.' Nobody else in the band knew about my scene with Scott and we were just silent with each other the whole time.

"Finally it came to Scott's turn to play and everybody freaked out over him. They thought he was great and they were all over him asking him to join the band. 'Oh no!' I thought to myself, 'Not him!' But then I thought about it and it dawned on me that we'd had that argument about a year ago, and the girl wasn't even my girlfriend anymore. So I figured the hell with it. By the time we left the rehearsal hall, he had me going to buy cigarettes for him because I was old enough to buy smokes and he wasn't. We have been close friends from that day to this."

In a more extraordinary turn of events, Bob ended up marrying Vicki Gorham, Scott's sister, the girl who intervened at the High Noon schoolyard showdown.

Bob was a high school senior by the time that the Ilford Subway got on track, and over a two-week period one Christmas, they went up to play in Mammoth where two very rich Beverly Hills kids were so impressed with the band that they offered to manage them. It seemed like a good idea at the time, but as far as a serious career move it was a steep climb up an icy slope.

"We ended up rehearsing for days and days in the back of this house where Dinah Shore used to live in Beverly Hills," remembers Bob. "I think that we played at the Century Plaza Hotel for the Jewish League Foundation and then the Daisy Club, which is the Hollywood version of the Speakeasy Club in London. We'd play for celebrities like Sammy Davis Jr., Dean Martin and Chill Wills. Kim Fowley was also hovering around us at that time. It was all pretty irrelevant stuff. We got produced by Terry Melcher, who also produced The Byrds, but nothing came of that. And then we were produced by David Mallett who had produced Ian Whitcomb, but again, nothing much to report."

The Ilford Subway came to the end of the line in the late sixties.

"I had just gotten floored by the music of people like Van Morrison, Procol Harum and Traffic," says Bob. "In the Ilford Subway we always did stuff like The Byrds and It's A Beautiful Day, so with these new influences in our head, Scott and I split. We just seemed to get invovled in an endless number of bands with other people that really never amounted to much. In fact, we used to spend more time sitting around in the back rooms of people's guest houses smoking joints and jamming when we were in the mood, with me on drums and Scott on bass."

A band was started by Scott and Bob that featured a close friend of Scott's on guitar. Apparently he was a real whiz kid, and it appeared that the band might make some sort of impact. Tragically, shortly after the formation of the group, he was killed in a motorcycle crash, something that would affect Scott very deeply.

"That incident devastated Scott," recalls Bob. "He decided the very day that he heard about the accident to take this kid's place, to try to get to where this kid would have eventually gotten to. Scott stunned everybody by dropping the bass, which he was very proficient at, and switching to guitar. That was a big departure for everybody because we now had to find a bass player, and as Scott wasn't very good on the guitar at that point, we sort of put things on hold for a while.

"Everybody sort of got hung up on summertime and the drug scenes that were going down, especially in Glendale. Glendale was just a hot bed of scandal. I didn't really get sucked into that scene because I always had a goal in my head of what I wanted to do and where I was going."

One thing that made Bob take a serious look at life in general was a hit and run accident that he was involved in around this time.

"I got hit by a car and it really levelled me out, I broke my leg and my face got smashed up. I was walking across the street and this guy in a stolen car just nailed me. I flipped up in the air and came down smack on the windshield with my face, which just swelled up like a balloon. I had no eyes, no nose, no nothing. It was just this big puffy thing. It was hard to just have fun after that and all of a sudden things got a lot more serious. I realized how easy it is to get killed and I just took off. I drove up the coast to Los Gatos to visit some friends. I knew a couple of girls up there and I just hung out. It was my only real hippy days, I guess."

So for a stretch of three or four months, Bob hung out in Bug Sur, frolicked in the creek, and spent some time with the same girlfriend that Scott and he had tangled over in the schoolyard. She was working as a waitress in a club called the Greasy Slew Duck Club in Santa Barbara. One afternoon he walked into the club and the band that was appearing there was hanging around.

"This guy from the band came up to me out

Scott Gorham, guitarist for Thin Lizzy with his sister, Vicki Siebenberg, backstage at Wembley's Empire Pool. Nov. '79

of the blue and said, 'Listen we've just gotten a gig in this club to play indefinitely and we don't have a drummer. Do you know anybody that plays drums?' I told him that I was a drummer and he offered me the job. All my gear was back down in Glendale so I drove down, picked up my drums and started playing with this band called R.H.S., which stood for Real Hot Shit."

Well, R.H.S. they might have been, but apparently their repertoire of Jeff Beck and Jethro Tull material didn't have crowds flocking to the bar, so most of the time was spent playing pool and drinking. Soon Bob headed back to Glendale and found that Scott had been busted a couple of times and was struggling. Eventually Bob, Scott, Derek Beauchemin (who played keyboards and would later become very close to Bob in other music projects) and bass player Rick Hart (now a recording engineer who recently worked with Pat Benatar) put together a band called Redeye, to play some Procol Harum-style material. The band, which played mostly in the Glendale area, was short lived, and one day Bob got a call from one of the guys that he had played with in R.H.S. asking if he'd like to come and audition for a group that was being put together at the Knickerbocker Hotel down in Hollywood.

"I was living in this house in Echo Park at the time and all the guys who lived there were dealing drugs. I lived in the garage. I just put up a few tapestries and had my stereo out there. Unfortunately, that's where these guys stashed their dope, so while I was out auditioning, the house got busted. The police had been watching the house and they moved in. They didn't find dope anywhere except in my room. I remember getting a call from this girl at the audition, which I passed, telling me not to come home because the police were there waiting for me. I checked into the Knickerbocker Hotel as Richard Kimball, a pseudonym I still use on the road, and turned into a fugitive.

"The court case finally came around and everybody got off. Apparently they would wave my passport in the air and say, 'Where's this Siebenberg guy?' They told the judge that I was a travelling musician and only stayed at the house when I was in town and that I really had nothing to do with it. Eventually it just kinda slid and when I reapplied for my passport, I had to make up this story that my passport had been in my jacket which I left at a party one night."

Playing at the Knickerbocker Hotel with this new band, Bob started to realize that the other musicians around him were not all that good. Over a period of time, he decided that one by one he would replace the musicians in the band with his own friends. The first guy to go was the guitar player, and in came Scott. Then the organ player got the axe and Derek Beauchemin joined. The singer, who had a voice like Tom Jones on an off night and wasn't really into British rock, must have been getting a bit nervous at this point, and for good reason as it turns out. Bob had found out that the singer he'd worked with in R.H.S. in Santa Barbara was working at the Hollywood Wax Museum. Before you could say, 'Who's that dummy I saw you with last night?' he was fronting the band, which was named Benbecula, apparently after an island off the Scottish coast.

Though the band was pretty hot, Bob had already decided that unless it got the chance to actually make a record, he was going to split for England and try and make a go of it over there. From his current vantage point, the music scene there seemed to be far healthier.

As it happens, Scott's sister Vicki was in England at the time, on a post high school graduation tour, and when it was time for her to come home, she stayed on for four or five months without her parents' consent. She phoned Bob and urged him to come over on his birthday on October 31. That was in 1970. Because of the problems with the drug bust and the uncertainty of the band, Bob didn't go, and eventually Vicki came back to Los Angeles and worked as a waitress.

"She was the first pioneer out of all of us," says Bob. "She was the only one that had actually been to England and spent time there. When Benbecula finally broke up, we sat down and said, 'Why don't we get out of here. We'll get married, I'll stop being in a band for a while and we'll go to London.' The plan was for me to go to music school there and do some teaching and session work on the side."

That's exactly what they did. They were married in March of 1971, and landed in London on April 30 that same year, with a suitcase and Bob's drum kit. They stayed in a hotel for a couple of days while they found a flat, and Bob started thumbing through the *Melody Maker* classified section for work as a musician. Scott was in L.A. at that point, working at ABC Records driving a forklift moving albums from one side of the warehouse to the other.

To stay in the country under a student visa, Bob continued to go to music school where he studied piano, flute and sax all the while constantly scouring the papers for a permanent position in a band. The government finally caught up with him and gave him six more months to

Bob's folks

stay in the country. In the meantime, Bob had been hanging out with a number of bands just to see which ones he could make some inroads with. Answering an ad in *Melody Maker* had gotten him a two-gig stint with the British pub band Bees Make Honey, after which he didn't hear from them again.

"The bass player for the Bees lived in Ealing Broadway, the London suburb where I lived at the time, and one day on the way to music school I ran into him. I asked him why the band didn't call me back, and he told me that they liked the way I played but I was just too loud. I said, 'Well you should have told me. I can fix that.' They were playing down the road in Brentford that Friday night and he asked me if I wanted to do the gig. Of course, I jumped at the chance and I just ripped up all sorts of underwear, taped up my drums with them and did the gig. I played with them for two and a half years and the thing really got going because we were one of the first groups to put Rock 'n' Roll into the Kensington Pub. As a lot of other groups like Ducks Deluxe, Kilburn and the High Roads, Brinsley Schwarz and many more started coming through, it turned into quite a scene.

"Out of all that came Nick Lowe, Ian Dury, and half the Rumour band. It was really quite a breeding ground. Frankie Miller would play at the Kensington and we'd back him during those days."

During his stay with the Bees, they made two albums that Bob drummed on - *Music Every Night* and *Bees Make Honey 1971/72*. Playing in the group was a great experience but their ambition was to be the best support band in London, and that fell short of Bob's aspirations. This was Bob's state of mind when he first crossed the path of Supertramp.

"Frankie Miller had done an LP with Brinsley Schwarz backing him, entitled *Once In A Blue Moon*," recollects Bob. "Frankie was about to set off on a club and college tour and the Brinsleys were off doing something else, so Bees Make Honey backed him up on those dates. We supported Supertramp, a band I'd never heard of, on a couple of the dates, and I guess the first time I ever saw them was at this little college down in Putney, which was our first gig with them. They had already set up their stuff when we arrived and the drummer was playing along with the guitar player. He was pretty good and I thought to myself that they might just be a good band. I didn't know it then, but it had actually been Rick playing the drums, because a few minutes later, the real drummer for the band, Kevin Currie, came in and Rick went over to the Wurlitzer. They were trying to teach this drummer a break in a song which turned out to be "Bloody Well Right," and he just couldn't get it. I could hear it coming every time."

That night they did their set with Frankie Miller and left before Supertramp played. The same thing happened at their next date but Bob did spend some time in a pub playing darts with Rick and Dougie.

"The next gig was at a club called Barbarella's in Birmingham, and because I had met the guys on our last date with them, I decided to stick around and see what they were like. I remember me and Ruan O'Lochlainn, the keyboard player for the Bees, standing right behind the bar and watching them. They came out and did a few songs and I was impressed. I liked the piano playing and the way Rick twitched around on stage, I liked Roger's voice and I thought the material was pretty good. At that point they were already doing songs like "School," "Dreamer" and "Bloody Well Right" along with some of the material from their first two albums. That was the last gig that we did with them.

"In talking with them briefly I realized that this was their struggling period. They had no idea where they were going. They had done a disastrous tour of Norway, all cramped into this van on icy roads with a few thousand foot drop on one side and snow slides on the other. Everybody got ill on the ferry coming home, they had hassles with their drummer the whole way, and they weren't happy with their sax player. They were at the point of just eking out a living, knowing that their record company wasn't happy with them, and wondering what the hell they were going to do.

"They'd come to the point that they couldn't go through auditions like they had before because they had gone through a lot of drummers to find the guy they had, and umpteen bassists to find Dougie. They were on the hunt for a drummer and I hadn't realized it, but Rick had spotted me on this little swing we made through England with them. Dougie, Roger and Rick would be behind the curtain backstage watching me to see what my attitude was and it seems that they found me to be the kind of guy that they wanted."

So Bees Make Honey returned to the Kensington Pub, which if you'll remember was one dipsy and two doodles from where Rick, Roger, Dougie, Russel, Tony and friends were making a new sport out of landlord-dodging at the Chateau Debris in Holland Villas Road. It was at the Kensington, after a few nights of dropping around to watch Bob play, that Rick and Roger approached Bob.

"One night as I was packing up my stuff," says Bob, "Rick and Roger came up to me and asked, 'How's it going?' I said, 'Fine, nice to see you.' They finally broached the subject. 'We've been listening to you really closely and we wanted to know if you'd consider coming over and having a blow with us.' I jumped at the chance, went over the next day, and started by doing the "Bloody Well Right" punches right off the bat. Then we blew through "Crime Of the Century," complete with the fills that I still do in that song, which are very much influenced by B.J. Wilson of Procol Harum. I've always liked him as a drummer. I suddenly had this sense of what I wanted to be doing as a drummer. I wanted to be dynamic and play with a lot of power, and up to that point I really hadn't had the chance to get into that.

"I remember at the end of the session Roger just kind of shaking his head and scratching his chin. It seemed to go really well. I went over a few more times and they eventually started hinting at the fact that they wanted me to join Supertramp. I was a little reluctant at first because they were really nowhere careerwise, and they were on the skids with the record company. I knew that they were living hand-to-mouth with their gigs. I was in the Bees Make Honey, being written up in the papers constantly, and working steadily. Everybody knew us and there was a buzz happening. So I told them, 'I don't know. Why don't we just keep jamming together for a while and see how it pans out?' In the end I found myself going over to the house to play darts and sit around listening to tapes of ideas that they had for their music. Soon it became obvious that I would really rather be spending my time with them and I decided that I would join."

The first place the band rehearsed to work Bob in was the Furniture Cave in Kings Road, and Rick would later comment, "I'd never heard such a loud drummer in my life. I couldn't hear anything but cymbals."

But, volume notwithstanding, and against the advice of his wife, Vicki, Bob was now the drummer for Supertramp.

He had finished his itinerary with Bees Make Honey, giving them two or three weeks notice, and was replaced by Fran Byrne, who would later become the drummer for Ace. At this point, as he and Vicki hadn't been back to California in three or four years, they went home for a while, turning their flat over to Rick and Steve Walker while they were gone.

In Los Angeles, they stayed with Scott, who they convinced to return to England with them in the hope that he could fill the role of guitarist in Supertramp, because when Bob left, it had been up in the air whether a sax player was going to be added to the band or another guitarist. By this time, Dave Winthrop, Supertramp's sax player, had stopped showing up at gigs altogether, so some decision as far as a replacement had to be made soon.

The tedious process of auditions began again, but one day, in a flash of inspiration, Dougie got on the phone to his old sax-playing band mate from the Alan Bown Group, John Anthony Helliwell. Unfortunatley, at the time, Helliwell was off playing the club circuit in Germany, so the band continued their search. But as luck would have it, John returned home a few weeks later and was invited to come down to a rehearsal at Manfred Mann's old studio in the Old Kent Road where they were currently working. □

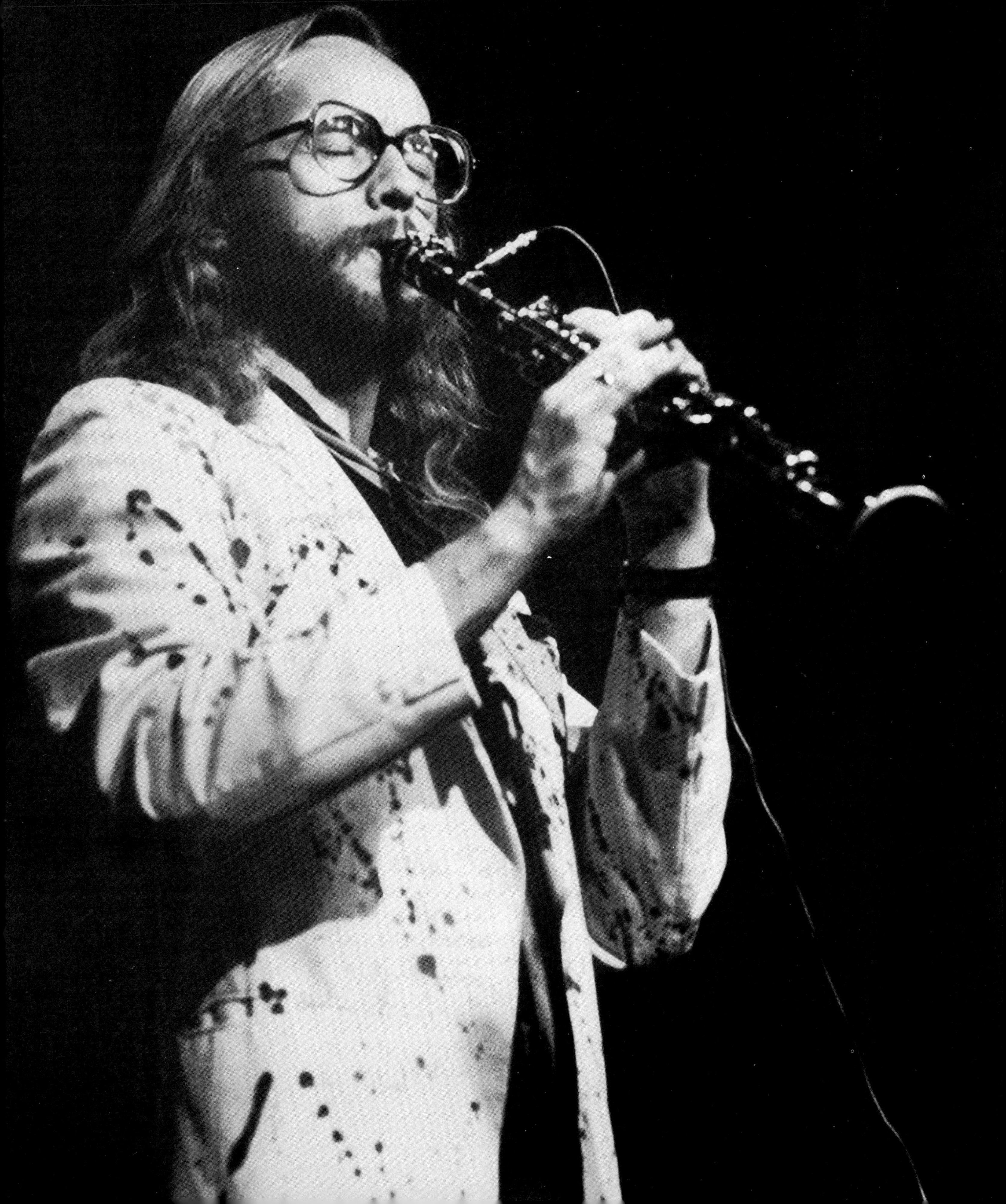

CHAPTER SEVEN

John Helliwell, 1966.

The short stint in Germany playing the American Forces Bases with a "20-stone multi-instrumentalist" by the name of Pete Lancaster, was obviously an interesting proposition for any musician, but for John Helliwell, it meant living apart from his wife Christine, who was still in England. After a few months, John had decided that he didn't like that situation much, and, in August of 1973, returned home to England. Almost upon his arrival in London, he received the call from Dougie inviting him to come down to one of Supertramp's rehearsals and see what developed.

"I knew Supertramp from their first two albums, and when I was in the Alan Bown Group we had played with them a couple of times," recalls John. "I do remember that I was very envious of them because I had heard that they had this very rich guy backing them, and I thought, 'Bloody hell! Here I am struggling and these guys have it really easy!' As I would find out later, things are not always as they seem on the surface.

"I had also gone to see the band when Dougie first joined them and I quite liked them but I didn't really think that they were too special. I remember the sax player Dave Winthrop because he was a very voluble guy and he used to collar me every time that I showed up. He'd get me in the dressing room and talk on and on about guys like Charlie Parker and some of the other players that we both admired."

After Dougie's call, John showed up at the rehearsal, played for a while and then sat back. Remembers Rick: "There was silence for about twenty seconds and then he told this joke about the Irishman who got a pair of water skis for Christmas and spent the rest of the year looking for a lake with a slope."

It cracked everybody up, and it was just a hint of the Helliwell-wit that would become such an asset in the band's live concerts. In short, John hit it off with Supertramp immediately.

When he got back home that day, John's wife Christine asked how it had gone. "I'm not sure," said John. "I think I'll go back down tomorrow and see how it goes." It went on like this for quite a few days, but soon he started to be drawn into some of the musical ideas that were being created by the band. During the rehearsals, they were doing songs like "Asylum," "Crime Of the Century" and "From Now On," and John started to get the feel of exactly how he would fit in. As far as anybody in Supertramp can remember, much like Dougie when he first started to play with the group, John was never officially asked to join. They just felt comfortable with each other as musicians and individuals. The final line-up of Supertramp would gell from that relationship.

John Anthony Helliwell was born in Todmorden, on the border of Yorkshire and Lancashire in England on February 15, 1945. A town of about 15,000, whose livelihood derived from the spinning and weaving of cotton. It stands at the meeting place of three valleys in the Pennines, through which roads set off to Halifax, Burnley and Rochdale, with the moorland hills rising mysteriously on all sides. Oddly enough, Todmorden was often referred to as Honest John's Town after John Fielden, who worked in his father's cotton mill in the late 1700s. He became very wealthy, yet he took it upon himself to plead the case for the welfare of factory workers in the area. On one of the hills stands Dobroyd Castle, the Fielden's ancestral home and one of the most imposing modern houses in Yorkshire. It was in a rural area, near the moorland setting of Wuthering Heights, that Helliwell grew up.

Of musical parents, and under the influence of his grandfather who produced Gilbert and Sullivan musicals at the local Hippodrome, John became aware of a great variety of musical possibilities at a very early age.

"My father used to be in a number of these Gilbert and Sullivan productions, and he sang in the church, as did my mother," recollects John. "When I was very small, they used to sing Gilbert and Sullivan around the house. By the time that I was a teenager, I hated the stuff, but since then I have seen some of their musicals and I actually quite like them."

A piano was introduced to the household when John was nine years old; it was to become his first serious instrument. "I played whatever it is you play when you're that age, and I did place second in a piano competition, but I gave it up after I got fed up with practicing."

A friend of the family that John used to visit would play him traditional jazz records by people like Kid Ory and Chris Barber. He heard Monty Sunshine play some clarinet solos on the Chris Barber records when he was only ten years old, but it made enough of an impression, even at that age, to prompt him to pick the clarinet as his instrument. He had already started to play the recorder and figured that the fingering couldn't be that much different from a clarinet, so over a two year period, he saved up the fifteen pounds needed to purchase one and started taking lessons from a guy who lived down the street. Eventually John became proficient enough to join the Todmorden Symphony Orchestra.

"We played Rossini overtures. And I remember that while I was with the orchestra, one of our main claims to fame was playing with a pianist by the name of John Ogden, who, the previous year, had won the world Tchaikovsky prize in Russia. We played Grieg's Piano Concerto with him at the Todmorden Town Hall."

By the time John was fifteen, he started to become more interested in modern jazz and saxophone players like Cannonball Adderley and Sonny Rollins. At this point, John managed to save up and buy himself a saxophone and played in a number of little groups at school.

A page from one of John's school workbooks contains a rather revealing look at how he looked at his life in those days. It was 1960, John was 15, and the English Literature assignment was to write an essay on what each student thought they would be doing ten years on. Under the heading "Myself in 1970," John's essay, verbatim, read this way:
*In 1970, I will be at the age of twenty five years; an age when I will have matured fully, and an age when I will be doing a job of some description. I will be living in an age of greater automation than this present era and greater efficiency in life as a whole. A few year previously I will have come out of the Royal School of Music and will be setting up for myself a career in the music profession - this will combine my pleasure pursuits with my work and enable me to enjoy thoroughly my occupation.
I will not be married: I consider it better not to get married before about the age of twenty-seven or eight, also I can have no attachments or be fixed in a home; I can have a good time with lots of different girls and boys. I will be what can be described as a 'roving performer of music' that is, I shall have no fixed job for a long time. I shall rove about the country doing what are known as 'gigs' with various bands and combos. I will also play classical music -as a soothing antidote to the riotous, noisy effects of jazz music with which I will be mainly concerned with in my profession.
I will not be living at home with my parents as my job prevents this, but I shall return home as frequently as possible and as often as my job permits. I do not know what the main fashions for men will be in those days but I shall probably be wearing clothes in a modern cut. One great point of my outward appearance will be my long hair and my beard; a close-cut, slim-looking fair beard, which will I hope attract the women. This, coupled with my 'cool' clothes and a shining golden alto saxophone will, I hope, cause quite a sensation.*

Well, John's personal *Mein Kampf* got a

John in Alan Bown Set.

John Helliwell in Alan Bown Set playing Forest Gate, 1966.

John and Alan at Cooks Ferry Inn, London 1966.

"satisfactory" rating from his teacher, who was well aware of John's musical aspirations from a group that he had formed called the TGS5, otherwise known as the Todmorden Grammar School Five.

"The headmaster wouldn't let us use the name," says John. "I had put this little group of kids together to play the Christmas party. We had a singer, trumpet, clarinet, guitar, piano and drums, and we did songs like "Chatanooga Choo Choo" and "St. Louis Blues." One day we were rehearsing and the headmaster came down to listen to us. After we finished, he called us into his office. 'I've been listening to this St. Louis Blues,' he said, 'and there are certain words in that song that I refuse to let you say.' Turns out, one of the offending words was 'baby', and he refused to let us say that so we replace it with 'loved one.' It was a real drag but that was the kind of school that I attended."

John continued to play in a number of amateur groups for the next few years, and though he initially had plans to go to the Royal College of Music, by the time he was eighteen, he had decided that he might like to become a computer programmer and have a career in computers. He left school after taking his A levels and then went off to Birmingham to work with Britain's largest computer firm ICL, training to be a programmer.

Music had not been left behind though. Through this two-year period working in computers, John joined a number of bands in the Birmingham area, including a dance band and his first real R&B group, The Dicemen. "We used to wear Beatles jacket and trousers so tight we often had to lift the guitarist on stage."

When The Diceman split up, the bass player went to join another Birmingham group called Jugs O'Henry and asked John if he wanted to join.

"Jugs O'Henry was more of a Blues group," remembers John. "During that era in Birmingham there was a lot of heavy musical action. The Moody Blues were just starting to emerge, and there was Carl Wayne and the Vikings, which would later become The Move and then evolve into the Electric Light Orchestra. There was Denny Laine with his group, Denny Laine and the Diplomats, and we used to play some gigs with The Spencer Davis Group featuring this young kid Stevie Winwood on keyboards, guitar and vocals.

"I used to do a jazz jam every Saturday afternoon at this pub in Birmingham, and there'd be all sorts of people showing up. Pete York, the

(From top clockwise) Alan Bown, Pete, Stan Haldane, Vic Sweeney, Jess Roden, John Helliwell, Jeff Bannister at the Golden Touch Club – Turnstall, 1966.

John Helliwell at the Marquee Club with Alan Bown Set, 1967

drummer for Spencer Davis used to come, and one day this kid, wearing a Harris tweed jacket sort of hanging off him, turned up asking if he could play piano. That was Stevie Winwood. Another day I was playing and this guy comes up and tells me that he liked my playing. He was a flute player and he wondered if I wanted to get together with him for a jam so that I could show him a few things on tenor sax. He lived just outside Birmingham in Dudley, and I went down and spent some time with him on and off. He played a good flute but his saxophone playing was just starting to take shape. That was Chris Wood who would later join Traffic with Stevie Winwood."

This was during the period of John's involvement with Jugs O'Henry and soon a major decision had to be made. Jugs had decided to turn professional and John had to decide whether he would continue to earn his ten pounds a week at the computer firm, or leave to make the grand sum of two pounds a week playing on the road with a professional band.

"I enjoyed computers but I thought I'd give music a go. We moved to London and got involved with the same management company that handled the Moody Blues and did some demos with Denny Cordell, who would become one of the major British producers of that era. The management people found us an apartment in London and supported us with five pounds each a week. We rehearsed a lot and played the odd gig but after a while it just sort of petered out and the money stopped coming from the management people."

It was January 1966 and John, who was quickly running out of money, had to make a decision to either go back to computers or get another job in a band. Covering his assets, he made an attempt at both. He applied for, and was accepted at a computer firm in Sweden, but at the same time he put an advertisement in *Melody Maker* that was headed, "Have Sax; Will Travel." As it turns out, the ad caught the eye of Alan Bown of the Alan Bown Set, a band that evolved from the John Barry Seven. (John Barry, primarily a composer, left to pursue a career in the film world, where he did a number of soundtracks for the James Bond films and many others. The remnants of that group became The Alan Bown Set.)

"I went along to play with the band in a freezing cold church hall. Played my sax which was falling to bits," remembers John. "Alan offered me some ridiculously small amount of money. They weren't earning much at the time but it was kind of an interesting band. So I had to make a decision again. Either I went to Sweden to work at the computer firm for some good steady money or I would stay in England and work with the Alan Bown Set. I opted for the music again."

The band, known as the Alan Bown Set before becoming simply the Alan Bown, worked all over Britain from six to seven days a week. Initially the band was an instrumental unit but then a succession of singers joined. Jess Roden was the first, and he was later replaced by Robert Palmer, who in turn was replaced by Gordon Neville, after Palmer quit to work in the group Vinegar Joe with Elkie Brooks. (Gordon Neville is currently one of London's top jingle singers and writers. He recently accompanied Sheena Easton to America to handle back-up vocals on one of her tours.)

"I was in the group for about five or six years but we really didn't have that much success on record. We had one single in the top 30 and made about six albums as we moved from record company to record company, finally ending up with Island Records. We had rotten management for most of the time.

"It was an exciting band to see in the clubs and we were doing Rock music with horns long before we'd ever heard of Chicago or Blood, Sweat & Tears."

Here's a few milestones along the way during the period that John joined The Alan Bown Set in February, 1966 and played his first gig with the group at the Royal Forest Hotel in Chingford:

July 29, 1966
"For sheer excitement there are few groups to beat the Alan Bown Set. In the overcrowded world of dance hall groups, they could be described as the 'apple in the apple pie' - and the cream too."
The quote is taken from a line in the B side of their new record which is out today.
Just how talented this London group are can be gauged by local audience reaction.
Bournemouth Pavilion audiences have long been labelled as the most discriminating in the country. Perhaps it is because they have seen so many groups that they are only prepared to rave about the best.
Yet the first time the Alan Bown Set played there a few months ago, they had the usually reserved dancers clapping, cheering and jumping on the stage to dance. Since that Sunday in February this year they have been twice more. News of their coming has attracted record audiences and they have been labelled by many as 'Bournemouth's favourite group.'
The dynamic presentation of their performance, good looks and excellent musicianship are responsible for this success story which has been repeated at dances all over the country. The group originally formed about fifteen months ago. Alan Bown, who was formerly with the John Barry Seven, hand-picked the other six musicians, and together they invested a lot of their money to get themselves going. A recording contract with Pye soon followed. Their first record, "Can't Let Her Go," was not a success, although it sold well on the Continent, but their next release entitled "Baby Don't Push Me," did slightly better.
Now with their new disc, "Headline News," out today, they could easily rocket up the charts. It is a catchy number, with a strong beat and the unmistakable brass and piano sound of the Set. The Set owe much of their success to the work of Alan himself. He arranges all their numbers, decides on their stage clothes, teaches them their dances and writes a lot of their material.
The line-up of the group is: Alan Bown, trumpet, vocals; Jess Roden, vocals; Vic Sweeney, drums, vocals; Stan Haldane, bass, vocals; Pete Burgess, lead guitar, vocals; Jeff Bannister, organ, vocals; and John Anthony, tenor sax.
Bournemouth Times, July 29, 1966

November, 1966
Peter Burgess replaced by Tony Catchpole on guitar.

July, 1967
"For our academic fans, John recommends the writings of Oscar Wilde, especially The Picture of Dorian Grey."
From The Allan Bown Set Newsletter, July, 1967

August 4, 1967
Police cut power on the band at a pub date in Acton after two numbers because they are too loud. The pub happens to be next to the police station.

August 13, 1967
Played with Cream, Jeff Beck, John Mayall, P.P. Arnold and the Denny Laine Strings at the Windsor Jazz and Blues Festival.

October, 1967
The Alan Bown Set becomes the Alan Bown and release the single "Toyland" on MGM Records, produced by Mike Hurst. This follows their split with Pye Records.

December 23, 1967
"The group was involved in a fight when they

Recording "Little Lesley" at Olympic Studios about 1968.

played at Dereham on 23rd December. Algie (one of the roadies) was taken to hospital but was released the following morning, John sustained a cut lip, and Jeff was hit on the head with a knuckle-duster. Steve (the other roadie) revenged them all by smashing a bottle in the face of one of the yobs, although he himself was stabbed in the back with a screwdriver. It is always unfortunate that when this sort of thing happens, innocent by-standers are very often injured too - during this fight, a young girl was slashed across the face with a broken bottle. The group is anxious to find out who she is, so if any of you know her could please ask her to get in touch with us. Thank you."
The Alan Bown Fan Club Letter -
January/February 1968

February 1968
Second single for MGM released entitled "Storybook."

April 1968
The Alan Bown Fan Club Newsletter reveals that John's height is 5' 10" and his collar size is 14½.

April 23, 1968
The album, *Outward-Alan Bown* is completed for MGM Records.

July 5, 1968
The Alan Bown's new single "We Can Help You" is released on the new Music Factory label distributed by MGM.

July 7, 1968
The Alan Bown appear at the Royal Albert Hall with Grapefruit, Bobby Goldsboro, The Byrds, Joe Cocker, The Easybeats, The Bonzo Dog Doo Dah Band and The Move. The Alan Bown profile in the concert program reads: "This seven-man group play largely their own material. To describe their act would be difficult without using words like psychedelic and underrated. Their intricate hand movements and arm wavings create an impression of continual motion and colour and their sound is both exciting and creative."

July 19, 1968
John fails his driving test but nonetheless buys a car that same day - an 1100.

July 20, 1968
The Alan Bown perform for the first time on television, appearing on the *Simon Dee Show* on the BBC.

July 1968
"I have a new love, the sea: I have fallen in twice in the last week. I fell fully clothed in the Solent

PLAYER OF THE MONTH
JOHN ANTHONY

THE Alan Bown! were, in some ways, pioneers of the soul explosion in this country, and although that's fizzled to some extent, they haven't dropped their trumpet/tenor foundation—just moved on to their own thing, which requires the added power of brass. We've featured Alan Bown himself in this series, and now it's the turn of Todmorden born John Anthony, Alan's partner in the blowing stakes.

John says that Chris Barber inspired him to start playing: "My first instrument was the recorder. I heard Monty Sunshine play some clarinet solos on Chris Barber records when I was 10, and that made me want to play. I saved for two years, managed to get £15 together, and bought a clarinet. Then I saved up again and bought an alto . . . and then a tenor".

"I had tuition on the clarinet and joined the Todmorden Symphony Orchestra. When I got the saxes I was doing semi-pro things with dance and jazz bands".

And then John left school, and started work as a computer programmer. "I still played in my spare time, and joined a group called Jugs o' Henry. We went to London after turning pro, but weren't very successful, and broke up six months later". After the split, John put an ad in a music paper, under the "Engagements Wanted" section, and it was worded strangely enough to attract the attention of Alan Bown, who offered him a job with the Set.

John has stayed ever since, and has just tasted chart success with "We Can Help You". But he feels that their singles aren't completely representative of what the group does on stage. "We're a very visual group," he says. "But you have to be good, musically, to put it across with any reaction". Although the Alan Bown! are commercial, John, like so many other group tenor players, falls back on jazz for inspiration.

"Modern jazz is my main love, but I'm also listening to good American groups, particularly Spirit, the United States Of America, Electric Flag, Blood, Sweat and Tears, and the Mothers Of Invention. I'm getting the words more now. There is a tendency to concentrate on the sounds as an instrumentalist, but that's not always the most important part of a record".

John, who plays clarinet, recorder and tenor ("a black Selmer Mk.6") in the Alan Bown!, is highly rated in the group world, but says he is: "Only just beginning. I improve by steps. I stay on a plane for a couple of months, and then move upwards as I develop new things. But I feel my musical horizons are rapidly widening".

October '68.

John (centre) at Sheffield Open Air Festival, 1970.

at 3 a.m. and went under, and got my legs wet at Aberystwyth...John and I are currently digging the Mothers Of Invention on John's stereo system. I buy the albums and John lets me play them on his gear for even better effect...I'm buying a jeep...I sang on a record with The Who called "Magic Bus" - it's on their next LP. John Entwhistle and I were playing soul sisters at the time...John and I are fast becoming the best car rally team - he navigates, I drive. We got home from Portsmouth the other night in ten minutes and we ran out of petrol too. It's true. I think. Well I'm only trying to help."
Note from Jess Roden to the Alan Bown Fan Club - July, 1968

August 19, 1968
John passes his driving test.

August, 1968
John Anthony (aka) Helliwell, is profiled in a press release from the Alan Bown's record company, The Music Factory. This pertinent data is uncovered:
Colour of Eyes: Blue
Colour of hair: Blonde
Hobbies: Literature
Favourite Colour: None
Favourite Food: Mousaka; Curries
Favourite Drink: Scotch and Coke
Favourite Singer: Billy Stewart
Favourite Actor: Donald Pleasance
Professional Ambition: To have a really well-made button hole every day
Personal Ambition: To be elected to the *downbeat* Hall Of Fame

October 1968
John named Player Of the Month by *Beat Instrumental Magazine* and is profiled.

1969
Jess Roden leaves the Alan Bown to form the group Bronco and is replaced by Robert Palmer.

November, 1969
The Alan Bown's "Gypsy Girl" single is released by Deram Records.

November 1970
The Alan Bown switches from the Deram record label to Island Records.

November 20, 1970
The album, *The Alan Bown - Listen* is released by Island Records.

1971
Robert Palmer is replaced by singer Gordon Neville and bass player Stan Haldane is replaced by Andy Brown.

San Diego, CA

July 1971
A new LP - *The Alan Bown, Stretching Out*, is released by Island Records. Chris Welch's review in *Melody Maker* read: "'Stretching Out' in the musicians' parlance means a chance to blow something improvised and maybe even arranged, with some elbow room and not too many glances at the clock. Freedom of this kind seems to have given the group their best ever chance to express themselves, and the results are pretty good. From all their years of playing, they have obtained much relaxed professionalism. Without being great innovators, nevertheless, the Bown men have long been into brass Rock arranging. The Bown problem was always settling down and developing a proper valid style. They seem to have achieved it here, with some original arranging ideas, not to mention excellent engineering. Particularly impressive is Andy Brown's bass guitar, and John Anthony's tenor work, heard to good effect on "Turning Point," a nine-minute blow."
Chris Welch, *Melody Maker*, August 21, 1971

John had entered into married life with Christine by this time and a number of changes had taken place in The Alan Bown. The bass player Andy Brown left the group (he would later do some work with Pink Floyd) as did guitarist Tony Catchpole.

"Dougie Thomson joined the group at this point to replace Andy Brown on bass along with a mad Scottish guitarist called Jim who used to drive the van," says John. "Everyone was terrified of Jim because he used to fight with people all the time, so he didn't last long. Dougie stuck around, and at the end, we all got really pissed off because things weren't going well and management was terrible. We got a deal with what we thought was a good agency and the money from the gigs doubled but the gigs went down from six a week to about one every fortnight. Finally, we all left Alan Bown and tried to form a group of our own. We called it Wizard (this was before Roy Wood's Wizzard) but the whole thing was rather abortive because the manager, who had helped to pay for the truck and half of the equipment, wouldn't let us use it and took it all away."

Wizard played a few gigs around London to fairly enthusiastic response but, because of outside pressures, nothing really came of it and they packed it in. There were a few lean months for John after that, compounded by the fact that he had inherited a pretty serious tax problem. Taxes that he thought had been paid while he was in Alan Bown, were, in fact, still outstanding with the Inland Revenue. He got a bill for close to a thousand pounds, and there was nothing much else he could do but supplement some nightclub work he was doing at the time with a job in the day as a dry cleaner.

"I was earning reasonable money but I could only stand that pace for a couple of months. I would go to bed at four in the morning after finishing my club gig and have to get up at seven to go to my job at the dry cleaners. I came home from that at four in the afternoon, went to bed for a couple of hours until my wife Chris woke

John's car suddenly burst into flames on the way to a gig!
Finchley Press, 1974

John backstage in San Diego, April 1979

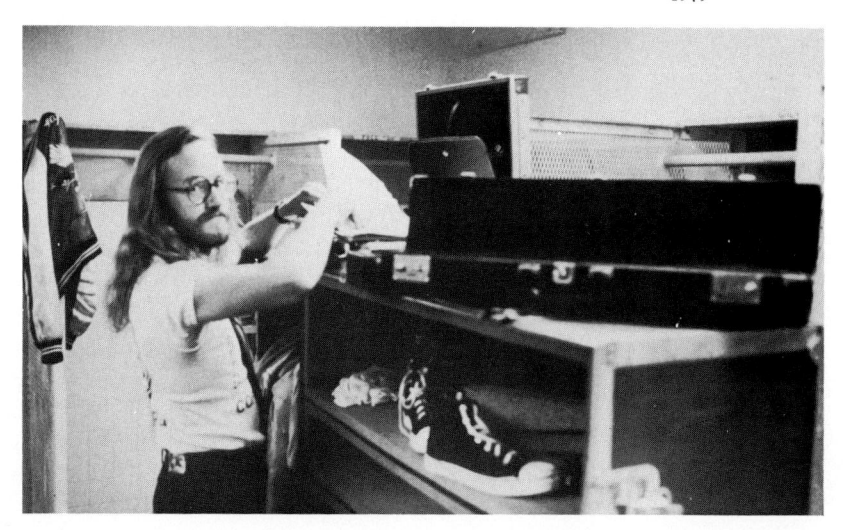

me up at seven for dinner, and then drove off to London from Maidenhead where we were living, to play the club gig. I did that until I'd paid off my back taxes."

He wound up his tenure with one club act and then went into Soho to play at a club called The Twilight Rooms which Dougie had just finished playing with a group.

"The Twilight Rooms was one of those places where the customers come in and ordered a twenty pound bottle of champagne and the girls would sort of sidle up to them and they had to buy them a drink. There was only three of us in the band and I was making thirty-five pounds a week, which was reasonable money in those days. We had to keep the music going continuously, so we each took turns taking a break. There were drums, piano and sax, so when the pianist took a break, I had to play piano, so there was just drums and piano. When the drummer took a break, the pianist couldn't play drums, so I had to fake it, because I couldn't play drums either. Sometimes we'd back a singer and then the strippers would come on and you'd get to know what number they wanted to strip to. Behind the stage was a partition of hardboard and when the stripper was ready, she'd hammer on the wall behind the drummer. At that point, we'd wind the number we were playing down and start whatever song they wanted."

Through a contact at that nightclub, John got some offers to go out on the road with a visiting American artist by the name of Arthur Conley, who had had the big hit in 1967, "Sweet Soul Music." John played with him for a few weeks and then from there he joined Johnny Johnson and the Bandwagon, a group known for the song "Breaking Down the Walls of Heartache" among others.

"I was part of the horn section in the Bandwagon and we used to travel with Johnny and his driver in his car, a very nice Rover, while the rest of the band travelled in the decrepit van. I did a few gigs with Johnny and then I got the offer to go to Germany to play with Pete Lancaster at a number of American Forces Bases. It was fun because it was a good, musical band. We used to also move our own gear so I kept fit lugging the organ and other stuff. That was my first small slice of Americana really, playing American air bases."

After returning home to England in August of 1973, John received the call from Dougie who was now working with Supertramp, and headed down to one of their rehearsals to see what all the fuss was about. □

Dressing room, Victoria, 1977

Victoria, 1977

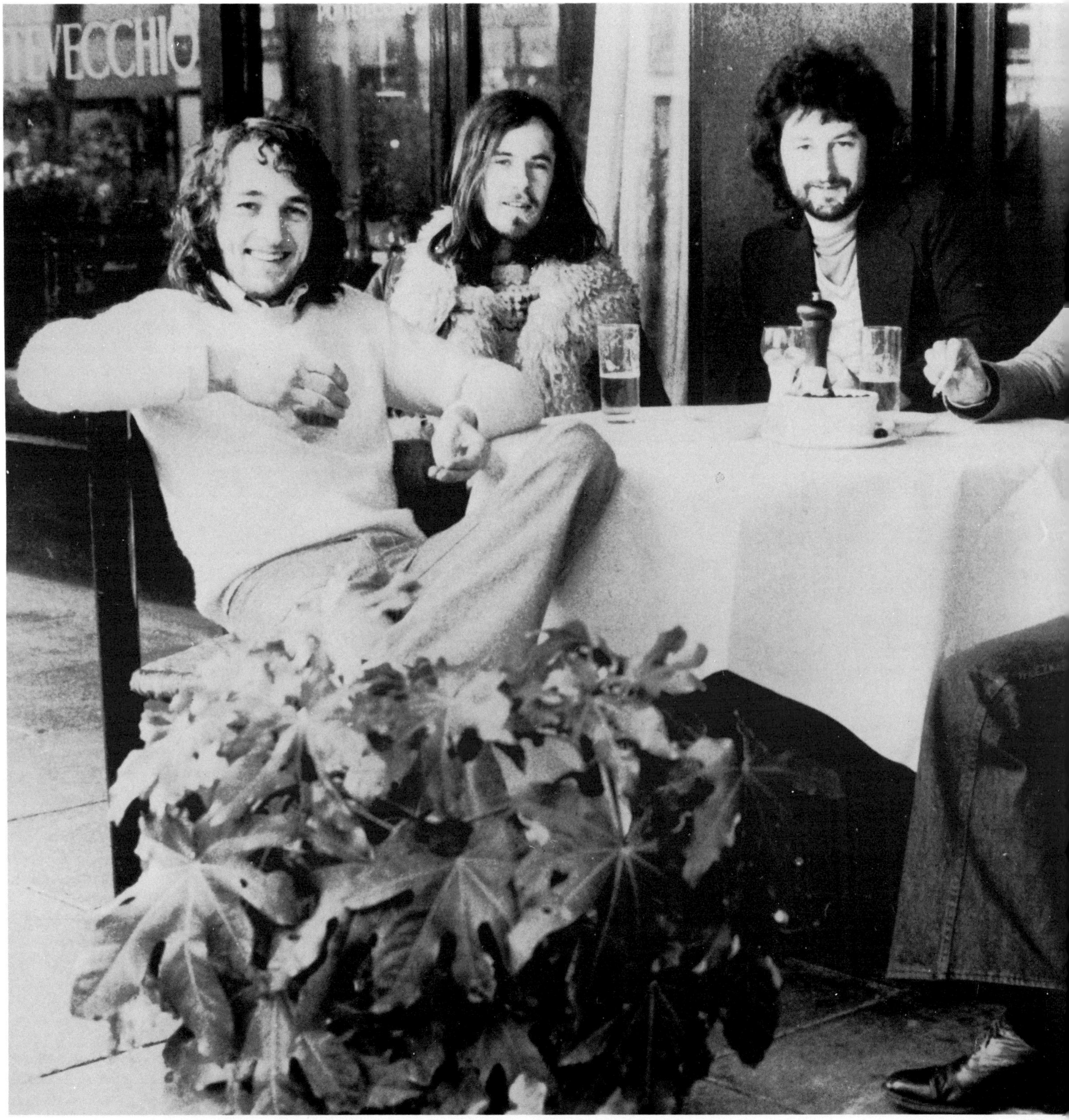
TEVECCHIO

CHAPTER EIGHT

There had been a point when things were getting to be a bit too much to bear for Supertramp. Serious consideration had been given, before the arrival of Bob and John, to just forgetting about the whole project and going their separate ways. It was Dougie who basically held things together during that depressing period. His enthusiasm saw the group through those stormy waters and made Rick and Roger see the folly of giving up when there was so much, on a creative level, going on with the band.

During the period that Supertramp was getting musically acquainted with John Helliwell in what was to be the final complement of the band, it was also very obvious that there was not much money to be had in rehearsing. It eventually meant that, for a period of time, most of the members of the group would have to get other jobs just to survive.

Bob had been back to America with his wife Vicki for a brief holiday and had convinced Scott Gorham, to come over to England with the hope of him joining Supertramp on guitar. When John fit into the mould so well, there was really no thought given to bringing anybody else into the band, so on Scott's arrival in England, he played in a pub band called Fast Buck, among others. Through Ruan O'Lochlainn, the piano player for Bees Make Honey, Bob heard that Gary Moore was leaving Thin Lizzy and that the group was auditioning guitar players. Bob passed the information on to Scott who went over to the audition and soon after joined the group. Scott played in Thin Lizzy until its apparent dissolution in early 1983.

For Bob, an extra job meant playing in a band at The Park Towers Hotel in Knightsbridge. "We'd play about five sets a night and I had about three solo spots in each set," remembers Bob. "If that wasn't bad enough, one night when we were playing our second set, do you know who rolled in? Carl Radle and Jim Gordon! They sat right in front of me! I was trying to be as good as I can...I just shit myself!"

John signed up with Manpower and got a job pumping gas, then went on to a factory where he screwed nuts and bolts together. "Roger couldn't believe it because I don't think he's ever done any other job but music in his whole life," laughs John. "I finally gave up the nuts and bolts job and went on the road in England with Jimmy Ruffin which tided me over for a while. Dougie, who now had a little girl called Laura, was also doing extra jobs working in a factory and playing clubs at night."

But Supertramp soon reconvened and moved

their rehearsals to a location under Kew Bridge in London.

"At that point, Russel Pope was really putting himself trying to bring the whole project together," recollects Dougie. "Russel was the roadie, the truck driver and the sound guy but there wasn't one specific talent you could put your finger on. It was his overall input to the project that was important. At that point, we were trying to find managers at the Chrysalis Agency and that wasn't all roses."

When the group finally felt that they had enough songs ready, they decided to confront A&M Records. One day, Rick, Roger and Dougie headed off to the A&M offices in London. "They must have thought we were coming to get out of our contract," smiles Bob. "I'm sure at that point in time they would have been all too happy to let us go." So sure was the record company that the purpose of the visit was for the band to terminate their contract, that they already had it typed up, signed and ready when the lads walked in the door.

They confronted Derek Green, who had just become the new manager of A&M Records in England, and explained that they had new personnel and a new musical direction and wanted to make another record. Green listened to the demo tape and said, "Okay, I'm going to put you together with our new A&R guy Dave Margereson so that you can build some kind of relationship with him and let him hear the songs you've got."

The artist and repertoire (A&R) director of a record company is the person who normally makes the initial contact with the artists in order to sum up their potential and recommend them for signing, so enter Mr. Margereson.

Margereson, an irrepressible and quick-witted character that Rick, Roger and Dougie took an instant liking to, had come up through the record industry ranks in London. He worked in the late sixties at CBS Records in London as assistant to Martin Humphrey who was the exploitation manager. He took over Humphrey's position in March of 1969 and later moved on to A&M Records.

They all sat in the office and put on the demo tape for Margereson, who listened intently as songs like "Asylum," "Crime Of the Century," "Dreamer," "School" and "Bloody Well Right," in their embryonic forms, bounced from the speakers. By the time the tape was over, Margereson was sold on the project.

"He really heard something in those songs," says Dougie. "In the end, he became an ally in trying to make it all come together. We redid our contract with A&M Records and Dave became the liason between us and the record label, getting us time in studios to work on the songs and finding us a rehearsal place."

For rehearsing, Dave found the band a cottage called Southcombe Farm a long way from London in the countryside of Somerset. It was here that the group, wives, cats, dogs, roadies and friends moved with the purpose of focusing their undivided attention on putting together their next LP for A&M.

"We still didn't have any money at the time," says Dougie. "I had my wife Christine and my daughter Laura, John had his wife Christine and Bob had his wife Vicki, so there was a bunch of us to support. Southcombe was a good idea in that it was economical for us all to go to one place where we could live very cheaply. Also, living so close to each other gave us a chance to get to know one another better.

"Southcombe didn't have very big rooms, but there were five or six bedrooms and it had an added-on section in the back where we stored all of our gear. We set the mixer and a little Sony tape machine up in the kitchen so we could tape some of our rehearsals as the songs took shape."

John continues: "A&M Records paid for the house and they sent us money so that we could go out and buy food down at the supermarket. The butcher would come around with a van and we lived next to a farm where we got fresh milk. Bob couldn't stand that. He called it cholera juice because he was used to milk in cartons or bottles.

"Russel was handling our sound then and Tony Shepherd was around, along with Ken Allardyce, who was a friend of Roger's. There were quite a few friends around as a matter of fact."

"The cottage was in the middle of no place," says Bob, "and we'd walk to the pub, which was about a mile and a half across the fields and down the road, but the isolation was good for us. It laid the foundation for us getting to know each other well under those circumstances, and to realize that we were all pretty different personalities. But I must admit, it was quite a shock to my system to have to share a house, a kitchen and a bathroom with a lot of other people."

Though the band had in the past produced their records themselves, it was very much in their minds this time around to find a producer that could work with them in the studio when they finally finished the material for the album.

One of the people considered in the beginning was Ian MacDonald, but after he visited them, the band realized he was not quite what they

Manager Dave Margereson.

Tony Shepherd.

were looking for.

It was during this period that the name Ken Scott suddenly jumped to the fore. The band had already recorded a single entitled "Land Ho," backed by "Summer Romance," which they had produced themselves. The record company hadn't been thrilled with the results and they asked Ken Scott to step in. "He remixed the single without even meeting us," remembers Roger. "We knew he had a good ear after we heard what he had done with it. He left his own mark on it."

Scott, who had previously worked with people like Elton John, David Bowie, The Beatles and John McLaughlin's Mahavishnu Orchestra, became the unanimous choice to handle the production chores for Supertramp. There was one small problem though. Initially, Ken was far from enthusiastic about taking on the project.

The band had sent him a demo tape of the songs which they had patched up and edited together from different mixes. Roger surmises, "He probably wondered what the hell he'd taken on!"

Ken resisted all invitations to come down to Southcombe to hear the band in the beginning. The first time he said that he had jaundice and the next time he suddenly came down with the mumps.

"It had to do with Pat's mother being psychic," says Roger. "Pat is Ken's wife and apparently Pat's mother had a dream or something that Ken shouldn't go down to Somerset that day. That's when he called us and said that he had the mumps. Three days later he phoned back and said 'Sorry, I was mistaken.' We didn't think anything of it until he confessed later."

Finally Dave Margereson did get Ken down to Southcombe to hear the band in rehearsal and he was impressed enough by what he heard to officially take on the project.

The band was at Southcombe Farm from November of 1973 to February of 1974, and that's where the album *Crime Of the Century* really started to come together. "Hide In Your Shell" was actually written by Roger while they were at Southcombe. Bob remembers the circumstances:

"The first time that we came together down there, we all ate hash brownies that somebody had made and I think that Rick was the only one of us that didn't have any. The rest of us just got fried and we were almost motionless. John literally couldn't reach his tea cup for about an hour. We were just zonked and eventually we went out to our little room where the gear was set up and Roger fired up "Hide In Your Shell" which we'd been loosely rehearsing, and everybody just layed into this sucker for the first time. It brought Rick from the other side of the house. He couldn't believe it. You could tell then that the song was going to happen."

Around Christmas of 1974, Rick's dad died and he had to go away for a while. After that, the band stayed at Southcombe for a few more weeks and then headed up to London to start recording the album in February of 1975, working at Trident Studios, Ramport Studios and Scorpio Sound.

"Ken had been a house engineer at Trident Studios in London," says Dougie. "He did Hunky Dory there and some stuff for Elton John. We started out at Trident and then moved on to The Who's place in Battersea, called Ramport. The last place we worked at was Scorpio Sound in London because Ken really liked the monitor system there. That's where we mixed the album."

Ken Scott was certainly no disappointment to the band as a producer as John would later explain: "Basically, the advantage of having a guy like Ken Scott to produce is that he knows the studio inside out. He added a million little things to our album. He gets stuff, particularly in the area of sounds and effects, to complement the music and fill the songs out, that we just wouldn't know how to get...things like the train noises in "Rudy" and the schoolkids in the playground in "School."

"He taught us a lot during that period," adds Dougie. "We contributed to the production in that we wanted it to sound great as much as anyone else but he was the vehicle."

Scott was also a stickler for detail as Bob was to find out.

"When we came up to London from Southcombe and started to record, we had our demo for the album," says Bob. "We had it pretty much visualized, or should I say, Rick and Roger certainly did. We rehearsed for a bit in London at Trident and then started the recording process. That was a new experience for me. I had recorded a bit with Bees Make Honey and a guy named Peter Straker, who came out of the cast of "Hair" in London, but that was just a session. You'd go in, set yourself up, take about ten minutes to make it sound reasonable and then hack through it. Here I was with Ken Scott who took three days to get the drum sound together - ten hours a day. It was a real education.

"We stripped my cymbal stands down, taped things up, put little rubber things around it to

(left to right) Christine Helliwell, Christine Thomson with Laura, Rick, Dougie and Roger in the background at Southcombe.

Southcombe farmhouse 1973.

Supertramp
CRIME OF THE CENTURY

Russel Pope.

hold the cymbals so they didn't clatter. He suggested getting some leather wheels to put between the pad and the wing nut. He listened to everything to make sure there were no rattles or squeaks. It was like being put under a microscope and it seemed to be an endless procedure. So here we are with Derek Green getting weirded out because we're not done yet and we're supposed to be done last week. Dave Margereson would come down and listen and tell us it was sounding great. He'd then go back to Derek Green and say, 'Listen Derek, you can't stop them now. Listen to this. Just think what it's going to be like when they're finished.' Derek would see that, give us two more weeks, and we'd be mixing away.

"Ken would mix in passages. He'd spend eight hours on eight seconds of music, and maybe on twenty seconds he'd spend a day. That's a bit of an exaggeration but it's not far from the truth. We'd all lay in front of these gigantic speakers and it would be so loud and so numbing that it would put you to sleep. You'd wake up four hours later and it would be the same twenty seconds of music. He was brilliant. He gave us a sound which I think attracted as much attention as the music itself. People don't know who I am, but I'll still go into an audio store to buy stereo speakers and ask them to put on a record that I might be familiar with to test them. A lot of times, they'll whip out the *Crime Of the Century* album. I know of guys with their multi-million dollar studios who use the record to make sure that everything sounds right."

The only real creative snag with the songs on the album came with "Asylum," which the band rehearsed over and over again at Trident when they arrived in London. For Rick, the song's composer, it was a frustrating experience because it just wasn't working the way he wanted it to. As time went on, Rick became more and more incensed, and luckily, just before he reached the breaking point, the song suddenly clicked.

"We recorded a long time for the norm in those days," says John. "We got really involved in it and spent from February to June of 1974 getting it together. A&M were paying for it every week and they were starting to get a bit nervous about the whole thing. Jerry Moss, The 'M' of A&M, came over from the States and we played him what we had finished. He was excited enough about what he heard to give his okay on the extra time in the studio. 'Let the boys take their time,' was his attitude and that really took some of the pressure off us."

While the *Crime Of the Century* album was being completed, in April of 1974, the single "Land Ho," previously remixed by Ken Scott, was released in England. It received tepid response from the public but *Melody Maker,* saw signs of promise in Supertramp. "Dozens of copies of this disc keep arriving by every post," wrote a *Melody Maker* writer. "Are they trying to tell us something? Well, first off, congratulations to the singers - you hear every word. It brings back memories of Procol Harum in their "Salty Dog" days - all hands on deck etc. But there the resemblance ends. A brisk, sparkling epic, with exceptionally well-recorded drums and saxes, make Supertramp sound like a promising team."

But meanwhile back at the studio, the band was going over some string arrangements with Richard Hewson, who then had given some rough ideas about what they wanted and some backing tracks and tapes to take home. One day, the band walked in and there was a 30-piece orchestra in the studio with Richard conducting. Though the string parts were tightly woven into the structure of the material, they were an embellishment that added significantly to the overall sound of the album.

The concept for an album cover was also being bandied about with the same eye to detail that marked the rest of the preparations for the release of *Crime Of the Century*. They brought a graphic artist by the name of Paul Wakefield down to the studio and had him listen to all of the songs so that he would have a better idea of the overall concept and direction the band was taking with *Crime Of the Century*, already decided on as the title of the LP because of its strength as a song and the fact that it was the last track on the album.

Wakefield went away and pondered a number of design ideas before returning to the studio with some rough sketches. The first graphic concept that he showed to the group was a set of bars, with hands behind them, set in a street gutter. Another was a sketch of a teddy bear with its insides hanging out. Out of the two they much preferred the idea of the bars, feeling that a disemboweled teddy bear wouldn't go over particularly well with the SPCSA (The Society for the Prevention of Cruelty to Stuffed Animals). With that settled, Wakefield went back to the drawing board and further refined the idea of the bars in different settings. When he came back, the one that appealed to the group the most was the set of bars with hands behind them floating in a star-studded night sky.

From there, Wakefield went into an art studio and had the bars made and did all the superimposing. The stars were actually holes punched into a black piece of paper with a light behind them. The art direction was handled by Fabio Nicoli.

Unfortunately, the *Crime Of the Century* LP was to be a single cover rather than a fold out which affected the total impact of the concept. The back cover of the album has a picture of Supertramp looking skyward. If it had been a fold out cover, the band would have been in one corner looking up at the floating bars rather than staring into space. The top hats and tails that the group is holding rather than wearing are meant to represent the trappings of civilized society. The image of hands grasping the bars floating through space needs little explanation. (*Crime Of the Century* did in fact become a fold-out album jacket later in their career when it was released as part of a special Audiophile Series by A&M Records.)

Crime Of the Century was released in September of 1974, with a full page ad in *Melody Maker* proclaiming: "Supertramp - Crime Of the Century. The promise achieved - a massive delivery...puts everything else away." If you are looking for unpretentiousness in a record company promotion office you'd better take Sherlock Holmes, a couple of good hunting dogs and a high-powered magnifying glass. Pretty weighty stuff this. Hype aside though, for the most part, the music press in England agreed with the record company's enthusiastic declaration.

Derek Jewell of the *Sunday Times* called *Crime Of the Century*, "...striking musically and in the philosophy it states, takes a very unexpected final turn."

Sounds raved: "There comes a time when you listen to an album and think, 'Christ, this band is going to be bloody big.' It's just a positive feeling bout the whole thing. Think of Genesis, the Beach Boys and various heady influences along with a smattering of Floyd and you have a basic idea of what the Tramp are about.

"Everything on their album is excellent - the production, the musicianship and the material. Loosely based on a concept (which I haven't figured out yet) this album takes you through a journey of musical and lyrical excursion. If you thought it was impossible to create something refreshingly new, give this band a listen."

Fred Dellar of the British music paper *New Musical Express*, was likewise impressed: "Own up - you'd written Supertramp off, hadn't you?

"To tell the truth, so had I. Their first album, which appeared in 1970, was a good enough effort, though I doubt if, saleswise, it did enough to keep Herb Alpert in bedsocks for a week.

RED HOT TRAMPS!

SUPERTRAMP take a giant step towards rock 'n' roll stardom this month when they hit the road for their first headlining British tour. But success has been a long time coming. The band was formed in 1971 but it was only two months ago that the album, "Crime Of The Century" made the MM chart — and that was their first hit.

And, suddenly, Supertramp have become hot property. Peter Bowyer, who is promoting the band's upcoming tour, commented: "I've had my eye on Supertramp for some time.

"Their concert at London's Victoria Palace in December was a sell-out and I believe they will enter the Yes bracket as one of Britain's major groups. They will break 'through in a major way in 1975."

The original Supertramp line-up folded in 1973, after two years without success. "I saw them just before the break-up and, from the two albums they had already made, I knew they had tremendous possibilities," said Dave Margereson, head of A&R for Supertramp's record company, A&M.

The new band includes three members from that original line-up — Richard Davies (keyboards), Roger Hodgson (guitar, piano) and Dougie Thomson (bass) — together with John Helliwell (saxophone), formerly with Alan Bown, and Bob C. Benberg (drums), previously with Bees Make Honey.

Pictured above, from left, are Roger, Dougie, Bob, John and Richard.

The tour starts at Sheffield City Hall on January 23, followed by concerts at Leeds Town Hall (24), Birmingham Town Hall (26), De Montfort Hall, Leicester (27), Manchester Free Trade Hall (29), Newcastle City Hall (30), Edinburgh Usher Hall (February 1), Kings Theatre, Glasgow (2), Oxford New Theatre (6), Brighton Dome (7), Guildford Civic Hall (8), Bristol Colston Hall (9), and Plymouth Guildhall (10).

Tickets for all the concerts will cost £1 — and they guarantee holders a reserved seat.

After the British tour, a series of American concerts are planned for the spring.

Melody Maker
JANUARY 4, 1975   12p weekly   USA 60 cents

teen toons

DISC TOP THIRTY SINGLES

#		Title	Artist/Label
1	(5)	OH YES YOU'RE BEAUTIFUL	Gary Glitter, Bell
2	(3)	YOU'RE THE FIRST, THE LAST, MY EVERYTHING	Barry White, Pye
3	(1)	GONNA MAKE YOU A STAR	David Essex, CBS
4	(9)	YOU AIN'T SEEN NOTHING YET	Bachman Turner Overdrive, Mercury
5	(4)	JUKE BOX JIVE	Rubettes, Polydor
6	(6)	PEPPER BOX	The Peppers, Spark
7	(2)	KILLER QUEEN	Queen, EMI
8	(10)	TELL HIM	Hello, Bell
9 ▲	(17)	MY BOY	Elvis Presley, RCA
10	(12)	TOO GOOD TO BE FORGOTTEN	Chilites, Brunswick
11	(8)	HEY THERE (LONELY GIRL)	Eddie Holman, ABC
12	(14)	WILD ONE	Suzi Quatro, Rak
13	(19)	LUCY IN THE SKY WITH DIAMONDS	Elton John, DJM
14	(11)	MAGIC	Pilot, EMI
15	(7)	NO HONESTLY	Lynsey De Paul, Jet
16	(13)	HOW LONG	Ace, Anchor
17	(25)	SHA LA LA	Al Green, London
18 ▲	(30)	GET DANCING	Disco Tex and the Sex O'Letts, Chelsea
19	(16)	JUNIOR'S FARM	Wings, Apple
20 ▲	(—)	TELL ME WHY	Alvin Stardust, Magnet
21	(27)	GOODBYE NOTHING TO SAY	Javels (Nosmo King), Pye
22	(20)	COSTA FINE TOWN	Splinter, Dark Horse
22	(15)	LET'S PUT IT ALL TOGETHER	Stylistics, Avco
24	(—)	LONELY THIS CHRISTMAS	Mud, Rak
25	(—)	IRE FEELING (SKANGA)	Rupie Edwards, Cactus
26	(18)	EVERYTHING I OWN	Ken Boothe, Trojan
27	(—)	UNDER MY THUMB	Wayne Gibson, Pye Disco Demand
28	(28)	ZING WENT THE STRINGS OF MY HEART	Trammps, Buddah
28	(24)	WHERE DID ALL THE GOOD TIMES GO	Donny Osmond, MGM
30	(—)	ONLY YOU	Ringo Starr, Apple

Two titles tied for 22 and 28

BUBBLERS

- SOUND YOUR FUNKY HORN — K C And The Sunshine Band, Jayboy
- DANCE THE KUNG FU — Carl Douglas, Pye
- THE BUMP — Kenny, RAK
- HEY MR CHRISTMAS — Showaddywaddy, Bell
- I CAN HELP — Billy Swan, Monument

PERSONALITY TOP TEN

DAVID ESSEX chooses his current favourites

1. IRE FEELING (SKANGA) — Rupie Edwards, Cactus
2. JUNIOR'S FARM — Paul McCartney and Wings, Apple
3. HOW LONG — Ace, Anchor
4. DREAMER — Supertramp, A&M
5. YOU AIN'T SEEN NOTHIN' YET — Bachman Turner Overdrive, Mercury
6. OH YES YOU'RE BEAUTIFUL — Gary Glitter, RCA
7. MY BOY — Elvis Presley, RCA
8. SHA LA LA — Al Green, London
9. MAGIC — Pilot, EMI
10. KILLER QUEEN — Queen, EMI

ALBUM TOP THIRTY

#		Title	Artist/Label
1	(1)	ELTON JOHN'S GREATEST HITS	Elton John, DJM
2	(2)	ROLLIN'	Bay City Rollers, Bell
3	(3)	DAVID ESSEX	David Essex, CBS
4	(6)	SHEER HEART ATTACK	Queen, EMI
5	(4)	SMILER	Rod Stewart, Mercury
6	(7)	TUBULAR BELLS	Mike Oldfield, Virgin
7	(8)	CAN'T GET ENOUGH	Barry White, Pye
8	(14)	COUNTRY LIFE	Roxy Music, Island
9		ELVIS 40 GREATEST HITS	Elvis Presley, Arcade
10	(9)	DAVID LIVE	David Bowie, RCA
11	(13)	STORMBRINGER	Deep Purple, Purple
12	(14)	BAND ON THE RUN	Wings, Apple
12	(10)	JUST A BOY	Leo Sayer, Chrysalis
14	(17)	THE DARK SIDE OF THE MOON	Pink Floyd, Harvest
15	(28)	SHOWADDYWADDY	Showaddywaddy, Bell
16	(23)	MUSIC EXPLOSION	Various Artists, K-Tel
17	(12)	PROPAGANDA	Sparks, Island
18	(11)	IT'S ONLY ROCK N ROLL	Rolling Stones, Rolling Stones
18	(21)	THE SINGLES 1969-73	Carpenters, A&M
20		BACK HOME AGAIN	John Denver, RCA
21	(16)	THIS IS	The Moody Blues, Threshold
22	(19)	STARDUST	Soundtrack, Ronco
23		MOTOWN CHART BUSTERS VOLUME 9	Various Artists, Tamla Motown
24	(27)	MUD ROCK	Mud, Rak
25	(24)	CRIME OF THE CENTURY	Supertramp, A&M
26		A STRANGER IN MY OWN BACKYARD	Gilbert O'Sullivan, MAM
27	(25)	THERE'S THE RUB	Wishbone Ash, MCA
28		HERGEST RIDGE	Mike Oldfield, Virgin
29		LET'S PUT IT ALL TOGETHER	Stylistics, Avco
30		WARCHILD	Jethro Tull, Chrysalis

SOUL TEN

1. (6) I CAN NEVER SAY GOODBYE — Gloria Gaynor, MGM
2. (—) YOU BELIEVE IN ME — Executive Suite, EMI
3. (1) GET DANCING — Disco Tex, Chelsea
4. (2) SHA LA LA — A Green, London

U.S. TOP 20 SINGLES

1. (3) WHEN WILL I SEE YOU AGAIN — Three Degrees, Phil Int
2. (5) KUNG FU FIGHTING — Carl Douglas, 20th Century
3. (1) I CAN HELP — Billy Swan, Monument
4. (6) ANGIE BABY — Helen Reddy, Capitol
5. (9) CATS IN THE CRADLE — Harry Chapin, Elektra
6. (7) DO IT (TILL YOU'RE SATISFIED) — B.T. Express, Roadshow
7. (4) MY MELODY OF LOVE — Bobby Vinton, ABC
8. (11) SHA LA LA — A Green, Hi
9. (2) WISHING YOU WERE HERE — Chicago, Columbia
10. (12) YOU'RE THE FIRST THE LAST MY EVERYTHING — Barry White, 20th Century
11. (15) JUNIOR'S FARM — Wings, Apple
12. (14) YOU'VE GOT THE LOVE — Rufus featuring Chaka Khan, ABC
13. (8) LONGFELLOW SERENADE — Neil Diamond, Columbia
14. (8) YOU AIN'T SEEN NOTHIN' YET — Bachman Turner Overdrive, Mercury
15. (20) ONLY YOU — Ringo Starr, Apple
16. LAUGHTER IN THE RAIN — Neil Sedaka, Rocket MCA
17. (19) I FEEL A SONG (In My Heart) — Gladys Knight and the Pips, Buddah
18. (18) I'VE GOT THE MUSIC IN ME — Kiki Dee Band, MCA Rocket
19. (—) AIN'T TOO PROUD TO BEG — Rolling Stones, Atlantic
20. (—) BOOGIE ON REGGAE WOMAN — Stevie Wonder, Tamla Motown

—December 7, 1974

And the band's drummer had a breakdown about that time - which really didn't help much.

"Between then and now there's been just one album and a few changes in personnel.

"And that my friends, is the history of Supertramp. Not impressive huh?

"But now they've come up with Crime Of the Century, which, whisper it not, has the makings of a monster.

"I suppose a lot of the credit for the band's apparent transformation must go to producer Ken Scott, who (Bowie fans please note) has surpassed himself on this occasion and shaped an album that grips you right from the first eerie sound of Richard Davies' mouth-harp.

"But the more I play Crime - and that's pretty often - the more I appreciate the strength of Supertramp's writing and playing abilities.

"The band have at last come up with something they can justifiably call Supertramp music - seventies rock that stems from many sources but funnels down to an almost orchestral sound that's impressive, though not pretentious.

"Among the high-grade tracks are Bloody Well Right, which moves from a meditative piano lead-in, punctuated by 'heavy' blasts, into a solid little bouncer, basically simple but schemed in diverting manner; Rudy, a song about a guy who's on a figurative train to nowhere, which comes replete with some Paddington sounds that would have pleased Izzy Brunel mightily; and If Everyone Was Listening, a pretty ballad and Beatle-ish in so far as Helliwell's clarinet gives it that kind of aura.

"Right then - fair dues to all those involved in *Crime Of the Century* - to Ken Scott, a mention in the New Year's Honour List, to Richard Davies, a gold-plated Steinway...and a fair share of the spoils to A&M, who have for so long placed confidence in the band."

The first single to be released from the LP was "Dreamer," and John Peel, a radio personality and music journalist of no small importance in Britain, had a few kind words to say in his column in *Sounds*:

"Taken from the LP Crime Of the Century - an LP which all good SOUNDSers will already regard with near superstitious awe. Supertramp are a skillful and imaginative ensemble and they should have had a hit with their fairly recent Land Ho! single. Electric piano dominates here, the vocals are high and light, occasionally ornamented with strong harmonies - hold on, Mr. and Mrs. Blackburn have just appeared on TV to prevail upon me to purchase gravy. I feel one of my attacks coming on. - Sorry, where was I?

Ah, yes, harmonies. Jolly good too. Supertramp runs through several changes here, all of them appealing, and, although this is scarcely going to be big, big, big in the discos, it should rivet lovers of good music whenever they gather together."

In an interview for *Melody Maker* during this period, John Bonham of Led Zeppelin raved about the Crime album.

But not everybody was overwhelmed with *Crime Of the Century*. Allan Jones reviewing the LP in *Melody Maker* was as caustic as battery acid:

"Cosmic alienation strikes again. So stand back out of the way because this, I fear, is nothing less than a concept album. And to make things worse, it's a confused and finally inept attempt at making some kind of statement. God, somebody has wasted a lot of money on this album. It sounds expensive, with all kinds of neo-symphonic aural fireworks. Trouble is that none of it really works. Supertramp have obviously been listening too closely to a lot of other people's records and have failed to reconcile the influences derived from other sources with a single inspiration of their own. They seem content to work on the most superficial of levels, hoping that if there's enough going on, the listener will somehow be convinced that he's being confronted with something quite extraordinary in terms of musical vision. They try everything in an attempt to conceal the essential vacuum behind the music on this record. Ken Scott ensures that it's all fairly listenable, for at least one run through. After that you're on your own. And it's not a particularly pleasant trip. The band themselves aren't without a certain amount of ability. It's just that their amibition has overtaken that ability. They lack a decent lyricist, or somebody to actually take control of their ideas and mould them into something more articulate. All they've succeeded in doing with this album is to consistently undermine any potential they might contain, and coming on like failed applicants at the Dmitri Tiomkin School for Overblown Movie Soundtrack Writers."

A viewpoint of *Crime Of the Century* actually being a concept album from beginning to end would arise a number of times in many of the written critiques of the LP during this period.

"Any album should be a concept just in the simple fact that if you make an LP, you should think about how it's going to affect the listener from beginning to end," Roger once stated. "We whittled down the number of songs we were going to put on the album from fifteen that we could have recorded. We decided on the eight, found the best order for them and the best balance. The first time that we heard the album right through, we were blown out because we didn't really know exactly how well it was going to work. It's a thought provoker, not a concept album. All eight songs were written at completely different times and put in an order where one song could answer the one before if you wanted it to. It's up to the listener."

Rick Davies concurs: "...it's not like *Tommy* or *Journey To the Centre Of the Earth* which are real concept albums. This is just a complete work which takes you from the beginning of side one to the end of side two. The numbers are linked in that they just sort of flow together. But it wasn't originally thought of as anything more than having the songs slightly related for good listening."

Adds John: "Reviewers seem to have gotten a far clearer idea of what it's about than we have. As we were piecing the material together, we could recognize the great connection between songs, but we didn't realize exactly what we'd done until we heard all eight of them, one after another."

About four years after the release of *Crime Of the Century*, Roger looked back on the LP and felt that, of all the songs that he and Rick wrote during that period (and for all intents and purposes, it was the last time that they would write together though all Hodgson/Davies songs continued to be co-credited), the title track of *Crime Of the Century* was most enduring for him.

"Probably that song will live forever," Roger stated. "I've had more people come up to me and say that that song touched them more deeply than any other. That song really came together when we were living together at Southcombe and just eating, sleeping and breathing the ideas for the album. The song just bounced between Rick and I for so many weeks before it finally took form.

"There were really some pretty dynamic forces at work when we were recording the album *Crime Of the Century*, some of them beyond our control. So many things fell into place both subconsciously and unconsciously. When we first heard the album from beginning to end, we were blown away because we hadn't realized what we had created. We knew that the songs individually stood up but we didn't know what the sum total would be.

"School" was one of the songs that Rick and I collaborated on. It was my song basically but Rick helped me with a lot of the lyrics. The piano solo was his, and it worked really well.

"Dreamer" was the result of a home tape that I did once. I had this tape recorder on which you could overdub and sing on top of your voice, over and over again. I just sang this song one day and put a lot of effects on top of it, as well as other voices. When we came to record the song for the album, we just copied the home tape. If you listened to the rough tape, you can tell exactly where the finished song came from."

Shortly after *Crime Of the Century* was released, Ray Townley of *Rolling Stone* broached the subject of the exact nature of the "crime of the century." At that time Roger suggested: "I think it has to do with what everybody is asking: 'What the hell is going on in this world?' A lot of people have asked if it's the Nixon thing, but it has nothing to do with Nixon."

David Harris of *Sounds* caught the band at one of their concerts during this period and had this to report: "A triple measure of Supertramp in a little over twenty-four hours is a pretty heady experience. They, alas, will tread one of two paths - the lonely to obscurity or the gilt-edged to recognition.

"The latter way is nothing more than they deserve. For Supertramp is a band for connoisseurs and right-minded people; a lovely combination of innovation and fresh tingle.

"I'm not sure that they were fully appreciated at gigs in Plymouth or Torquay on successive nights. The telly provided a third fill - as though to reaffirm their consistency - when the *Whistle Test* featured them.

"Plymouth was a revelation. Utilising a huge backdrop to a spotlight flooded stage,

Supertramp were superduper, playing nearly everything from Crime Of the Century. It was a date that gelled like peaches and cream - much to do with the use of four keyboards - ordinary and electric pianos, an organ and a string machine that was beautiful as a kind of refined mellotron.

"The band relied exclusively on an eloquence and elegance so sadly missing in this misshapen electronic age. They did Dreamer, the new single, Rudy and lots more from Crime.

"After being off the road for an infinitely long time, it is good to welcome Supertramp back. Supporting them was the excellent Steve Ashley and a more-superior film of Mike Oldfield's *Tubular Bells*."

John Walker of *New Musical Express*, was at their gig in Preston in December of 1974.

"By playing a confident game of musical chairs on stage, the band make total use of facilities. With keyboards dotted all over the place, they need all the manpower they can get.

"They get it from the two members who double on keys as well as the contributions of Richard Davies sitting beneath a yellow parasol and trapped on three sides by organ, electric and grand pianos.

"Their perfect example of instrument-sharing methods came when windman John Helliwell, calmly holding a chord on the mellotron-mimicking synth, realised an oboe solo was due and was expertly relieved from Keyboard duties by Roger Hodgson who obviously considered That Vital String Sound more important than his guitar at that particular point. They didn't leave any audible crack in the music.

"Helliwell is the band's answer to Paul Madely wandering roundstage like a lost child discovering new things - striking bells, clapping into mikes, harmonising, and on odd occasions, trying-out the instruments assigned to him. He even feels it his duty in spare moments to conduct his two fellow-singers, Davies and Hodgson.

"Dougie Thomson never appears bored by the generally-uncomplicated Supertramp bass duties which are often confined simply to laying notes over the bass-drum beats.

"Davies, who begins most of the numbers on his own, is just as at home singing to his own piano playing as he is blasting along with the rest of the band.

"There seems to be more happening now for a band who deserved more credit than they ever got for past efforts."

After seeing the band at Reading University, Brian Harrigan of *Melody Maker* reported:

"...Roger Hodgson on piano and vocals, impressed particularly. He has an expressive voice and an interesting keyboard style.

"The overall impression of the band's set was that they still have something to learn about breaking down the barrier between performer and audience.

"Obviously, their type of music is hardly the framework in which a band could enter the 'I want everybody to clap your hands and stomp your feet' syndrome...

"At the end one had the impression that Supertramp have been influenced by the later work of the Beach Boys.

"The idiosyncratic drumming - and that's meant to be a compliment - the repeated open chords on piano and harmonies, all put one in mind of say, Holland or Carl and the Passions. And that is quite a compliment."

One thing that the band has felt very strongly about from the outset is encores. Often when the band didn't come out for another once around, the audience actually started booing them.

The witty Mr. George Bernard Shaw once commented on encores this way: "In every average audience there is a certain proportion of persons who make a point of getting as much as possible for their money - who will encore, if possible, until they have had a ballad for every penny in their shilling, with the orchestral music thrown in as a makeweight. There is also a proportion - a large one - of silly and unaccustomed persons who, excited by the novelty of being at a concert, and dazzled by the glitter and glory, madly applaud whenever anyone sets the example. Then there are good-natured people who lend a hand to encourage the singer. The honest and sensible members of the audience, even when they are a majority, are powerless against this combination of thoughtless good-nature, folly and greed.

"There are doubtless many concert-goers who encore from a genuine desire to hear over again a performance which has just given them great pleasure. One cannot help wondering whether their consciences ever ask them why they permit themselves to do at a concert what they would be ashamed to attempt elsewhere. Imagine the sincere encorist consuming a Bath bun and asking the confectioner to give him another for nothing because the first was so nice.

"It is, however, of little help to dwell on an abuse without suggesting a remedy. The simplest one would be to send round the hat with an announcement that as soon as the singer's terms for one song had been collected, the encore would be complied with."

Roger Hodgson told Brian Harrigan of *Melody Maker* back then: "We don't do encores. We feel that we have a balanced set which comes to a natural conclusion.

"Even if the audience was demanding an encore, we wouldn't do one. That's not because of a 'couldn't care less attitude' because we care a lot about the audience. We try to communicate with them and set up a bond between them and us.

"We don't do encores because we feel by the end of the set we have done our best. If we could be sure that we could find something that would be a natural improvement on the last number of the set then we would do it.

"But there would be no point in playing an encore just for the sake of it."

John would later comment: "It happened a couple of times, when we have actually agreed to an encore, that when we went off, the crowd has actually refused to leave. After fifteen minutes with the houselights on, they were still stamping and chanting. The guys feared a riot, so we went back on and did some more. I think that they're terribly overplayed. The audience has come to accept the fact that you go off and then you come back, because everybody does. It's not a bad thing but you can see it's so planned sometimes."

At one point in their touring in England, Supertramp had a visitor from A&M Records in the U.S. who would be the catalyst for charting the band's course across the Atlantic to North America.

"An A&M representative by the name of Pat Luce came to a gig we were playing in Brighton because she'd heard a lot about us," recollects Bob. "I think she came over for Jerry Moss because she was the head of special projects at the time. This little dynamo comes whipping into our organization, saw a few shows, and the next thing we know, we are on our way to America.

"There was a hub-bub at the time about how we couldn't go as a supporting act because of the amount of work it takes for us to set up our sound and lights so the decision was made for us to go on the road in America as headliners, a place where at that point, nobody had heard of us."

A&M were very helpful in solving part of the problem by injecting enough money into the band to allow them to bring their whole show over to America and absorb the losses as they broke new territory in the various cities that they played in the U.S. and Canada.

As the album had started moving up the charts in England, Dave Margereson, the person who was instrumental in arranging for the band's re-signing to A&M Records and one of the people most responsible for their current good fortune, left the security of his job as A&R Director of A&M in England and stepped into the quicksand world of artist management. He guided Supertramp's career under the auspices of his newly-formed company, Mismanagement. Only Margereson would have dared to tempt fate with a name like that.

"We all thought he was mad," remembers Bob. "Here we are with this LP that we think is good but who knows? He's got what seemed to us at the time to be a cushy life. His life was entertaining people and he wanted to drop that and be our manager! You've got to hand it to him because he saw it from the beginning. I was really impressed because he actually knew Joe Cocker."

When Supertramp arrived in America, they did quite a bit of promotional things like visiting radio stations and doing interviews but also, they had to face the harsh reality of headlining concerts in an area of the world where they were not a big draw. That minor detail was dropped in the lap of Frank Barcelona the president of Premier Talent, one of the biggest booking agencies in America.

The first concert that they played in the U.S. was in Milwaukee and the demand for tickets was less than spectacular.

"I think we had pre-sold about 200 tickets, so we all took to the streets and just gave out tickets," says Dougie. "People couldn't believe it. It's amazing how outrageous someone gets when you try to give them something for nothing. If you charge them a buck for it they'll take it, but if you give it to them for nothing, they figure there's a catch. I think we ended up getting a crowd of about eight or nine hundred on the night of the gig. That story repeated itself through many places in North America on the first tour. The second time out, those numbers multiplied ridiculously, so it worked, even though it cost us money."

Bob remembers a similar situation in Indianapolis.

"I remember standing outside the Circle Theatre the first time through, giving out tickets. You'd walk up to somebody and literally say, 'What are you doing tonight?' They'd answer, 'Ah, nothing. Why?' Then you'd tell them that you were in the band playing at the Circle Theatre that night. They'd ask the name of the band and when I told them, they'd usually say no thank you.

"Our second gig in Buffalo drew quite a large crowd because apparently a local deejay had been playing the flip side of "Dreamer" which was "Bloody Well Right," and it had become a hit in that area.

"I knew something was starting to happen because I would phone my friends in L.A. and they told me, 'Hey, we hear your band on the radio and even down at the local Licorice Pizza record store. They've got a poster of your LP. You guys must be doing pretty good.' I'd tell them I didn't know. I was just out there hitting things every night."

As part of their three and half week, 25-city tour of the U.S. and Canada, Supertramp made a stop-over in New York on April 11, 1975 for a concert at the Beacon Theatre. They headlined, with Chris de Burgh opening for them, and a reviewer for *Cashbox* magazine, one of the major American-based music trade papers, saw much potential in their debut performance in New York.

"Playing to a decent sized house in New York, Supertramp performed an unusual set, featuring tight arrangements and fine musicianship and vocals," he wrote. "A bulk of the material was from the A&M group's latest Crime Of the Century LP and was characteristically subtle in shifts of dynamics and tone colors. Particularly impressive were the technical aspects of the show, with expert gimmick-free lighting tied closely to musical changes and one of the cleanest sound systems to hit the concert road recently.

"The show opened dramatically with an umbrella emanating a reddish glow and covering a band member playing an eerie tune on harmonica, seguing into an effective band entrance. The major difficulty with the remainder of the performance, whose best moments included the new single Bloody Well Right and Crime Of the Century, was a tendency towards undue repetition of certain patterns. A humorous interlude was provided by one member's (Rick) solo piano rendition of A, You're Adorable, performed in a jacket lit with Christmas tree lights, a less subtle example of the sense of humour that this outfit maintains throughout much of their show. The final tune - Crime - featured a 2001-like film of space, out of which the cover art from the LP (hands gripping jail bars) gradually grew larger throughout the piece. Supertramp is a major attraction in

England, and the apparent success of this first U.S. tour points to similar recognition in the not-too-distant future on these shores."

One of the real surprises for the band on their first trip to Canada, was the reaction that greeted them in Montreal and Toronto. Montreal was their first stop and they drew over 4000 rabid fans, mostly French-speaking, to their concert at the University of Montreal.

"That was probably the first time that I saw all the lighters and matches in the arena," says Bob. "The curtains opened in Montreal and there was this panorama of lights. I remember getting the drum roadie to check it out because he's stationed down behind the drums and can't see anything. He stood up and just freaked. We were both there at the drums just turning to jelly and we hadn't even started yet."

The band played Massey Hall in Toronto, an important date in that the head office of A&M Records (Canada) is located there. Their meeting with some of the people that worked at the company was to be momentous in a number of different ways later in the bands career. It was here that they met Charly Prevost, the person who handled publicity on a national level for the company. The band took an instant liking to him, and shortly after he would join the management team - first as the band's road manager, and later working with the management company in Los Angeles on the overall coordination of their career.

It was just prior to this period, before the tour began in Milwaukee on April 4, 1974, that I first met Supertramp one rainy Sunday afternoon at the A&M publicity offices that were located in a house on Madison Avenue in Toronto. Over a cup of tea, we talked about their first impressions of America and it amuses me now to see that so new was our acquaintance, that in my notes, I refer to Rick as "beard," Roger as "other" and Dougie as "Scotty". Our conversation went like this:

Rick: One of the things that we noticed in America was how they are always going on about 'product.' That's the way record people refer to albums. To them it's 'product.' Last night we went to this dinner with deejays and it was just mind-boggling the way they go on about 'product.'
Dougie: You're not from a radio station, are you?
Writer: No.
Dougie: Good. I didn't want to slag off radio stations if you were an announcer or something. (He laughs) Radio seems to be just geared for advertising here. We heard about stations taking singles and speeding them up to about 48 or 49 rpm so that when people listen to another station which is playing the song at the regular speed of 45, they didn't sound as good. Imagine that escalating, one going faster than another until everyone sounds like Mickey Mouse.
Writer: Well, it's not unusual for radio stations to edit singles for their own use either.
Rick: He's not joking!
Dougie: They've chopped about with our single "Bloody Well Right." We have a repeat going at the end and they've cut that off and they've also edited the beginning. In England, it's just as it is on the album but the deejays here have been sent an edited copy. Television is just mind-boggling as well. The adverts come in without any warning. You'll be watching a show and all of a sudden the ad is there and you think it's just a change of scene in the show. It's hard adjusting to it from England because they only have one commercial channel and when the ads come on, there is a definite break. It's only once every quarter of an hour. At the end of a show here they have a lot of adverts and then they come back just for the credits.
Writer: But overall, how do you like America?
Roger: It's a bit mind-boggling.
Rick: More for the people than the actual place.
Dougie: New York was very busy, but we quite liked it. The food is unbelievable. It's so abundant. You get twice as much as you can eat on a plate.
Roger: A lot of it is the worst food I've had anywhere. It's not natural.
Writer: Have you tried a McDonald's over here yet?
Roger: I don't eat hamburgers. I wouldn't eat them.
Dougie: Roger's a vegetarian...
Roger: I wouldn't set foot in there anyway...
Dougie: The rest of us eat meat and...
Roger: We've been eating in good restaurants.
Dougie: I've had one really good steak and steak's are an American specialty really. The rest of the food's been rather synthetic. It's all well-presented and all that.
Roger: All the vegetables and lettuce and so on are just too good to be true.
Rick: The frightening thing is, I'm sure you can see it in the people.
Roger: It reflects the way everything is. Everything's false. We've been feeling the effect of it in the last four days. Maybe it has got something to do with the routine we've been keeping.

Roger shows his soccer form.

Dougie: No, it's lack of exercise, I think.

Roger: Yeah, lack of exercise and eating all that junk. You can feel it.

Rick: We saw quite a heavy campaign on TV about it. It was absolutely mind-boggling. Sixty percent of all Americans over 35 have got some sort of coronary heart trouble.

Writer: How much of your own strong beliefs are packaged in the music on *Crime Of the Century*?

Rick: The point of the album is for people to sit down and just enjoy it, not take any gospel from it.

Roger: The only thoughts that a listener provokes are his own so he's finding out about himself. I'm really conscious of a new generation that is coming up after ours. They're just being palmed off with shit, most of them. That's a shame to watch because after all the acid generation and all that energy that was happening then, just seems to be going out the window.

Rick: In the last four days, it's just been incredible. Somebody said, 'Everybody wants to be a star.' And it's true. They all want to be known, you know. Radio people keep talking about their listener figures or I handed so and so our album. They're all looking for an identity of some kind. Perhaps they feel lost or something. There are so many people there.

Roger: That's the whole thing about western civilization. Being a success.

Rick: I've only seen a few days of it so perhaps it's a bit stupid to talk.

Roger: When our manager, Dave Margereson, comes over here to America, he used to play a game called 'Spot the subtlety.' I can see what he means now. It's unbelievable.

Dougie: England's really had its run as far as music and everything. I should think that about six years ago you could have come to America and played a lot of crap and got on really well if you were British.

Roger: England is very lethargic at the moment. Maybe complacent is the best word.

Rick: It's either lethargy or riots.

Writer: Obviously you're formulating plans in your head for the next album?

Dougie: The tunes are all in our heads for the next album and we're all ready to go in and record them. (Roger looks over at Rick and laughs)

Dougie: We rehearsed last month so we're ready to go in and record.

Roger: Our big problem is that the songs are there but we've got to go and finish them off. Finishing off a song can take months.

Rick: Let's just say we're going into the studio because it's booked.

Roger: We're not supposed to say where we are going to record.

Dougie: Anyway, it's going to be in L.A.

Writer: What about the stage show? Are you going to shoot off rockets and things?

Dougie: No it's a little more subtle than that. We've got lights but they blend in with the music.

Roger: If rockets had something to do with the music, then we'd use them.

Dougie: We just perform the album with some new songs in the middle and finish up by playing "Crime Of the Century". There are no encores. It's a complete piece of music and you can't really come back and do things after that. It'll kill it. As long as the public knows the reason that we are not doing encores. It's not because we think we're big time. It's because we've thought about the whole thing, that we don't do it. We have to get that across.

Rick: Chuck Berry apparently needs another thousand dollars before he goes on for an encore.

Dougie: We're different and people will eventually come to accept the fact that they've seen a proper concert and I think we should stick to that.

Late in the tour, the band finally hit Los Angeles where they played at the Santa Monica Civic Centre on April 25, 1974. It had been a concert that the whole band had looked forward to but perhaps no one was more excited than Bob who was returning home after a long stay in England.

"I had left L.A. and now I found myself back," says Bob. "I was not so much glad to be back but here I was at last, employed in an up-and-coming band in the area where I spent a lot of time jumping from band to band looking for the right combination."

"It was awesome how vast America was," adds Dougie. "I remember what a thrill it was finally getting to L.A. We played the Santa Monica Civic and it was packed. It was a real buzz."

Harvey Kubernick, a correspondent for *Melody Maker* in America, was at the Los Angeles concert and he sent this report back to England.

"For Supertramp, this was a very important gig. One that could either make or break them in the U.S. Back in seventy and seventy-one, they had been local underground favourites, but could not raise enough enthusiasm throughout the country to substantiate a trip across the

Atlantic.

"They then faded into obscurity with nary a word until last fall when Crime Of the Century was released. It took off slowly but has been selling well during the last few months.

"So the stage was set. Here was a band, previously almost unknown, headlining at the prestigious Santa Monica Civic on their first tour. Only two other groups, Wizzard and Nektar, have done this recently. Wizzard passed the audition and Nektar bombed. But the Civic was sold out, and one could feel the electricity of the crowd when opener Chris de Burgh left after an unexpectedly short set.

"The lights went out and moments later the audience roared its recognition to the opening lines of School. The band seemed a bit nervous at first with keyboardist Rick Davies hitting a few clunkers but after the thunderous applause for Bloody Well Right their second offering, the group seemed to realize that the crowd was with them all the way.

"The band's three focal points, Davies as leader, reedman John Helliwell as spokesman, and vocalist-guitarist Roger Hodgson as the star, have a lot more to offer an audience than any one-man-band, while drummer Bob Benberg (a local lad making his homecoming) and bassist Dougie Thomson give the band a solidarity and punch the previous editions of Supertramp seemed to lack. Benberg was particularly impressive. His drumming is fundamentally solid yet aesthetically interesting, and he was miked so well it sounded almost as if he was hitting the heads of the mikes.

"It's the Davies-Hodgson compositions, however, that are the lifeblood of Supertramp. Davies has a simple, old-fashioned keyboard technique, while Hodgson's flowing guitar lines and beautifully fragile falsetto vocals on songs like Dreamer, give the band a real flair. Meanwhile, Helliwell provides the finest saxophone melodies I've heard since Keith Gemmel was blowing for Audience several years ago.

"The visuals worked well throughout the set and the performance was clean, tight and highly professional. Bloody well right, indeed!"

Richard Cromelin of the *Los Angeles Times* was also on hand.

"Having foregone such standard preliminary rituals as playing to a few devotees at some club or second-billed to Edgar Winter, Supertramp took over the Santa Monica Civic Friday for its first local appearance. It turned out to be one of those unanticipated knockouts, the sort of thing that would renew anyone's sagging faith in the unpredictability of rock 'n' roll.

"Supertramp's name must immediatley be added to the litany of '60s-style pop bands (along with 10cc, The Raspberries, et al.), by virtue of its captivating, winsome melodies, quality singing, command of dynamics, sense of song structure, beautifully layered arrangements and overall inventive approach. The band reminds one of 10cc at several points along the way, which means that the basic point of reference is prime-time Beatles.

"The British quintet is remarkably adept at moving from light, happy refrains to full, somber, quasi-orchestral segments, from spare voice-and-piano passages to surging ensemble rock 'n' roll. The entire show is marked by a rejection of indulgence and ponderousness and by a flawless feel for space and motion. Every solo is integrated into the entirety of the song, each song into the highly unified set.

"Supertramp's presentation is crisp and to the point, displaying excellent taste in its employment of effects (notably the clean stage setting, superb lighting and a judiciously utilized short film) and in the modest but sufficient establishment of individual personalities.

"Its music is immediately charming, then varied and sophisticated enough to maintain the spell, and its surface accessibility is enriched by the intriguing nature of its many esoteric aspects. The audience response was appropriately ecstatic, not only approving the performance but revelling in the awareness that, finally, something new is in the air."

The band members at this point had gotten little apartments in Venice Beach on the outskirts of Los Angeles. They were ready to set out on the road again to make the most of the excellent reaction that they were starting to get in concert. Unfortunately, this momentum was about to hit a snag. On a drive from Seattle to Vancouver for a concert, they took a short break on the side of the highway. Roger and Tony got out of the car and in their high spirits, started putting on a clown act.

"Roger and Tony got onto a tree stump and were fooling around," remembers Dougie, who apparently caught the whole incident on his super 8 camera. "I was playing with the zoom lens on my camera and I panned over to pick them up in the viewfinder just as they fell off the thing. Roger put out his hand and went, 'ouch!' so I panned down his arm to his hand. We just laughed about it and didn't think anymore of it. We got into the car and resumed the drive to Vancouver. We stopped again and we could see

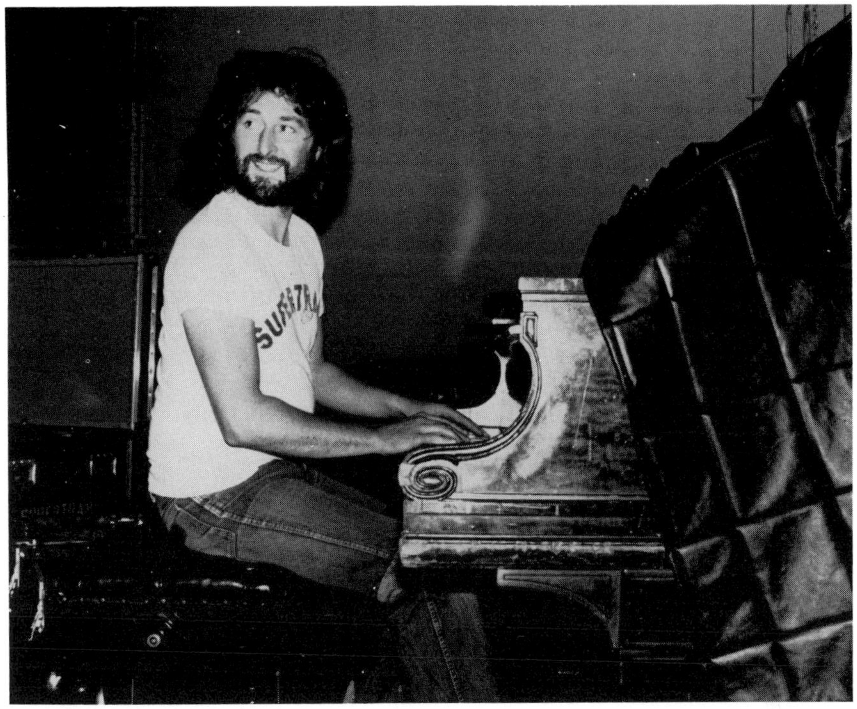

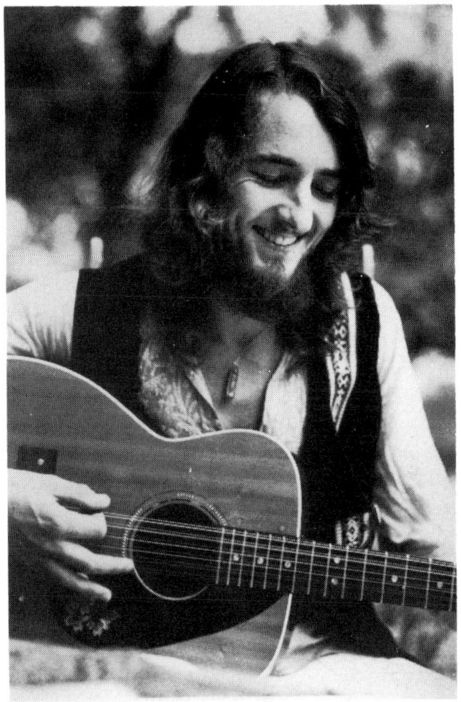

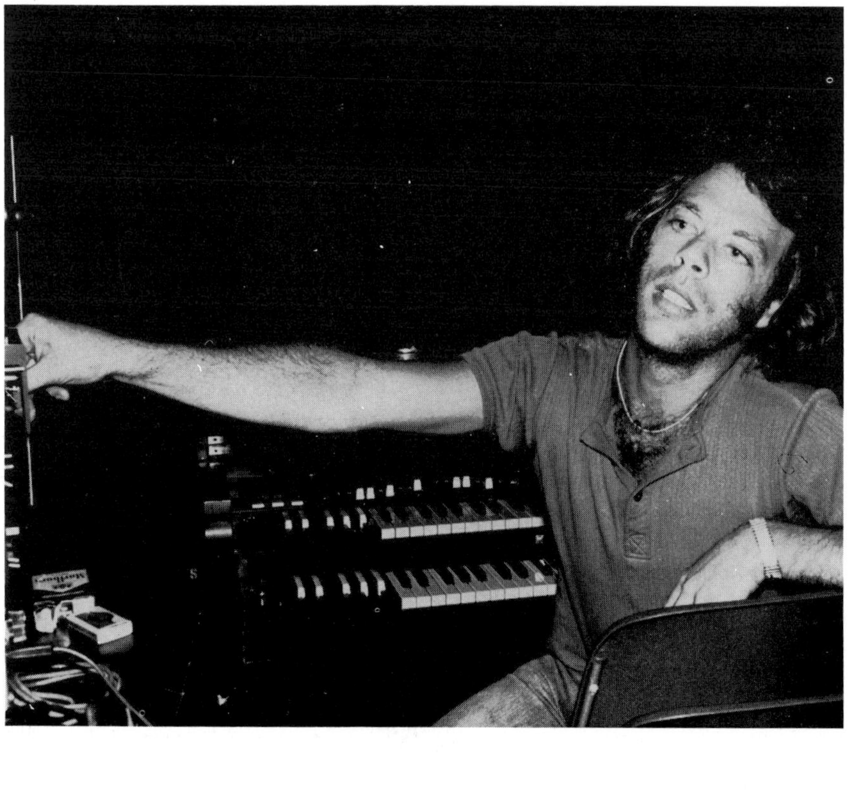

Roger sitting there holding his wrist - the great expanding wrist. By the time that we got to Vancouver, that hand was twice the size of the other one. We actually saw the film back later and laughed about it."

It wasn't funny at the time though. The rest of the band's dates were cancelled and they headed back to Los Angeles.

"When Roger fell off the log and fractured his thumb, it really put the muckers on the whole thing," says John. "Bloody Well Right" was just starting to get going as a single and the reaction to our concerts was great. We went back to Venice Beach and hung around for a while, waiting for Roger's thumb to heal. We did our one and only television show, *The Midnight Special* with Roger in a cast that he had painted pink and a long sleeved shirt so that nobody noticed."

The pressure was starting to build from the record company for them to start recording another album. The band figured, as long as they were sitting around, they might as well start on it. There were some tunes ready to record but there was no real concept of a finished album. Ken Scott was in Los Angeles and they went into the studios on the A&M lot in Hollywood, located almost on the corner of LaBrea and Sunset Boulevard. That was the summer of 1975.

John had left his wife Christine in England, very pregnant, at the start of the tour, and he couldn't be there when their son Charles was born in April of 1975. When it became obvious that they were going to be spending more time in the U.S. than originally planned, she came over with the baby to live with John down in Venice Beach.

"We had to go up to Hollywood to record," says John, "so I bought a bicycle and I used to ride it 15 miles each way to the studio every day. I wasn't in shape when I started that but after a while it made a big difference. When we all lived at the beach, within walking distance from each other, we'd get up, go straight down to the ocean and have a dip, sit around in the sand for an hour or so, have breakfast and then head out to the studio."

"It was a much more fragmented thing," according to Dougie. "We did half of it in Los Angeles and then went back to England and finished it there. Career-wise we had to get it out and get back on the road. The pressures started to mount and Rick wasn't very happy during that period. Crime had really just started to pick up momentum when Roger screwed up his hand and ideally we would have liked to continue touring and built it to a bigger record."

In the autumn of 1975, the group packed up and moved back to England with producer Ken Scott to put the finishing touches on *Crisis? What Crisis?* at Ramport Studios.

Tony Stewart, a writer with *New Musical Express*, did an interview with Rick and Roger in January of 1975 after seeing them in Sheffield, and went back to his typewriter to author a rather snide, but comical, overview on the two writers behind Supertramp. Under the Headlines "Successful Pop Group acknowledges absolute ignorance!!" "Supertramp 'We dunno' bombshell rocks Rock World!!" and "Journalist stymied!!" he wrote:

"The album Crime Of the Century is Supertramp's own sardonic, and at times downright derisive, brand of existentialism. Accordingly, one would expect its two main creators to at least be a little bit contemptous of life. One might even be unsurprised were they to launch into entertaining invective, not to speak of out-right cynicism.

"But Richard Davies and Roger Hodgson are not a bit like that. Davies is a stolid, laconic individual, prone to long bouts of silence, obviously bemused by the current interest Supertramp are creating with their chart success. Hodgson, by comparison, is garrulous, bright and helpful in manner - though he, too, is pretty non-commital, especially when discussing the band's music.

"But if they decided to become a pair of comedians one suspects Davies would be the strong, silent type, and Hodgson his eager-to-please side-kick. They'd be a Wow with a Routine.

"As it is they have no routine at all and this particular interview was the proverbial blood-out-of-a-stone job. No matter.

"On stage, though, the situation is somewhat different - as Supertramp's successful opener to their current tour at Sheffield City Hall illustrated. There it's perfectly fine to look a shade mean 'n' moody, and of course, there are the other visual (not to mention musical) distractions, notably chirpy saxophonist John Anthony Helliwell smacking his lips together so that they sink into his face like he'd forgotten to slip his dentures in.

"Towards the back of the stage there's the wasted-looking and slightly dour Scots bassist Dougie Thomson, who sways in time to the music like a cork floating gracefully on water. To his right, the short-haired, reserved American

Jerry Moss of A&M.

drummer Bob C. Benberg.

"Musically their act - based to a great extent on the Crime album - is excellent. Although they have an introverted image, they pace their set smoothly, running through a multitude of instrumental changes, as they steadily gain momentum, eventually attaining a suitably climactic conclusion with their title track of the elpee. **(Tell me more, Tone - Ed.)**

"Supertramp are a truly remarkable band. **(Thank you - Ed.)**

"As I've already mentioned, neither gentleman is prone to making profound (or come to that, very interesting) statements about their album, and although Hodgson would prefer not to play to audiences at all, they both have an altruistic approach to performing and recording.

"'You play music you enjoy,' comments Davies, 'and hope people are going to enjoy that.'

"That, in itself, is at loggerheads with the apparent content of the album - which seems to me to be a perceptive view of society, nevertheless expressed in disdainful terms.

"But all that remark prompts from Davies is, 'Maybe. Yeah.'

"'I tell you what,' offers Roger. 'Reviewers have got this album much clearer than we have. We didn't actually realise exactly what we'd done until we heard all the eight songs one after another.

"'When I first heard it I was blown apart. I don't know why...but it does have that effect on you.'

"What is it all about though?

"'Really I think that's what it's about,' Roger says, referring to my assessment of the set. 'If it means that to you...'

"'...That's the crunch, isn't it??' adds Rick. **(Maybe. Yeah. - Ed.)**

"What does it mean to you?

"Roger: 'It means something completely different to me than it means to Rick.' **(Go! Go! - Ed.)**

"Rick: 'What it means to me is feeling right about everything that's going down at that time you're doing it. That's all it means to me.' **(This is really fantastic - Ed.)**

"Which means absolutely nothing to me, so again I ask him what he means. There's a long pause as he considers this question.

"'That the lyrics are right for the song,' he eventually answers. 'That the arrangements are right for the song. That the mood's right.'

"'What does the album as a whole mean to you?' Roger asks of Rick.

"There's a minute's silence finally broken by Roger.

"'It's a difficult question,' he says. **(You might say that, by now - Ed.)**

"Eventually, it's discovered Crime was not intended as a concept album; that the two musicians are too close to it to rationalize its content; that they are pleased with its commercial success - 'because it enables us to carry on.' That both musicians are exceedingly bloody vague.

"'It's dangerous to be unvague,' comments Rick. 'It's the only way to be. Who could you quote, a musician, someone you respected, who wasn't vague?'

"I name a musician. But Rick only comments. 'That approach doesn't appeal to me.'

"'I think we could tell you what each song is about,' Roger says helpfully. 'As a concept, which wasn't particularly planned. I think the reason it's taken off is half the music and half the sign of the times, really. Crime Of the Century really does go with what's happening in the world today.'

"Surely by saying that you are admitting you have a view as to what Crime is about?

"'Well I do, but Rick doesn't. I think the way the world's going is everyone's responsibility. That's what the last track, which Rick wrote, says.'

"Other questions probing their philosophy are sadly unfruitful, and are greeted by blank expressions. So it only remains to ask just how they feel after so many periods of despondency. Are they now optimistic?

"'I don't know,' responds Rick. (I should have been ready for that, but I wasn't.) 'I'm really convinced,' he continues, 'somebody's going to get ill and screw the whole thing up.'

"He laughs.

"So you're the eternal pessimist?

"'Yeah. I go to sleep thinking about fuses and things. It does tend to get to you after a while and it becomes very hard to relax.'

"There's another long pause as we all ponder on this statement.

"Each of us reluctant to commit ourselves further.

"I politely wait to see if another bombshell will be dropped.

"The atmosphere is, dare I say, electric with anticipation.

"'It's a great band,' Roger comments, almost to himself. 'It's got a load of potential. How much of that potential is allowed to get out, only time will tell.'

"I don't know about that either." □

Supertramp
CRISIS? WHAT CRISIS?

CHAPTER NINE

Rick looks on as Roger works at the mixing board.

It had been Ken Scott who had wanted to return to England to mix the *Crisis? What Crisis?* album and put the finishing touches on recording some of the songs. The pressure was on and from Los Angeles Supertramp worked their way back to the east coast playing a number of concerts in Texas, up the east coast of America, ending up in Montreal.

Close to 12,000 people showed for that Montreal concert, the largest crowd the group had played to up to that point. It was a gratifying testimony to just how big the band had become in Canada. At that point, the *Crime Of the Century* album had sold well over 100,000 copies in that country and was just the start of a long-standing love affair between the land of the maple leaf and Supertramp.

Back in England, the group were to start a world tour in Britain, beginning in mid-November of 1975. It was now September and there was much left to do in the recording of *Crisis? What Crisis?*

"Crisis was not an easy album to make because we were kind of unsure about what to do," remembers Bob. "We knew we had got our foot in the door and had tasted a little bit of success with *Crime Of the Century*. It was at the point where we were either going to be one-hit wonders or we were going to be able to pull off another good album.

"After the rehearsals in Los Angeles, we went into the studio with Ken Scott with a loose idea of what the songs were going to be instead of having a demo of the LP from beginning to end. We formulated the album in the studio and, in fact, at one point, we had to stop production, go away and cook up a couple more tunes. It was during that period that "Ain't Nobody But Me" was written.

"The atmosphere was also different recording in Los Angeles. In London, it's usually rainy and dismal outside so the climate makes you want to stay inside, makes you want to socialize and get your head down into doing the music. In Los Angeles, it's kind of hard to pull yourself off the beach and go into the studio. We'd all kind of dwindle in at different times, having been in the sun too long and often already tired. It was our own fault really. The atmosphere was just different. We were recording the album on the main lot of A&M Records so there was all this hub-bub and business being conducted just outside the studio door. We put up a note that said, 'Closed Session' but, of course, everybody thought that it didn't mean them. So everybody would be dropping in to see how the lads were doing.

"We finally pulled out of there and went back to London to finish off at Ramport Studios and Scorpio Studios in the autumn of 1975. But even in England, things were a bit helter skelter. Roger would be doing vocals at one studio while they were doing mixes at another. I think it shows a little bit in the album."

Now, given this set of circumstances, you might think that the album title *Crisis? What Crisis?* was inspired by the group's current state of mind, but actually, it was the return to England and the continuing economic crunch they found there that brought forth the idea for the album's title and subsequent graphics.

"That same year we returned home, things really started to turn downhill in England," remembers John. "We'd been living away from it for a while and weren't really aware of the situation. When we went back it seemed that all of the newspapers in England had headlines in the paper each day that had some mention of a crisis. It was Rick that came up with the name *Crisis? What Crisis?* and one day, when we were sitting around Scorpio Studio, he came in with this sketch of a guy in a deck chair under an umbrella with all this chaos going on around him."

Based on this idea, Fabio Nicoli, Paul Wakefield and Dick Ward designed the final art work for the album cover.

It was not an easy design as more than thirty photographs were put together with the model that appears on the front cover sitting in the deck chair. A number of trips were made up to Wales to take pictures of factories and miners' houses before the cover took its final form.

When the cover was finished, Dave Margereson took Fabio Nicoli out for supper one night to celebrate. Nicoli, best described as a bon vivant with over-the-top tendencies, was a perfect match for Margereson, who on occasion has been known to let his eccentricities hang out. They chose a Russian restaurant for dinner and for some reason, as yet unexplained given that the moon wasn't full that night, they decided to try all 16 brands of vodka available on the drink list. The result was predictable and somewhere between the borscht and the beef Stroganoff, Nicoli raised his glass, cried out, "To Supertramp," downed the contents and flung it at the wall. The glass shattered and was forgotten about by the shocked waiters who were at this point treating the table with fearful detachment.

They finished their meal and as Nicoli was making a brave attempt to stand up, he slipped and fell, cutting his wrists on the broken glass on the floor. He had to be rushed to hospital where they had to almost rebuild the muscles in his wrists. He was incapacitated for a few months after the incident and fully recovered.

During the recording of Crisis, a couple of journalists visited the band in the studio as they struggled to put the finishing touches on the LP. It was October of 1975 and the beginnings of a British tour were looming ever closer in mid-November.

Chris Charlesworth of *Melody Maker* was the first visitor and it was immediately evident to him that Supertramp was not the type of band to let something as insignificant as deadlines bend their perfectionist tendencies out of shape.

"Supertramp are not people who rush things," wrote Charlesworth in a flash of understatement. "Neither do they court publicity or move before they are quite ready. With all the dedication of nuclear scientists, they have been piecing together their next album, carefully planning every stage of the process.

"For the last month they have been at Scorpio Studios behind the Capital Radio building in London's Marylebone Road, or at EMI's Abbey Road, supervising the addition of string parts to this very special fourth album.

"You'd have to stay late to catch them though: the five musicians arrive late and stay much later. The album's not finished yet - or it wasn't last week - and it hasn't even got a title, other than The Crisis Album, to which it is being referred.

"They're a quiet bunch, Supertramp. They're an arranged band in the British tradition, relying on precise routine in their stage act, just as they do in studios. Little is left to chance, which partly explains the considerable delay since the galaxy of publicity that suddenly hit them early this year.

"Unmixed, incomplete tracks are difficult to judge, even with a dab hand like engineer Ken Scott working the board, but the next 'Tramp album sounds impressive, even in its fledgling state. As a rough guide, it's less severe than its immediate predecessor, freer and looser, with more attention paid to melodies than strict musical virtuosity and complex arrangement.

"Is the follow-up, another concept recording as 'Crime' appeared to be? 'We've been trying to explain that 'Crime Of the Century' wasn't a concept album,' said Roger Hodgson. 'It was just that it went together so well on stage that it

Charly Prevost (left) with Doug Chappell, national promotion director for A&M Records of Canada.

appeared to be.'

"'They may say this is a concept,' said Davies, 'but this is much less planned, purely because we haven't had as much to do to it as we had with Crime. It will flow from beginning to end, though, in much the same way.'

"But the new album won't form the basis of a stage act as 'Crime' did. 'We won't be doing this album straight through,' said Hodgson. 'It'll be a mixture of material on this new tour, sort of half old and half new.

"'Recording for us is a painstaking process, though. With Crime we had no standard to keep up at all, as we didn't know how good it was going to be or how successful, and now we have. With this album, we have to take everything a stage further and try to get into unique vocal sounds which means experimenting.'

"Davies admits that the success of 'Crime' came as something of a shock to the band after their previous lean years. 'You're in a different sort of league. But as soon as the initial thing is over, and it only lasts for about ten minutes, you just carry on as before.'

"'With Crime, we were in a farmhouse for three months rehearsing and we knew it before we went into the studio,' said Hodgson. 'But with this album, we didn't have any rehearsal time because of the schedule which has been very crazy ever since. It was almost lucky that I broke my hand in America because that gave us a month off.

"'We're not a band that can do an album in a month. It's a really big project for us.

"'Sometimes recording can get depressing because it takes an awful long time these days,' said Davies. 'It may be better technically, but it's changed an awful lot. We're all pulling in the same direction but it's just frustrating that we can't get the sound that we want.

"'We find that we can get a guitar sound in one studio, but when we go to another, it sounds completely different,' said Hodgson. 'We started the album in Los Angeles which was a complete fiasco. We were there for two or three months recording and for the time and money we spent, we didn't get much out of it. But since we came back over here, it has got back together again.'

"Then John Helliwell arrived, and he proved slightly more talkative than his two colleagues. 'The new album is not quite so strict as Crime. The chords are sweeter and not quite so dramatic. This album is a result of knowing each other better through being on the road together.

"'Some of the songs are amalgamations of things that have been knocking around for the last five years before I was even in the band.'

"'We've always been a touring band and over the years things have built up that we have written,' said Davies. 'Until this band, we haven't been in a position to record these things. The other band wasn't really good enough, but this one gelled so we can play these songs now.'

"'We tended to find that playing Crime on stage got a little heavy which was why I played the piano and looned around a little half way through,' offered Helliwell. 'This next set won't be quite the same because we'll probably sandwich both sides of Crime around some new songs.'"

Pete Makowski of *Sounds* visited with Roger and Dougie during a very hurried lunch hour before they went back to recording.

"While Marc Bolan could be seen strutting into the London Weekend buildings amidst a flock of staring faces, parading his green rinse, just around the corner two figures entered Scorpio studios in a blur of anonymity. There are no screamers waiting to greet the arrival of Supertramp's Roger Hodgson and Dougie Thomson, only producer Ken Scott and a couple of tape operatives to remind them that they have eight more tracks that need mixing for their forthcoming album.

"With a tour beginning in November there's also a new show to rehearse, which might explain why Hodgson and Thomson looked positively exhausted. Supertramp have been on the road continuously since the release of Crime Of the Century - an album which brought this band from obscurity to the limelight in a short space of time. Now the band find themselves back in the studio with a new baby to nurse.

"While Hodgson prepared a cup of dandelion and honey tea, Thomson told me some stories about their recent trip to America: 'It was really weird at one gig. We were sent a bunch of black roses by these guys who came to the show dressed in suits with their faces painted white. They said that the album had changed their lives.'

"It's also an album that has changed the Tramp's lives and after three years of writing, rehearsing, recording and performing the album, the group feel relieved to be able to have new material to integrate into their live performance.

"The new album is entitled Crisis? What Crisis? 'We thought of thousands of names,' said Hodgson, 'in fact, if there are any bands looking for album titles, we've got loads. We were going to call it Second Offence but that sounded quite

Roger and Rick in a
pensive mood.

Dougie and Roger at
the recording console.

Bob Siebenberg

meagre compared to something as spectacular as Crime Of the Century.

"As opposed to Crime, where the songs were co-written by the two songwriters of the band - Hodgson and Rick Davies - this album features individual compositions. 'Rick and I see life from opposite sides of the spectrum. That's why our songs balance out so well on an album. We've got some ideas for weird links between the tracks but the biggest problem with this album has been the time. Most of the songs on this album are at least a year old. Some of them are four or five years old. But I don't think we'll do another album like this, we'll take a long break before we go into the next one. We've wasted so much money because we weren't really prepared for this album and we have to write things in the studio and that's why we've been so long doing it.

"'We really look forward to presenting the new material on the road. Before, we just took the whole album out on the road but this time we look at it as a selection of songs, so we can pick and choose and we'll be able to think of the live thing as a set.'"

A single, "Lady," was released from the album and then at the end of November 1975, *Crisis? What Crisis?* finally saw the light of day. As far as press reaction, Rick seemed to have some misgivings about how this current project would be received. "I expected a slightly harder time with this album," Rick commented. "I expected it to be good for Crime and not for this one. But the press are funny. There's only a few people that you've got confidence in as far as what they think and sooner or later they blow it for you by saying something completely silly."

As "Lady" hit the streets, *Melody Maker* did the Critic's Tarantella on it. "No relief from the dreadful here. Supertramp remind me of Simon Dupree and the Big Sound for some obscure reason. There's a similar inflated quality about Lady which recalls Dupree's Kites. This single is from Supertramp's forthcoming album *Crisis? What Crisis?* and indicates no real development from Crime Of the Century or their last single, the surprisingly successful Dreamer. Ken Scott's production is typically extravagant and manages to construct a facade of continuity upon the curious arrangement with lurches in too many directions for comfort. The vocals are strident and lack any real strength. A possible hit on the strength of Dreamer, but it deserves only moderate success."

Tony Stewart of *New Musical Express* was the first to express an opinion on *Crisis? What Crisis* in print. "Supertramp aren't the type of recording band who demand immediate attention; they're very much an acquired taste," wrote Stewart. "Either you learn to consider them performers of rather enticing songs, or merely regard them as anonymous musicians making equally anonymous music.

"In appreciating their songwriting skill, however, it should be remembered that quite honestly they're hardly excellent musicians.

"They have limitations, and although they tend to work within these confines there are moments, particularly Richard (sic) Hodgson's irritatingly brittle guitar solos during Sister Moonshine, when they unsuccessfully attempt to step outside them.

"John Helliwell, generally a very fine musician with an assortment of excellent ideas, is also guilty of this with the particularly bland sax contribution to Ain't Nobody But Me.

"Of course, these inconsistencies are symptomatic of a brash confidence, which if channelled properly makes for a better feel on the material. Well this at least seems the case with pieces like Lady and Another Man's Woman.

"But, leaving aside these limitations, Crisis does find 'Tramp broadening out instrumentally, allowing, for instance, both Helliwell on clarinet and the superb Dougie Thomson on bass to develop themes more extensively.

"And yet, the album is, like Crime, based on Davies' and Hodgson's panache for writing good melodies, with Bob C. Benberg providing his distinctive rhythmic feel to most of them, something best illustrated by the tracks Sister Moonshine and Another Man's Woman.

"As an album, Crisis is generally excellent, both vocally, instrumentally, and a Ken Scott (and Supertramp) production.

"The album concludes on a high with the beautiful love song Two Of Us, which also, incidentally alludes to the determination of the Davies and Hodgson partnership to carry on, despite their earlier disenchantment."

Geoff Barton of *Sounds* saw the LP this way: "It's a hard task to follow and improve upon an album of all-round excellence like Crime Of the Century, but Supertramp have done it. Just. Crisis? What Crisis?, while being rather less of an opus, less of a conceptual whole than Crime, still hangs together remarkably well.

"What I find most admirable about Supertramp is their ability to slowly build, then enlarge and elaborate upon a theme with (by today's standards) the minimum of instrumentation. Over Roger Hodgson's unusual Woolworth-like organ plunking sounds, themes are explored to their utmost. Lady, for example, the band's latest single, starts inoffensively and unremarkably, yet grows in stature progressively, to eventually take on almost operatic quality. Very much like Dreamer, admittedly, and not without Harleyesque chants and vocals phrasing, it's the most obviously commerical song on the LP. It seems likely that it was cut with the intention of it being the single.

"The rest are less immediate. Crisis begins gently, with distant car horns beeping and far away whistling impinging on your consciousness like the first sounds of dawn. Whispered vocals also encroach, conjuring peaceful images, reminiscent (of all people) of the late folk duo Tir Na Nog.

"'Easy does it, easy does it,' sings the voice, appropriately, and the whole thing becomes altogether more spritely, taking on a more postive direction. The number leads into Sister Moonshine (louder, more intense, with fluid guitar) almost before you know it, and the LP finally begins to shape up.

"Supertramp with impeccable care, layer small sound over small sound, which coupled with a precise sense of musical dramatics, makes the album wide-ranging and complex.

"Finally, a choir sings, strings weep, vocals become breathless and a cinema soundtrack quality pervades.

"Same holds true for side two: while being less concise, the songs are both elaborate (Two Of Us) and witty (Poor Boy - slinking Thirties stuff with muted trumpet/duck quacking and overall antiquated feel).

"Good as this album is, I have a feeling that Supertramp may have overreached themselves this time around and exhausted current ideas. They'll have to come up with something rather different next time, I suspect, to ensure continued success.

"But meanwhile, here's an album with which, as the title suggests, you can lock yourself away in a room and forget about Chrysler troubles (how am I going to get that body panel for my Hillman Imp?), about bombs in London, about England's poor football performances and other similar crises, and simply enjoy."

In America, the three highly influential music trade papers, gave there typically bland, yet postive, appraisals of *Crisis? What Crisis?*

Billboard commented: "The second LP from the group that went high into the charts their first time around, is another mix of rock, jazz and electronic instrumentation with unusual blends of lead and harmony vocals. One of the few groups with anything really new to offer to surface in the past few years, the quintet thrives on intricate arrangements, moving the vocals in and out almost as if they were instruments of their own. Several cuts sound almost 50ish which is fun. But the majority of the set is their own unique sound."

Wrote *Cashbox*: "One has always taken it for granted that music backed by electronic keyboards and other manner of things to come technology must be rooted in the future. Supertramp on Crisis? What Crisis? proved that it is possible to musically have the best of both worlds. Blues, as well as folk and latent pop influences spearhead a very clear outing as various vocal diversions and some fine horn excursions play effectively off the aforementioned keyboard runs."

Record World jotted: "An album that deserves attention on the basis of title and cover alone, yet the Crime Of the Century boys have the musical chops to back it up. The originality of their basically raunchy sound is largely in John Anthony Helliwell's wind instruments. Provocative are Sister Moonshine and A Soapbox Opera."

It was during this period that a new personality was brought into Supertramp's inner circle. Charly Prevost, whom the band had met during their first North American tour while he was working as head of press and publicity for A&M Records in Canada, joined the band as their tour manager. Prevost, a fully-bilingual French-Canadian, penned the band's biography for A&M Records on the release of the Crisis album and pretty well summed up the group's state of mind on the eve of their first major tour of the world.

"For Supertramp, much has transpired in the year since the acclaimed Crime Of the Century was released," wrote Prevost. "Success has made demands on the group members unequalled in their careers to date. How they have survived this initial rush and how they are facing the future is really all that these words can be about.

"They cherish and nurture the aura of mystery that's as much a part of Supertramp as Crime Of the Century is. By their own choice, the individuals in the band reveal little about themselves other than their musical backgrounds. Rick Davies' and Roger Hodgson's music is the vehicle they use and is what initially

Bob and Rick talk to fans backstage.

brought them all together - but it couldn't sound the way it does were it not for the combined efforts of the rest of the band: Dougie Thomson, John Anthony Helliwell and Bob C. Benberg.

"My initial personal contact with them was at the start of their first North American tour. I was a publicist for A&M in Canada at the time. Crime was spreading like wildfire across the country and the band was due in for four concerts. It was with anticipation that everyone was awaiting their arrival. Whatever apprehension I might have felt beforehand quickly dissolved into a genuine and growing warmth once we'd met.

"My experiences with Supertramp are relatively recent, but I've been a part of good and strange times - sometimes simultaneously. More than 15 people travel together and contribute to the show. Hassles are varied and constant and keeping tabs on it all creates a strange sort of pressure that could ruin the wrong people. Manager Dave Margereson, the first A&M employee to join Supertramp, contributed his personality and energy to make it all work. Dave was the A&R person for A&M in Britain until about a year ago when he was asked to become manager. His character has greatly contributed to Supertramp's collective state of mind.

"One of the more obvious aspects of the state of mind is Supertramp's constant drive for improvement. Recently Dave and I became ecstatic over a particular concert and couldn't wait to share our feelings. Little needed to be said: the sound had been superb, the sellout crowd had left wanting more, but the dressing-room scene was very sombre following the show. The group felt that they could have played with more inspiration and that the PA could have sounded still better! This scene has been repeated with great frequency in recent months - perfectionists are never satisfied.

"This feeling - not surprisingly - is apparent in the studio as well, where even more care is taken to make sure everything sounds right and fits in the correct place. Recording a 'Tramp album is a long and arduous process. The creation of this finely textured and inventive music requires a great deal of painstaking attention to detail. Although it was hardly mentioned openly, when the sessions for Crisis? What Crisis? began early this summer, all participants were conscious of Crime's shadow over this new project.

"Enter Ken Scott, master producer and honorary 'Tramp. His intimate knowledge of the studio again lent itself to properly defining the new songs. Aside from the immaculateness of the performances and production, one can't compare Crime with Crisis - the gap in emotions is too wide. Crisis has captured another absorbing side of Supertramp."

With *Crisis? What Crisis* in the stores, it was time for the band to look forward to the most extensive concert tour of their career, an excursion that would take them through Britain, Europe, the U.S., Canada, Australia, New Zealand and Japan over an eight month period between November of 1976 and June of 1977. □

KODAK SAFETY FILM 5063
→4A →5 →5A →6 →6A →7 →7A
8 →8A →9 →9A →10 →10A →11 →11A →12 →12A
→18A →19 →19A →20 →20A →21A →22 →22A
23 →23A →24 →24A →25 →25A →26 →26A →27 →27A
28 →28A →29 →29A →30 →30A →31 →31A →32 →32A
33 →33A →34 →34A →35 →35A →36 →36A

CHAPTER TEN

Roger tests equipment.

Even while Supertramp was putting the finishing touches on *Crisis? What Crisis* in the studio, the crew had moved out to the Shepperton studios, about 30 miles from London. The group would follow for last minute rehearsals and preparations for the British leg of the world tour that was to kick off in Bristol on November 12.

Shepperton is one of England's biggest movie studios and while the Supertramp crew was working in one area of the complex, *The Omen* starring Gregory Peck and Lee Remick, was being shot in another. Watching the shooting of a fifteen second segment of the film, in which the dog gets impaled on a picket fence, must have been partially inspirational for the crew. That fifteen seconds took one whole day to shoot (complete with the drugging of the dog, of course). It was the kind of eye to detail that the Supertramp crew were coming to appreciate in their current circumstances.

They had turned their section of the studio into a regular workshop where sets were being built and equipment - seventy-five percent of it brand new - was being tested. There was also the small matter of figuring out how much room all this gear was going to take up so that they had some idea of what sort of truck would be needed to transport it.

This would be a crucial part of the planning because the efficient packing of the equipment in the truck could save hours in loading and unloading as well as protect the equipment from damage caused by any rattling around of loosely-packed gear.

When all the equipment cases finally arrived, Russel Pope drew lines on the floor to represent the dimensions of a forty-foot truck so they could see exactly how they could pack the gear most effectively. They stacked it and restacked it until the jigsaw puzzle seemed to fit together. Apparently everything was set for the arrival of the truck.

When the group finally came out to Shepperton, the crew would spend the day working and then the band would show up for rehearsals at about seven or eight in the evening. The crew would leave and get a well-earned rest. The group had not played together since they headlined one day of the Reading Festival on August 23 almost three months prior and now there were only ten days of rehearsals before they set off for Bristol on November 12.

The hall in which they rehearsed at Shepperton had a stage about sixty feet square. This was the area where a lot of the audio was done for the most of the movies made at

Shepperton. The band would play until five in the morning each day usually to an audience of one - Charly Prevost, their newly acquired tour manager. Charly would sit in the middle of the cavernous auditorium in an armchair. "I was overwhelmed. I was quite new to all of this and while the band was playing I'd suddenly realize that I was the only one in the world listening to them. The only time that my reverie was broken was when Bob would stick his hands out from behind the cymbals and make a motion for me to roll a joint. I'd roll the joint, take it on stage and pass it around then go back to my front row seat."

One of the few outside visitors to drop by during that hectic period before the start of the British tour was a journalist by the name of Leonard Setright. The band first met him when he had come to the Reading Festival in the rain that summer and been very inquisitive about the group's sound system. An interview was arranged and one Sunday, Setright showed up at Shepperton.

He was about forty-five years old and a former World War II ace who was currently the automotive editor for *Penthouse* magazine. He certainly stood out in the Rock and Roll landscape around the studio dressed in grey flannels, a jacket with a flower in the button hole, shirt, tie, polished black shoes and every hair in place looking as dignified as a wealthy country squire who wrote only as a hobby. Setright had been sent all of the Supertramp albums earlier and seemed quite conversant with the band's music and asked many questions about the meaning behind some of the songs. The odd thing was that he didn't bring a note pad, a pencil, a cassette machine or anything with which to record the interviews. He just came in, watched everybody, including the crew, work for four or five hours without saying a word and then went to each member of the band and the crew and asked them what they did, what led to it and what they were doing at that moment. Soon he was ready to leave and they took him to the main gate. He was riding a 1200cc Kawasaki motorcycle that he was testing for an article. As they watched, Setright got into a yellow motorcycle suit and helmet, started up the motorcycle, and was off giving everybody the old RAF salute as he zoomed off down the road.

Everybody talked about Setright for months after their meeting with him because he was such a unique character. He was the type of writer who tries everything and then goes away and writes about it. Rock and Roll was new to him and he looked at it the same way as parachuting, flying a glider or deep sea diving.

The evening of November 10 came and the next morning eighteen people along with twelve tons of equipment were set to leave for Bristol for the beginning of what would be an eight month world tour.

Besides the five band members, the characters in order of disappearance included:
Dave and Cass Margereson, Managers
Charly Prevost, Tour Manager
Russel Pope, Sound Technician and Mixer
Tony Shepherd, Lighting Designer
Ian Trevor Lloyd Bisley, On Stage Monitor Mixer
Brian Kelly, Electrician and Lighting
Steve O'Connor, Stage Manager, Electrician and Lighting
Kenny Thomson, PA and Stage Set-up
Ken Allardyce, On Stage Set-up and Guitars
Norman Hall, On Stage Set-up and Drum Kit
Dave Connor, Transportation
Patrick O'Doherty, Transportation
Joan Armatrading with her back-up band, The Movies, accompanied Supertramp on their British and European tour.

November 11 (4:00 a.m.) - Charly gets a call from Russell. He's still at work with the crew at Shepperton loading the truck and not all of the equipment will fit into the one truck. The band is scheduled to leave for Bristol that morning so arrangements are hurriedly made to secure a second truck. Later that day, the entourage leaves London on the way to Bristol. Dave Connor is driving one truck and Pat O'Doherty is at the wheel of the other. The band and the rest of the crew are travelling by coach driven by Lenny, a non-member of the Supertramp crew, but a person who would become a much-loved and indispensable part of the organization in the weeks ahead. With a rousing send-off from the people at A&M Records in London the coach heads off to Maidenhead to pick up John and then presses on to Bristol for their first concert of the British tour.

November 13 - Arriving at Colston Hall in Bristol, the crew finds that because the trusses are triangular pieces of metal which are long and heavy, they have great difficulty in getting them through the load-in doors. The only practical solution seemed to be to take them in through the front doors but the manager didn't want to hear about it because he was afraid the equipment would scratch the marble steps. An impasse was reached until someone in the crew

Charly Prevost from his stint as Director of National Press and Publicity for A&M Canada 1974.

took the manager out for a coffee for a few hours. While they were gone they brought the equipment in through the front. The group played the concert that night and the consensus seemed to be that it didn't go too badly considering it was the first gig. Loading the gear out after the concert was a major operation and they didn't get finished until four in the morning. It also became obvious that they were going to have to replace the smaller truck with a larger one because as things stood now, the gear was loaded five layers thick. Meaning that as well as everything getting crushed, it was also very difficult to load and unload. By the end of the night the crew was very tired and swearing up a storm realizing that they had a 210 mile drive to Lancaster University that day for a concert that night.

November 14 - Arriving in Lancaster, the crew went immediately to the university to start setting up while the band checked into a little bed and breakfast hotel called The Mayfair in Morecambe, a few miles away from the gig located on the ocean. The concert that night took place in a very small gym packed to the pylons with avid Supertramp fans. It was an exciting night and a terrific gig all 'round.

The usual routine after a concert would see everybody return to the hotel and have a late supper at the restaurant but Morecambe was such a small town that there was nothing open by the time that they got back. Even the road crew who would normally have sandwiches, cookies, tea and milk waiting in enormous quanitities were out of luck. Charly, sizing up the situation, realized that the only source of food at that hour was the kitchen of the hotel in which they were staying. He slipped into the kitchen and made off with a side of ham, several yogurts and anything else he saw that you could chew and swallow. He distributed the food and smugly went off to bed. The next morning after breakfast, the lady asked him how he had enjoyed his little snack. Apparently she lived right behind the kitchen and had seen the whole thing.

November 15 - From Lancaster, it was on to Leeds University about 80 miles away. Russell had had what seemed to be a cold for a few days but when the group arrived in Leeds it was obvious it was a little more serious. The dressing room that night was in a cafeteria downstairs that had a number of booths. Bob, Rick and John were playing their ongoing game of darts in front of a specially built flight case that had clothes, an amplifier and other props in the bottom and a dart board built into the top. Laying in one of the booths was Russel, completely dressed with a coat, scarf and toque, wrapped in a sleeping bag and three blankets. It had not been an easy proposition to find a doctor to come out to the gig but Dave Margereson had located one who had prescribed some medication for what he had diagnosed as viral pneumonia. He also gave the ominous warning that if Russel didn't do something about his condition, he might never work again. Russel was the only sound person that Supertramp had, and though there were a lot of volunteers, there is only one Russel and he insisted on mixing the sold-out show that night. Though he was constantly on the verge of passing out from the medication and hot toddys he had been taking, when the concert started, Russel was behind the mixing board, bundled up in various pieces of clothing, sleeping bag and blankets with the doctor standing behind him in case anything untoward should happen.

Brian Harrigan of *Melody Maker* had come up from London to see the band at Lancaster and Leeds and had this to report: "They're quiet-spoken, reserved and have, with the exception of reeds-man John Helliwell, no stage presence. They recognize this and compensate with an extensive light show and judicious use of curtains, backdrops and similar visuals.

"And they attract the sort of audiences who will sit quietly during a song, mouthing the words but remaining still until the end when they erupt into roars of enthusiasm.

"Take a young man called Tim Easton, who caught the band at Leeds University. He's 19, a student of microbiology at the university and as staid as they come. He regards himself as a serious person and is a great fan of Supertramp. He was one of the few people to buy their pre-Crime Of the Century single Land Ho. He likes them because of "their thoughtful music." There's plenty in there to get your mental teeth into. It's intelligent music, he says.

"'I guess I don't really know who our fans are,' says Benberg. 'Some older people, a few little kids. We're hitting everybody in some way or other. Dreamer brought in the younger ones.'

"Singer/guitarist/keyboardist Roger Hodgson agrees. 'We got a letter from someone saying that Dreamer is their 18-month-old kid's favourite record. Somehow I don't think that's typical.

"'Polite audiences? You wouldn't have thought that if you'd seen us at Lancaster University last night. They were all up front

Rick at the dart board.

Ken Allardyce at Victoria Airport.

stamping out of time with the music. Then some idiot leapt on the stage and started screaming 'Mob Rule' down the microphone. I hope he wasn't a Supertramp fan.

"'Obviously, if you have a hit single, it's going to attract all kinds of people.' Including some who decided to do a Tarzan act on the band's curtains at Lancaster.

"'Ripped 'em to shreds, the silly buggers,' grumbles bassist Dougie Thomson. 'I don't want to see people like that in our audiences again. Fortunately we don't get them very much. In America we got a strange lot.

"'Some guy phoned our manager at eight in the morning after we'd come back to Britain. Phoned him from Chicago or somewhere. 'Get Rick and Roger on the phone,' he was mumbling. 'They changed my life. They're the only ones who know the meaning of it all.'

"'He said he'd call again but this time he'd reverse the charges because we could afford it. What a nerve.'"

"At Leeds University, they were only the second band to sell out this term. The other was Roxy Music.

"About 2500 students and outsiders crammed into the confines of the university hall to hear about 90 minutes of Supertramp music - and they loved every bit of it. They were quiet during the number, roared at the end and leapt to their feet for Dreamer like one of those high-speed films illustrating the growth of a corn field.

"The band weren't all that enthusiastic about the audience because they felt they were a little rowdy. To be sure, they tried Helliwell's patience during one announcement to such an extent that he shouted 'Bastards' at them. But that was only between numbers. The 'Tramps, however, like to be heard at all times.

"The band displayed perfectly the traits which have attracted such a large following. The set they played was like a jigsaw.

"They performed six numbers each from Crime and Crisis, alternating between each album, ensuring that the familiarity of one song, such as Bloody Well Right, offsets any resistance that might be engendered by a new one like The Meaning.

"The arrangements are similarly carefully worked out. Benbeg said earlier, 'We aim to reproduce as closely as possible the sound we produce on stage to the record. I think we do pretty well.'

"They do, and are only surpassed in this by 10cc. To be truthful, this is hardly the most exciting approach to take to a concert. Furthermore, it leads the audience to watch out for the difference between the live performance and the studio version. But, they do it well, meticulously reproducing the same tempo, relative volume and even solos.

"Sister Moonshine displays their close affinity to the Beach Boys, who themselves, rate among the elder statesmen of arranged music. Benberg's drumming includes familiar hallmarks like a heavy use of tom-toms, snare shots off the beat and a relative absence of cymbal work. Benberg is by no means a mere human metronome. He explores the dynamics of his kit, feeling out its limitations and thinking all the time.

"Likewise, harmonies on this number were well worked out and each member of the band took a part. Occasionally, Hodgson's voice cracked a little under the strain of the more falsetto notes and a bum note crept in here and there - albeit, rarely.

"They attracted a knowledgeable audience. Davies has only to walk on stage and put a harmonica to his lips and they applaud instantly - they all know it's School from Crime Of the Century. Similarly, the very first piano chords of Bloody Well Right gets the same knowledgeable reaction.

"'In Glasgow on the last tour,' says Benberg, 'all the girls sang along with Roger on the opening verse of If Everyone Was Listening. It really gave you a shiver.'

"At Lancaster, Helliwell, as usual, acted as front man. The rest of the band leave it to Helliwell to set up a rapport with the audience and he does it quite well. He adopts the persona of a slightly, upper-class, continually amused would-be superstar. He speaks in clipped tones but hadn't really had sufficient experience to overcome the shouters who infiltrated the hall. Usually, he doesn't have to worry about them.

"'Here's an old single of ours,' he murmurs and the hall surges to its feet, aware that it could only be Dreamer. They sing along through the whole song, rather self-consciously as though they're perhaps a little embarrassed at being seen showing such emotion in public.

"Supertramp slide from that to Rudy and the audience keeps singing. Lady from the new album finished the set and there's a long wait for the expected encore, which of course is Crime Of the Century.

"The concert was an unqualified success in terms of response but Supertramp were a little ragged at the edges - the loss of their sound engineer through illness explains that partially. He's an integral part of the band, attending every recording session and discussing with them the equipment he needs to reproduce their

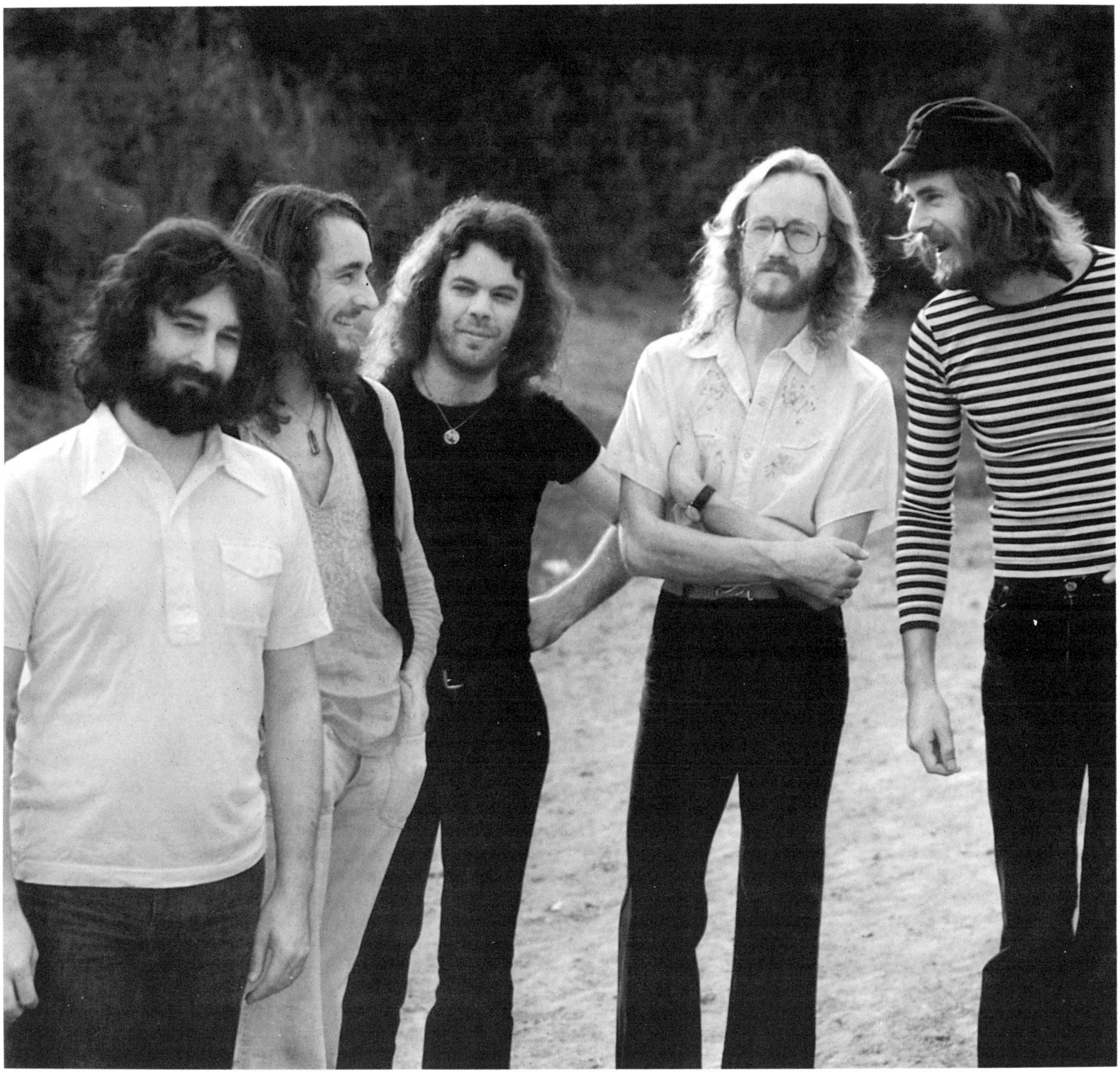

recorded sound. They're a calculated band, without any question.

"After the show, the monosyllabic Davies returns to the game of darts which the concert interrupted. The rest of the band chat among themselves for a few moments about the gig, which they agree was just a little too rowdy.

"Benberg explains: 'We prefer people to just listen. Sometimes we've noticed in concerts that they wait until the very last note has died away before they start applauding. We really prefer to play in a theatre situation where people are seated and have very few distractions. If you wanted to describe us in a nutshell, I guess you could simply say we're a theatre band - a group of guys who like to play in a proper concert hall atmosphere.'

"Hodgson agrees. 'There's a mellow vibe about the band. I suppose we're all pretty introverted but that's the way it is. It shows in the music -it's simply, well, mellow, I can't think of a better word to describe it.'"

After the Leeds show, things were shaping up in a pretty chaotic pattern. The concert ended late which really put the pressure on the crew who had to catch a train at 2:20 a.m. to get to London for the concert at Croydon's Fairfield Hall the next night. They couldn't drive the 200 miles and make it in time because they had already spent the last few nights without sleep driving to the first three concerts. Each day of the concert in Britain the load in time was ten o'clock in the morning. There were two shifts. First the light crew would go in and set up the lights and three hours later, the sound crew would go in and set up the PA. It was to be Charly's baptism by fire and with seconds to spare he got the crew to the station and onto the train.

Back at the hotel in the restaurant after the show, Bob almost burnt the place down when his lighter suddenly exploded into flames. Perhaps Bob wasn't as shocked as he should have been. The same lighter had set fire to his finger on the plane flight back from the U.S. earlier.

November 16 - Because of its proximity to London, the Croydon gig was a fairly important one for the band. The press would be there in full force and they found out that A&M's Jerry Moss would be in attendance along with the promoter of most of their British dates, Peter Bowyer.

On the first tour of England that Supertramp had done for Bowyer, the promoter had worn a white suit to each one of the concerts. As a bit of a joke on Bowyer, this time around, the band stipulated in their rider, a document attached to the usual contract indicating the group's technical and backstage requirements, that the promoter had to wear a white suit. Of course, this stipulation was only meant for the eyes of Peter Bowyer, but somebody had forgotten to take out the clause when the contract was sent to other promoters. Figuring it was just another eccentricity from a Rock band, a number of other promoters at the university actually called up and asked if they had to wear a white suit to the concert. Supertramp had their quirks but choosing a promoter's evening wear was certainly not one of them, beyond the inside joke with Bowyer.

November 17 - After Croydon, it was off to Brighton the British seaside resort to play a concert at the Brighton Dome, an impressive structure that looks very much like the Taj Mahal. Brighton is teaming with holiday makers in the summer but this was November and the place was deserted. They were the only guests at the Royal Crescent Hotel, a stopover made particularly memorable by the bar that had a pool with baby sharks in it.

It was here that Lenny the coach driver got caught up in the spirit of things. It was becoming plain that things were not going as smoothly as they could as far as loading in and loading out each day and it was decided in Brighton that some sort of change had to be made to the system. The equipment was taking too much time to set up which meant that the band's sound checks were always late and after the concert, the crew wouldn't be finished loading out until the wee hours of the morning.

After the gigs, Lenny had normally taken the band back to the hotel and stayed there but this particular night, he dropped the band off at the hotel and came back to the gig. Everybody asked him what he was doing there and he answered, "Well man, we've got a new system to work out." He was told that it wasn't his problem but he persisted: "We're all in the same boat together for the next few months." And saying that he took off his jacket, rolled up his sleeves and started working with the crew loading the trucks and directing traffic. He turned out to be particularly good at directing the flow of equipment, one of the most important aspects of loading and unloading because everybody is into their own thing. Lenny won the admiration, love and respect of everyone for his selfless attitude that night.

Norman Hall, Russel Pope, Ian Bisley (the road crew).

November 19 - The band had a day off on the 18th before driving to Bournemouth for a concert at the Winter Gardens on the night of November 19. For some reason, *New Musical Express* writer Tony Stewart made his way down to Bournemouth from London that night to attend the concert and under the headline: "Are you ready for the breathtaking visual dynamism of Supertramp?" he later wrote this about that night's concert: "Although not a visually stimulating act, or one which on stage is likely to scorch your eyes, Supertramp do present a show which on a musical level is almost completely satisfying . . .

"Basically, as their show at the Bournemouth Winter Gardens on Wednesday night illustrated, they're merely extending and developing their recorded work, adding to the dynamics, but rarely moving too far away from their own concept of strong melodies.

"To a certain extent it's true their act is not particularly adventurous, and they're also perhaps limiting their own range by choosing to aim for a polished professional performance, rather than attempting to spark off each other with some spontaneous playing.

"Not only is this an artistic restriction, but it's also a commerical one. Because quite simply if you don't enjoy their records you won't enjoy their concert show. And though their standard of musicianship is high, it's exposed only to the degree the songs allow.

"Still, John Helliwell finds plenty of opportunity to lay into some excellent sax and clarinet work, while his mellow smooth style contrasts well with Roger Hodgson's more abrasive guitar technique. Supertramp have nonetheless established a distinctive style, the most obvious feature of which is rhythmic electric piano, the basis of both "Dreamer" and "Lady".

"Yet the scope of their style is much broader, due in the main to the multi-instrumental capabilities of the three front men, Helliwell, Hodgson and Rick Davies.

"Davies, primarily a strong vocalist with a mellow timbre to his voice, moves from organ to electric piano, with the occasional trip to a grand sitting at the back stage, while Helliwell works with a complete range of saxophones and wind instruments, with the occasional dabble on the string machine or electric piano.

"Hodgson concentrates mostly on guitar, while adding his impassioned vocal (not unlike Winwood at times) to such pieces as "Hide In Your Shell", with the odd scurry of electric piano.

"With such abilities the various combinations of sound are considerable, to the point that Helliwell, as he admitted later, at times couldn't remember which instrument he was supposed to play during a particular passage.

"Their stage act however, also illustrates fragile elements in their overall concept, and some immaturity as a working unit.

"Firstly their material, pulled from both Crime Of the Century and Crisis? What Crisis? all dates from a particularly creative period of Davies' and Hodgon's two years ago with nothing much since. The lack of onstage improvisation stifles one source of inspiration, and the pressure of touring as a successful band means they'll be unable to find the time to write in any other environment.

"According to them, when we talked after the gig, this doesn't worry them as they feel the songs will eventually develop into distinctly Supertramp entities. Even so the work of drummer Bob C. Benberg and bassist Dougie Thomson often invites comparison with Procol Harum."

November 20 - It was a 55-mile drive from Bournemouth to Portsmouth where the band was to play their next concert at the Guild Hall and for Roger a special homecoming performance.

There was a two day break between Portsmouth and the next concert in Newcastle far to the north but there was no time to lay around and recuperate. The next morning, Charly and the band members caught a train up to Glasgow where they were to do a special radio show on Radio Clyde the evening of November 21. In Glasgow, the group was just about to check into the Albany Hotel, when they heard someone calling them from the bar. They turned around and found a reception committee of almost everybody that the band knew in Glasgow - the members of Nazareth; Bill Fahilly and Derek Nichols, their managers; Dougie's brothers and other assorted relatives. The interview at the radio station wasn't until midnight so by the time they showed up everybody was in pretty good shape. There was also wine and beer waiting at the radio station so you don't have to use much imagination to figure out the band's collective state at this point. During the interview, the group played "Goldrush," a song that they used to open their concerts with before "School" but has never been recorded. They had tried to record it in the past but it never quite came off in the studio but this particular night they were talked into doing

Russel and Norman.

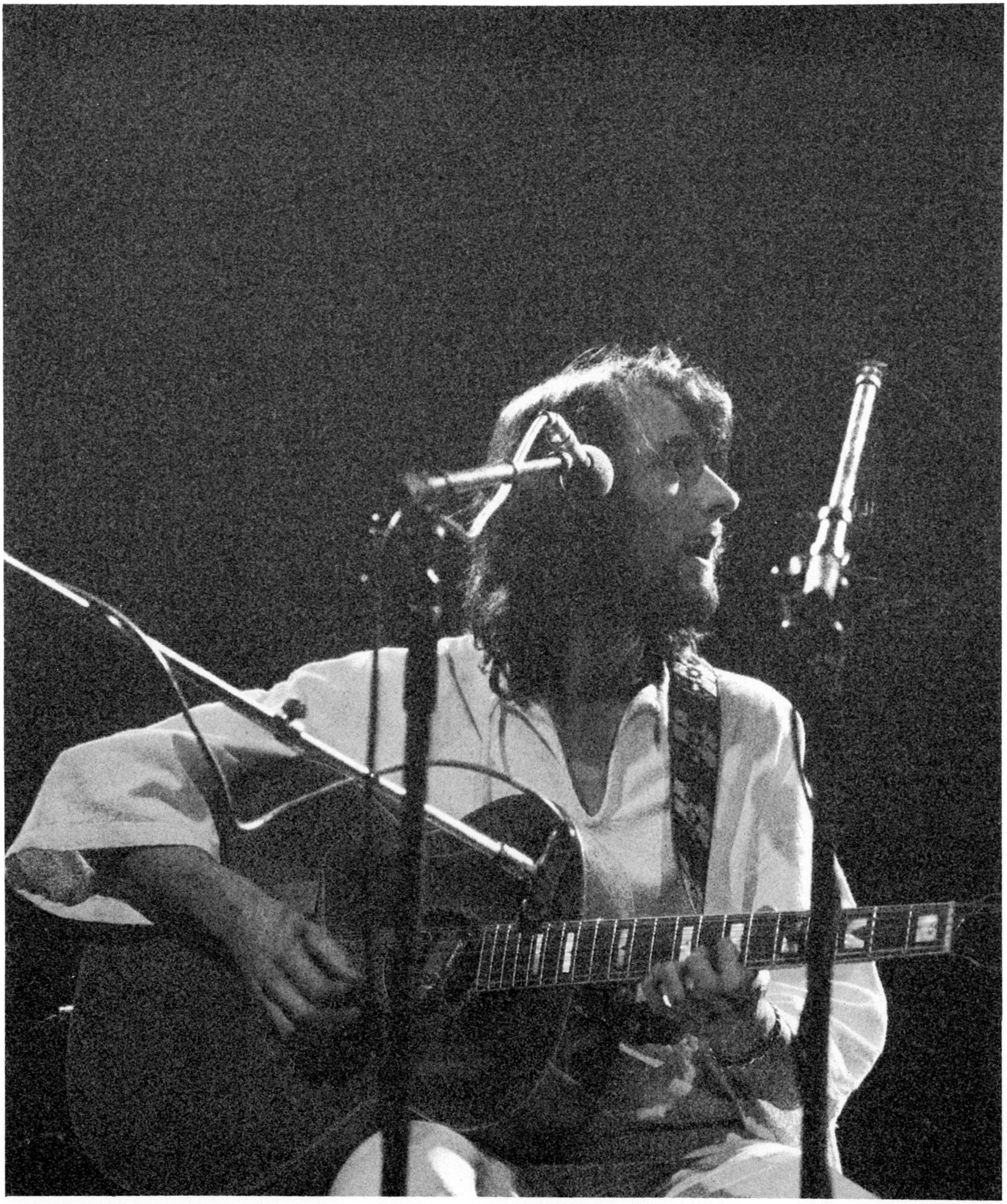

the song to a live radio audience. The interview seemed to go on for hours and by this time, Bob specifically is very pissed and very quiet. Suddenly the interviewer turned to Bob and asked him what he thought of Joan Armatrading who was opening all of the Supertramp shows on that portion of the world tour. Bob was always making jokes about Joan and he slowly looked up at the interviewer in his drunken stupor and made some inane comment and Rick fell off his chair. The interviewer looked at him as if he'd just crawled out from under a log and the local promotion guy from A&M Records started giving the sign for the interview to end because he felt the band was sounding a bit out of the picture at that point. It seemed to everybody to be the type of thing that would make good radio in Glasgow but nonetheless they finished up and headed back to the Albany Hotel where Nazareth and their crew had just got back from their gig at the Appollo Theatre and were back in the bar. A short time after, Charly decided to head up to his room because they had a train to catch in the morning. About an hour later he was laying on his bed reading a book when he heard a knock on the door and two A&M promotion guys came in holding up Bob who was beyond sanity. There was a train to catch at eleven o'clock and it's now four o'clock. Bob stayed and talked for a few minutes then he left. A while later the two A&M guys were back with Bob but this time they'd taken his pants away so he'd stay put. That didn't stop Bob. A few minutes later he went back down to the bar. He was brought back to Charly's room by the two very uptight A&M reps and finally went back to his own room. Somehow, Bob managed to get up the next morning in time to catch the train to Newcastle.

November 22 - The band played the City Hall in Newcastle and the next day went on to Edinburgh to do a show at the Usher Hall before returning to Glasgow once again for a concert at the Apollo Centre.

November 24 - On their arrival at the Apollo, the crew was a bit dismayed to find the stage about nine feet high; everything had to come in through the front door and be lifted onto the stage. A number of locals were recruited to hoist the equipment and in the end

Lenny's bus.

Len Wright

it went pretty smoothly.

Glasgow audiences can get pretty rowdy and, besides the fact that it was Dougie's hometown, it's important to play well there because if you don't, the audience shows its displeasure and can get pretty ugly about it. They were told about a riot at an Alice Cooper show one New Year's Eve. Apparently it was sort of the attitude, "You think this is violent. We'll show you what violence is." And they broke up the place.

The concert was a sell out and after the show the group was presented a gold statuette for the accomplishment. They had been the first group in quite a while to sell out the Appollo. With many of Dougie's relatives and friends in attendance, it turned into a pretty emotional night.

There was more insanity back at the hotel after the gig. Nazareth was still in town and most of the band's Glasgow friends showed up. At this point, if the heavy concert schedule wasn't getting to them, the partying certainly was.

November 25 - On to the Caird Hall in Dundee. It was snowing a little bit as they came into town and the hall proved to be quite a quaint little place. "A bit like playing a convent," Charly would later comment. "You could smell the varnish and wax and the place was spotless." (Nazareth had just played there a few nights before.) During the concert that night it was obvious to the band that everything was starting to gell nicely. Dundee was a bit of a turning point.

Back at the Tay Centre Hotel after the concert, the group was visited by Tony Burrows, the artist relations person from A&M in London, and Stewart, one of the A&M promo guys who had been concerned about Bob's drunken state in Glasgow. They were sharing a room and at about three-thirty in the morning they went up to bed. But not everyone was tired. Charly, Norman Hall, Kenny Thomson and Dougie were in a rather mischievious state of mind and somebody hit upon the idea of filling up some garbage bags full of water and dumping the contents in a place other than the North Sea. They had somebody go up to Stewart and Tony's room and ask for Stewart. He came to the door in his jockey shorts and before he could blink, they let him have it with a deluge of water. It completely ruined the room. The mattresses were soaked, the curtains were dripping and there was water all over the carpets and streaming down the hall. Everybody was drenched. It was to be the birth of the Aquaman who would pop up in a different persona throughout the rest of the tour.

November 28 - It was a two-day drive to Cardiff in Wales for Supertramp's next concert at the Capitol Theatre on November 28. The first night they stayed at the Royal Angus Hotel in Queensway just outside of Birmingham and played a little soccer in the shadow of the ruins of an old abbey that had been burnt down in the 1700s. It was a cold and misty day and they were sinking up to their ankles in mud, but the match went on. Almost everybody came down with terrible colds that day as they continued the drive to Cardiff.

They all arrived the day before the concert and stayed at the Cardiff Centre Hotel. At eleven o'clock the next morning everybody was rudely awakened from a deep sleep by a fire drill. Charly had been out and returned to the hotel, running into the hotel manager on the way to his room. "You guys are really nice," the manager told Charly, "but there's a red-haired guy who's a real turd. During the fire drill, he came down and was screaming and swearing at me in his underwear." It seems that Dave Margereson had not taken at all kindly to being awakened by a fire alarm - a false one at that.

While the fire drill was in progress, everybody came out into the street and as they were looking up at the hotel, Ian Bisley and Brian Kelly suddenly appeared on one of the balconies dressed as women. They started screaming for help and Ian was doing his excellent impression of Queen Elizabeth to an almost hysterical audience below.

The Cardiff concert turned into quite a wild night. In the middle of the second song "Bloody Well Right," a fourteen or fifteen year old girl jumped up on the stage, dove over the piano and got Rick on the floor and was almost raping him. She was finally led off by Norman Hall but throughout the show, people were hanging off curtains and the lighting tressle was swinging back and forth quite ominously.

Charly realized that to avert any trouble after the show, it would be a good idea to get the house lights on as soon as possible. "Crime Of the Century" faded and the curtains closed and Charly asked this old Italian who was working the lights to turn them on. He didn't move. Charly asked again and still nothing. By this time, Charly was furious but the angrier Charly got the more angry the lighting guy got. Roger walked by just as Charly had reached the end of his rope and was swearing at the top of his

Manager Dave Margereson playing "Silly Buggers" backstage.

lungs. "Need a hand," asked Roger a usually peace-loving personality. The guy flicked the switch.

November 29 - The Birmingham gig the next night at the Odeon presented less than idyllic conditions for both the band and the crew. The load-in for the two trucks was down a narrow side alley so they had to turn around and back down it to get to the back doors. Also as it turned out, the night the band played was the first anniversary of the bombing of the pub next door by the IRA in which three people had been killed. The security that night was severe and everybody had to go through a body search before they entered the theatre. There was a nine-foot drop between the front of the stage and the audience, making it very hard for the band to get any energy at all from the crowd. All in all it was a pretty non-descript concert.

November 30 - The Manchester concert the next night at the Palace Theatre almost turned into a bit of a fiasco when it was discovered during the sound check that the organ and the Wurlitzer piano had gone on the blink. Manchester is over 100 miles from London and that was going to be the closest place where either one of those instruments would be readily available. The concert was scheduled to start at seven o'clock and that afternoon Dave Margereson drove off to London in a truck to pick up a new organ and Wurlitzer. By twenty to seven there were about 2200 people standing outside in the pouring rain. The band had done its sound check and the rest of the equipment was set up on stage. Just as it was being decided whether to cancel the gig or not, out of the fog and into the smog drives Dave with the spare parts. It all gets thrown up on stage, Joan Armatrading does her opening set and the Supertramp show starts on time. Everybody was a little nervous because they didn't have time to check the new equipment but the worry was for nothing and it turned out to be one of the best shows the band had done in the last 18 months. The band was on a roll and the next night's gig at the De Montfort Hall in Leicester on December 1 was also one of the most memorable concerts the band has ever performed.

December 2 - Supertramp moved on to the Hanley Victoria Hall in Stoke-On-Trent on December 2 and again the road crew had reason to do a little wall kicking when they found out that the access to the hall was through a little tunnel about three feet wide. The hall itself was like a church with three balconies and wood panelled. Dougie and Charly had reason to be excited though. They are both real buffs on war machinery and across the street from the hall was a greenhouse with a Spitfire in it that had been piloted by a woman during the Battle Of Britain.

December 4-5 - Sheffield City Hall was the next concert on December 4 and then the Coventry Theatre on the 5th of December. The weather by this time was playing havoc with the health of quite a few members of the crew and the band. Rick and Roger were constantly fighting off colds throughout this period; however their spirits were probably lifted a bit with the thought of spending a few days in London which would include two concerts at the Hammersmith Odeon on the 6 and 7 of December.

December 6-7 - The Hammersmith shows were like a homecoming. During the number "Hide In Your Shell," it had been a tradition - starting with the recorded version on the *Crime Of the Century* album on which Christine Helliwell and Vicki Siebenberg collectively known as The Trampettes sung the harmonies - for friends of the band to do the back-up vocals on the song. During the previous tours, when Gallagher & Lyle and Chris de Burgh had opened for the band, they would come out and sing the harmonies. On this tour, Joan Armatrading's back-up band The Movies, were recruited. Julian, the conga player, John, the guitar player and Jamie, the drummer did the harmonies and with each night, they would dress a little more elaborately for the spot. For the Hammersmith gigs, Charly went out and bought them bathing suits and sunglasses like the guy on the Crisis album cover. An ounce of hash was the bribe and they went out on stage dressed like that for the two nights. Seeing as it was London, they also used two gorillas at the end of the song Asylum. Charly took the part of one, eating a banana.

It was a rewarding two-night stand with most of the critics showing up for one or the other of the concerts. They hit the cover of *Melody Maker* that week and received generally favourable reviews in the Rock press.

In *Sounds*, Phil Sutcliffe sized up the show this way:

"I have never known an audience that seemed so devoted to a band as the congregation at Hammersmith the other night. Nearly every

"Asylum" being performed in London.

number rated an outburst of applause as if they were Sinatra on the opening bars of My Way. The reasons are quite different, though, I imagine. I sensed an audience which has recognized a considerable new talent and wants everyone including the band to know that they are valued, that they must stick around for a long time and make a lot of music for us 'cos we need it in this crisis (what crisis?).

"So Supertramp are loved - and that's a surprise. Because they are one of the coolest bands in the big time. John Anthony Helliwell is the only one who seems to have any personal rapport with the crowd and perhaps his puppet-like mock show bizzy gestures say it for the rest of them; that's just not their scene. Even their lighting is almost entirely on stage i.e. no long beams from the back of the auditorium linking them and us.

"And their music, delivered with supreme precision as it was, is rarely hit-you-between-the-eyes stuff so the reaction of the comparatively impartial observer is hardly one of excitement. Except of course when they played their two singles Dreamer and Lady. Whether or not they were purpose-built hits, they really do it and were the highlights of the set to me because the sweat came busting out on my brow and that's when this musical animal knows when he's enjoying himself . . ."

December 8-10 - The band spent their first day off in London before driving to Hull on December 9 for their gig at the ABC movie theatre the following night. It was one of those gigs where hardly anything had been arranged properly by the promoter and the truck drivers got busted because the only access to the hall was through the bus terminal and to park both semis there caused havoc. There wasn't enough power in the hall so a generator had to be brought in. There were a lot of last minute details and the show wasn't sold out. Goodbye Hull, hello Preston!

December 11 - Preston was the gig that everybody feared and nobody wanted to do. The band had played there before and it was no picnic. The gig was on the third floor of a building and all the gear had to come in by an elevator after the trucks drove in through a small tunnel. When you've done four or five difficult gigs in a row, everybody's really tired and trying to save their energy. The guy who runs the hall doesn't want to know about your problems and certainly won't compensate for the extra time it takes. It was a beautiful hall, though it's probable that no one in the crew was noticing the scenery at this point.

December 12 - In Liverpool, Supertramp played the Empire Theatre on Lyme Street. A pretty impressive place because every act that has ever visited Liverpool has played there. The hall is right across the street from the ferries that come in from Ireland and the pub at the terminal is the only place outside of Ireland that you can get real Irish Guinness beer. Driving into Liverpool, the first billboard that they saw was advertising a Beatles revival that had taken place that summer.

December 13 - To get to Ipswich for the concert at the Gaumont, Dave and Charly chartered an airplane for the crew for the 300 mile flight from Liverpool, a distance that would have been impossible to drive in England in one day. In Ipswich, normally a summer resort area, the concert was to begin at seven o'clock and the last bus ran at ten. Charly called the terminal and asked for the manager who agreed to hold the bus for an extra twenty minutes. This was also the day that Charly lost Bob, Rick and John. They played pool and darts together, so normally, if you couldn't find them, they were usually at the local pool hall. The sound check was set to go and Charly went on a search of the local streets and finally found the trio hiding in a pool hall just down from the hall.

December 14 - The gig at Great Yarmouth's ABC theatre was destined to provide some light relief even though at the outset it looked like another royal screw up by everyone who had anything to do with the gig. Nothing was together. The dressing rooms were terrible and the place itself was a dump. The manager of the place kept coming backstage and rabbiting on about how great it was to have groups of Supertramp's stature coming to Great Yarmouth because it would give the place a good reputation and get bigger groups to come up.

Behind the hall where the gear came in there was this long alley wide enough for one car. The gate was closed at the top of the alley because the crew had piled all of the empty equipment cases there. Both trucks were parked on the street and the local policeman kept coming up, writing tickets and sticking them on the windscreens. They were totally ignored by Pat and Dave and this guy was getting really upset. He wanted them to park the trucks but it was almost 15 miles to the lorry park and there was

Chris De Burgh and Jeff Philips, Brighton, England.

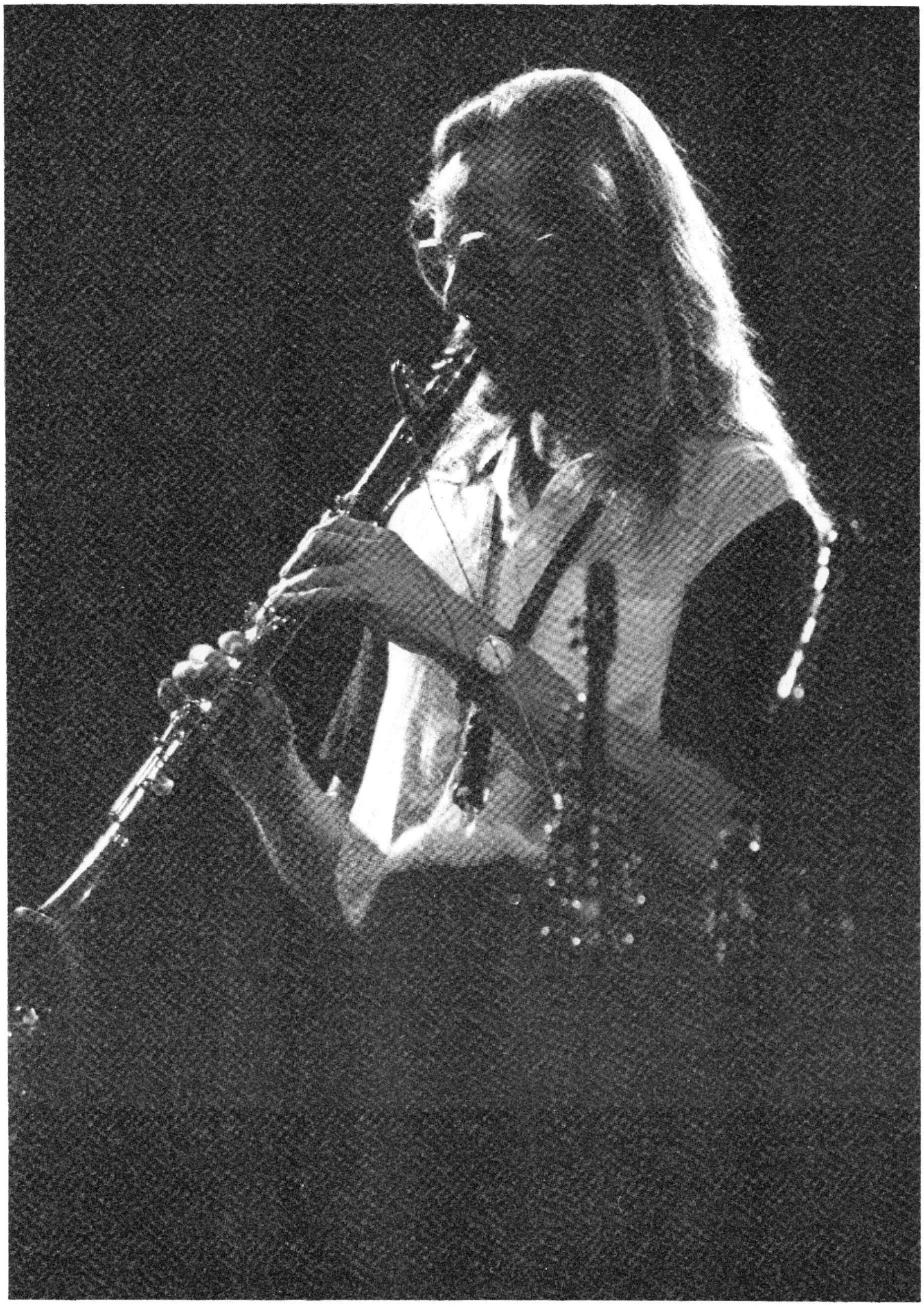

more chance of pigs flying than Pat and Dave moving the trucks that far away from the gig. The promoter was supposed to have arranged for permits for the trucks but he hadn't. When he showed up in his white Rolls Royce, he took one look at the alley where he usually parked, saw it was cluttered with cases and started whining. Before he could continue, a couple of the members of the crew deposited another pile of cases into the alley. The Rolls stayed on the street.

After the concert, the band came out to find Lenny in a screaming match with the policeman about the coach. He wanted it moved. In front of the coach was Pat's truck and behind it was the police car. The cop kept writing out tickets and Lenny kept tearing them up. The cop was fuming at this point and he went over and started hassling Pat in his truck who was waiting for the coach to leave so he could back into the alley and get the gear. He wanted Pat to take the truck to the lorry park and he kept yelling at him until finally he told Pat to get into his car. They were both sitting in the police car and the cop was writing out another ticket. Everybody was on the coach by this time and they were watching all of this go on. Suddenly Lenny, who was beyond reason he was so pissed off, got into the coach, put it into reverse and stood on the accelerator. The cop heard the tires of the coach squealing and looked up in time to see the coach coming at him. He dropped his pencil. Lenny stopped two inches from his bumper and then after ripping up all the tickets and throwing them out the window, took off down the road with everybody leaning out of the coach window with their fingers in the air showing him that in their minds he was number one. Pat got stuck with a ticket but as far as anyone can remember, it was never paid.

December 15-16 - On the way to the next gig in Plymouth which was a 337 mile drive, the band got stuck in fog on the way through London. Roger had decided to drive Pat's truck down to Plymouth and with the thick mist it took about six hours to move one mile through London. For a while the Supertramp entourage stopped and Roger went for a walk and when he came back he had picked up a terrible cold and had a rough time for the next few days.

The memorable thing about the Plymouth gig was a guy called Killer who was a one-man security force in the town. He had killed a kid at a gig once and had gone to court but nobody testified against him because everyone in Plymouth was afraid of him. He was about six foot three with a crew cut and real heavy duty. He used to sit in the front of the stage and periodically patrol the area. That night he told everyone, "I'm really worried about these kids. There's going to be a riot and I'm going to have to break a few heads." He intimidated everyone.

December 17 - The next gig was at the Paignton Festival Hall and the group stayed at a little bed and breakfast place called the San Remo Hotel in Torquay. There was a piano in the lobby that hadn't been tuned for twenty-five years at least and Rick sat there and played "Crime Of the Century" on it. There was a fantastic dining room only open at specific hours and the next morning, very early, Supertramp, Joan Armatrading and her group The Movies and another A&M group Hustler sat in the dining room having breakfast. There was a Spanish waiter, who hardly spoke any English and screwed up all of the orders. The manager was rather dignified looking in a tux. Suddenly the manager noticed that the waiter was making a right cock up of things, and thinking that nobody could hear, he took him behind the kitchen door and started screaming at him. There is a comedy series called *Fawlty Towers* that features John Cleese as a hotel owner who is always having run-ins with his Spanish waiter and as everyone in the room caught sight of this poor waiter looking at them through the little window in the door to the dining room, everyone cracked up at the same time as they suddenly saw the similarity to the TV show in the situation they now found themselves in.

December 18-19 - From Plymouth the band went up to Swansea to play the Brangwyn Hall and then headed for Southampton, the second last date of the British tour. Roger's mother Jill came out to the gig with his two sisters Caroline and Eve. Peter Bowyer, the promoter of most of the tour, showed up to introduce the band. Just before Joan Armatrading and The Movies came out for their opening set, Peter went up to the mike and started the intro: "Ladies and gentlemen before we welcome Supertramp I'd like to present Joan Armatrading and her group The Movies back from a successful tour of America . . ." He paused for a moment, a gorilla tapped him on the shoulder, he turned around and the gorilla let him have it square in the face with a bag of cream cakes. Peter turned back to face the audience, who didn't know how to react, and he finished the introduction. As he was walking off the stage somebody threw a bucket of ice water at him. It was to be only the

Coming off stage.

beginning of a wild night.

It was a special night for Roger because Southampton was very close to his home town of Portsmouth and John introduced him on stage that night as local-boy-makes-good to a thunderous ovation from the crowd.

It was also the night that a couple of guys from Ryder Truck came down from London to put the heavy on the band for the rest of the money that the band owed on the truck rental, "Or give up the trucks." As they had one more concert to do in Southend, the latter suggestion was out of the question so the band was faced with coming up with quite a large sum of money on the spot even though they had reportedly paid 95 percent of their bill for the British tour. A lot of name calling went on but it was finally resolved.

As it was Peter Bowyer's last concert with the band, a reception was held back at the Polygon Hotel. Peter had had a few drinks during the show and by the time he got to the reception he was well on his way to oblivion and ended up having a champagne spraying duel with Dougie. The hotel manager was working the bar and was not at all impressed. Everything finally calmed down and Peter went up to his room, rather intoxicated.

In the meantime, Charly and Brian had decided it was time to do something to Mike Stone, Joan Armatrading's manager. Brian got a skeleton key from the front desk under the pretext that he had lost his, and he and Charly headed for Mike's room with the original idea of sticking all his furniture to the ceiling with heavy duty glue. They tried it but the ceiling was too high and they didn't have a ladder and not enough bodies. In the end they decided to hide every stick of furniture and luggage in his room. They put the bed in the closet and took all of his luggage and put it somewhere else. When they left the room there was nothing in it. When Mike got back he was convinced that everything had been stolen.

That was not the end of the high jinks. From Mike Stone's room they went over to visit Peter Bowyer. They knocked on his door and when there was no answer they walked in and found Peter passed out on the bed, fast asleep. They carefully took off the covers, grabbed the mattress and carefully dragged it out into the hall with Peter still lying on it in a pair of briefs. They locked the door behind them and left, leaving him snoring away in the middle of the hall in his underwear and no cover. Dougie, Kenny Thomson, Norman, Brian and Ian were involved at this point and as they ran down the hall, Peter got up on one elbow and said, "I'll remember this!" The next morning at about a quarter to seven, Charly got a call from Peter who was down in the lobby. "You'll never be safe," he told Charly. "I'll get even if it takes twenty years." He had apparently woken up at about seven out of his stupor and realized that his key was locked in the room. He had to go to the lobby in his underwear to get a key. He was a good sport about it though.

From Southampton the band headed for Southend where they would play their last concert on the British tour at the Korsaal. All the wives, children, friends and relatives came out to the West Cliff Hotel and to the concert that night. Southend is a summer resort town which meant that in December it was virtually deserted. The concert hall was a dirty little place that hadn't been used since summer and there was no heating in it. Few arrangements had been made and it was cold and depressing being there. You could see your breath in the dressing room. Still, it being the last gig of the tour, everyone was anxious to get on with it.

After the show, there was a party back at the hotel, and once again there was mischief in the air. The band was there with their families and some A&M people from London as well as Mike Stone, Joan Armatrading and The Movies. Earlier in the tour, Charly and Brian had bought a number of canisters of shaving cream that they had saved for just such an occasion. While everybody was sitting around talking, eating and getting drunk, the shaving cream was being passed back and forth between Charly, Russel Pope and Brian who were quietly squirting great gobs of the stuff on pie plates. As Mike Stone walked in and was bending over the food table, Charly slipped up to him and he was the first to get the shaving cream pie in the eye. Just as everybody in the room was reacting to that, Russel went up to one of the A&M promo guys that they'd had a run in with in Glasgow and let him have it. To say the least, he was pissed off and made an off-handled threat of physical injury to Russel but realizing he was in a heavy minority, the matter dropped.

The party continued and it got later and later until the manager of the hotel showed up at the door. He asked them to keep the noise down and to pay any damages. As he was about to leave, Bob started to run from one end of the room to the other to demonstrate that he could jump over the food table, clearing all the drinks and bottles. He missed by a few feet and landed square in the middle of the table, sending food, drinks and bottles clattering to the floor as it collapsed under him. He got a beer bottle in the eye and it looked like he had been in a fight. He was growing his beard again and looked just terrible as he stood up and faced the manager, who shrugged and told them not to worry about it as he left the room. Everyone was in hysterics.

December 21 - The band drove back to London in a 26-seat coach filled with friends and relatives. In the back of the bus, Charly, Dave and a couple of the members of the band were trying to have a business meeting as the bus bounced along. Bob, hungover with a vicious looking black eye from the night before, tried to sleep and had very little success. The band finally made it home and had a few days off before Christmas in advance of setting out on the European and Scandinavian leg of the Crisis tour.

In Europe, besides playing their normal concerts, the band also had a fairly rigorous promotional schedule as well. As usual, it was a very exhausting excursion for both the band and the crew but there were a number of memorable highlights along the way that would keep everybody's spirits high. Predictably there would also be some bizarre incidents as well.

At one of the early gigs, just outside of Brussels in Belgium, Charly arrived at the hall to find that the stage for the night's show had been built out of tables along one wall. On closer inspection, Charly doubted the solidity of the make-shift platform and talked to the promoter about it who assured him that the stage would hold eight tons. Charly jumped on the stage to check it out and the whole thing collapsed under him. Charly had gained a little weight on the road but he wasn't even close to nudging the scale at eight tons. The band played on the floor that night.

Amsterdam was absolutely Supertramp crazy. They played to a sell-out crowd at the Concertgebauw on January 12 and the demand for tickets was so great that they added another Amsterdam show at the Congress Hall by the Rye, four days later. After the show the first night, a few of the members of the band and crew rode around Amsterdam on bicycles, visiting some private clubs and exploring the canals until about six in the morning.

The Berlin concert had been highly anticipated by everyone in the group and they got an early start from Amsterdam the morning after the second concert for the ten hour drive to the German capital. On the bus, some of the members of The Movies, who without Joan Armatrading, this time were doing the European dates with Supertramp, and Charly were engrossed in a rather sophisticated board game called Diplomacy that has been known to last for weeks given the right players and circumstances.

After five and half hours, the coach hit the German border and then as it was getting dark at about eight o'clock they had reached the corridor to East Berlin. All the lights were turned off in the coach as they reached East Berlin because everyone wanted to see the wall, the machine guns and land mines. Dougie and Charly were very much into military history so for them the sight of abandoned Russian tanks and monuments to Stalin was quite an exciting experience.

Besides the ongoing game of Diplomacy in the back of the coach, there was also an interminable card game in progress between Bob, Rick, Russel and Dave Margereson. It had been going on throughout the ten hour drive and was still in full swing when they hit the first border crossing into East Germany. A middle-aged guard boarded the coach scowling and checking everybody out. He had a rifle and it was quickly established that this wasn't a guy you'd want to get into an argument with. He was just about to walk off the coach when suddenly he turned and went over to where Bob was sitting. He looked over his shoulder at the cards that were in Bob's hand and without a word grabbed the cards from him. Startled, Bob looked up at him. The guard, stone-faced, pulled out a card, laid it down on the table and won the trick. He gave the cards back to Bob, gave everyone a smile and got off the coach. After the tension of those few minutes under scrutiny it was a magic moment.

The band played a pretty decent sold-out show in West Berlin and the next day, having some time to themselves, they took the coach for a tour of East Berlin. Throughout the tour, the group had amassed a pretty impressive collection of good Danish porn magazines which at this point were scattered around the coach. As they entered East Berlin through a maze of walls, tank traps, machine guns, barbed wire and guard dogs they came to one of the checkpoints. Once again, a guard boarded the coach and, spying the magazines, confiscated all of them telling them that they couldn't take them into the People's Republic of Germany. He put them all under his coat and walked into the washroom. "They're not for me," he explained when he boarded the coach again. "They're to be destroyed."

The guard guided them through the corridor to East Berlin where they spent the morning exploring before heading for Munich, a place that had some special memories for Rick, who had spent a lot of time there during the days before Supertramp was formed.

In Munich, besides playing a concert, the group was scheduled to do a TV show that was to be shot at an old abandoned warehouse on Dachaustrasse, the site of the gas works during the second world war. The TV shoot turned into a pretty riotous experience. The TV people had supplied the group with a lot of instruments because for some reason they didn't want them to use their own and as a special effect, halfway through one of the songs, they released an amazing amount of foam that eventually enveloped the whole band in a virtual tidal wave of suds. As the floor became more slippery, the camermen with their back packs were having increasing difficulty keeping their balance. At one point, as one of the guys was shooting Rick during a piano solo, the cameraman slipped and fell over the Wurlitzer which ended up on the floor smashed into a million pieces. People were slipping, sliding and falling all over the place but extraordinarily enough it turned out to be a pretty good looking film.

German crowds can get pretty rowdy sometimes and at that night's sold out concert, in a 1000-seat hall, there was a riot as a large crowd of people remained outside unable to get in. There were lots of broken doors, broken glass, broken jaws and uptight people that night which in terms of performance, turned out to be a pretty hot night for the group.

In Hamburg the next day, there was a myriad of hassles getting the gear into the hall because the promoter had forgotten to tell them that the symphony orchestra would be recording in the hall until late in the afternoon. It was a panic getting everything set up in time and unfortunately The Movies had to forfeit their opening set.

After the show, back at the Parkhoch Haus Hotel, Dag, the keyboard player from The Movies, and Rick sat down at the piano in the bar and proceeded to entertain everybody until the place closed. Calling themselves Ricky and the Rockettes, they cracked jokes, played a lot of old cabaret numbers and got everyone to sing along with them. It was a very relaxed, mellow and special moment in the middle of a rather hectic tour that was destined to get even more chaotic before its completion.

The band played their last German concert in Hanover on January 24 and arriving at the Holiday Inn before the show, there was a surprise waiting for a couple of the members of the crew. Throughout the tour, there was a mythical band that everyone would talk about called The Byzely Brothers Band named after Ian Trevor Lloyd Bisley who was one of the many geniuses involved in the technician crew. He had this imaginary band that was actually made up of various members of the road crew. In Hanover Charly had a sign put up on the Holiday Inn marquee that read, "Welcome The Byzely Brothers" in English on one side and in German on the other. Ian and the other guys were surprised to say the least.

The Road to The Albert Hall

Following the European leg of the Crisis tour, Supertramp were scheduled to play a number of dates in Scandinavia before heading back to London for a farewell concert at Albert Hall before heading for America. It was the middle of winter and, as Rick and Roger could attest from prior experience in Norway where they had to abandon their bus in a snow bank during an earlier visit, the area was not particularly suited to touring at this time of year.

Nonetheless, the band headed for the ferry on the north German coast that would take them to Copenhagen for the first concert on the Scandinavian leg of the tour.

Arriving in Copenhagen, the band checked into the Plaza Hotel and found that Roxy Music was also staying there and was playing a gig at the Tivoli Gardens across the street that night. The group had a chance to catch the last part of their set before they headed back to the hotel where everybody including Rick and Russel got quite drunk on a vicious brew called Elephant Beer. In somebody's files there are some incriminating shots of Bob and Dougie running naked through the hotel and riding up and down in the glass elevators.

Supertramp played to 1200 people at the Tivoli Gardens, a show made notable by the fact that it was the first time that they had played "Soapbox Opera" live. At the sound check that afternoon, Roger spent some time at the string machine working on a song that would eventually be called "Even In the Quietest Moments." Roger would sit by himself sometimes and at other times Rick would join him on drums and together they would work out different bits of the song. Rick was sick at this point and spent a lot of time in his room with the saxophone he had brought on tour with the intention of learning to play it.

Roger Hodgson.

The band prepared to leave Copenhagen on January 28 for the last of three gigs - Lund, Oslo and Stockholm - before heading back to England for their farewell concert at London's Royal Albert Hall, a week away. There was a certain amount of uneasiness in everyone about the prospect of facing a very tight schedule in the next seven days in an area of the world in which the weather could be very unpredictable. The distances between the cities, not to mention the trip back to London, was significant and the successful completion of the tour would very much depend on everything running like clockwork.

The crew took a ferry the next morning and the band took a hydrofoil through Copenhagen harbour to the west coast of Sweden where they took a bus for the relatively short ride into Lund. The trip through the harbour was breathtaking. It was a beautiful, clear day but bitterly cold and everyone wrapped up as warmly as they could in order to stand outside as long as possible just to feel the breeze and have a look at the cruisers, destroyers and submarines of the Danish navy that were currently at anchor.

They got to Lund to find that the crew was extremely pissed off. The load-in to the Olympum was probably the most difficult that they had faced to this point. All the gear had to go through a tunnel about a quarter of a mile long and then through four sets of doors, down the length of the hall and hoisted up onto the stage. The trucks had to come down an incline, into a garage, but as they were too high to fit they had to be unloaded at the top of the ramp which added another 150 metres to the run. The crowd was very receptive that night so it partially made up for some of the aggro.

The next day, everyone set off for Oslo, about 400 miles away, and on arrival checked into the Grand Hotel. At the 1200 seat hall at which they were to play, a collective groan went through the road crew. The access to the venue for the equipment was by way of a large basket lowered down the side of the building. It was only large enough to take one piece of equipment at a time. There were a few tons of equipment sitting in the trucks and, as luck would have it, it was the coldest day in Norway in 25 years.

The coach was parked a few blocks from the hotel and the trucks were parked in two separate locations close to the hall - Dave Connor's truck with the lighting gear was parked so that all he had to do the next day was to open his doors and unload and Pat's truck with the stage gear was sitting outside the KLM Airlines office a few blocks away.

Lenny had tried to start the coach that evening but it was dead. As it wasn't needed, he decided to leave it and work on it the next day.

Everyone spent the night at the hotel and the next morning the lights were unloaded from the truck. Instead of being finished by 11:30 in the morning as was usual, it took until mid-afternoon because it was much slower working in the freezing conditions. Not to mention that the gear had to go 35 feet up the side of the building. The gig at Lund had been hard and then there was the long drive to Oslo. By this time, the crew was pretty uptight.

At this point, Norman came running in to report that Connor's truck with the stage gear wouldn't start. Everybody headed over to where he was parked and after three hours of working on the engine, it finally started but wouldn't go into gear. Thinking that the transmission was frozen, they tried a blow torch and boiling water, but nothing worked so it was decided to call a large tow truck to pull the semi and its eight tons of equipment to the gig. It was getting to the point where discussions were already going on about scrubbing the concert but the tow truck arrived in time and the slow process of moving the gear into the hall began.

As the tow truck was leaving, Charly noticed that Pat's truck which had been unloaded, was parked over a metal grill which was buckling under the weight and if allowed to sit any longer, it would collapse and break the axle of the truck. They tried to back it up but it was sheer ice and there was no traction. The tow truck was summoned again and two hours and another hundred dollars later, Pat's truck was pulled to safety. Things were further complicated by the fact that it was the last day of taxes in Norway and the people there pay their taxes *at* the tax office, so the traffic in downtown Oslo was bad and tow trucks were being called everywhere.

At this point, it was time not only to worry about the gig that night but also the drive to Stockholm the next day. The transmission on Dave's truck was shot so something had to be done to get a replacement tractor to pull the trailer with the lighting equipment. Upstairs in the hall, the process of unloading was going very slowly and it was becoming more and more obvious that the concert would have to be cancelled. It would have taken the crew until at least 10:30 that night to finish setting up. The concert would have lasted until 1:00 in the morning and the way things were going, it would have taken the crew until eight to get loaded up and on the road for the drive to Stockholm. It would have been outrageous to have asked the crew to do that so the gig was scrubbed. When Ian Bisely found out, he was so pissed off that he lifted a heavy table and threw it against the wall. His reaction was indicative of the kind of pride that the crew took in their contribution to the Supertramp organization.

The band was consulted and they agreed it was the only thing that they could do. There were a lot of panic calls to the promoter and everybody was extremely depressed. The gig had been sold out and the band felt that they owed it to a lot of people in Norway, including the record company, to do it, but the decision was really out of everyone's hands.

The next morning everyone was supposed to make the 350 mile drive to Stockholm very early but Lenny had gone out to start the coach and got absolutely no response from the engine. Pat went out to his truck but he had as much luck as Lenny. As a precaution, the band booked on the train that was leaving for Stockholm at 11:00 that night and in the meantime, to cut costs, they all checked out of their rooms and left their baggage in Charly's room.

A new battery had been found for Pat's truck and as Lenny was putting the wires on it, it exploded, narrowly missing his face. Another battery was installed and finally they got the truck started. They worked on the coach for the rest of the afternoon and by 8:30 that evening got it started so the group decided to drive to Stockholm with Lenny rather than take the train.

It was time now to worry about Dave's truck that needed a new tractor to pull the trailer. A call was put into ITS, the biggest transport company in the world, and arrangements were made to have the tractor brought down to them. By the time it arrived everybody was sitting in the coach playing cards and listening to music waiting to hit the road. But there was another snag. As they tried to hook the tractor up to Dave's trailer, they found that the electrical contacts and hoses were different so they had to modify all of the parts.

It was about 28 below zero and as they worked on the truck, the coach, without warning, started to spew water out of the radiator. One of the lines had frozen and the water had backed up. They couldn't keep the coach running any longer so it was turned off for a while. When the trucks were both ready to go, the coach was restarted and some new fluid was put in. For a while anyway, everything seemed to be okay and they drove off to a gas station to get fueled up and pick up some snacks for the long drive. It was about one o'clock in the morning and everyone was in a state of bewilderment and depression, feeling that there was a force much greater than themselves trying to prevent them from leaving Oslo. It was late and a long drive to Stockholm overnight.

Suddenly as they were sitting at the service station, the coach started to spew water again. After working on the radiator for a while with a blow torch to try to thaw it out, the coach started up again. It went about two blocks this time and again the water started spilling out of the radiator. The trucks had gone so there was nothing else to do but go back to the Grand Hotel in Oslo and check in for the night.

The only way left to get to Stockholm was by plane which left at 7:30 in the morning. They booked on to that and settled down for a night's sleep.

Miraculously everybody was up in time the next morning to check out and say a very reluctant goodbye to Lenny. He would have loved to have been at the last gig of the tour after being with the group through thick and thin over the last four months but he had to get the coach back to England and get it fixed. He was booked on the same ferry that the trucks were taking after the Stockholm gig and in the meantime he had to get the coach back in running order.

Dave Connor abandoned the motor that didn't work and everybody headed for the airport. They made the plane in time and suddenly, as they were all sitting there preparing for take-off, Ken Thomson jumped up and said, 'Shit, I've forgotten my passport in the air terminal!' They got the flight attendant's attention and they got the plane, which had already started to taxi down the runway, back to the gate. They put the stairs down and Ken ran across the runway while the plane waited with the engines running. The door was locked when he reached the terminal but he pointed to the passport sitting on the seat and one of the terminal employees handed it to him. He ran back to the plane which finally left Oslo.

That was Sunday morning February 1 and Bob's wife Vicki was expecting their first child any day in London. Bob was hoping that he could be there so he was anxious to get to Stockholm, do the gig and leave right after.

The trucks arrived in Stockholm on time but there was one slight problem. The guy who drove Dave's truck from Oslo to Stockholm had no passport with him and it was up to him to get the truck over to the ferry after the gig that would bring the gear to England. There would be another tractor to meet the trailer when it arrived in England to take it to the Royal Albert Hall in London. The timing was going to be extremely tight.

The group played the gig in Stockholm that Sunday and on Monday the trucks prepared to leave for London. It was a long drive to the ferry crossing at Bremerhaven. The ferry had to be taken by the trucks by Tuesday because there were only two running each week and the one later on would have been too late to have gotten the trucks to England in time for the concert on Thursday night, February 5.

The gear had to be set up on Wednesday afternoon so that the band could do the show on Thursday. The group and most of the road crew took a British Airways flight to London after the concert while Roger, Rick and Charly stayed behind to do some press on February 2. That was also the day that Jessie Siebenberg was born, Bob and Vicki's first child, at the Hammersmith Hospital in London at 7:30 in the evening.

At the ferry docks in Bremerhaven, the trucks had to catch a boat that left at 5:00 p.m. Dave's truck, which was being driven by the Norwegian, made it to the ferry on time as did Lenny, who had driven the coach down from Oslo. Lenny was standing by the railing of the ship at quarter to five and there was no sign of Pat with the light truck. If Pat didn't make it on time, the Albert Hall gig would have been put in jeopardy. Apparently Pat had really put the hammer down on the way from Stockholm, picking up about a hundred speeding tickets and driving virtually day and night. He arrived at the docks at about ten to five and had to clear customs. The guard told him that it was too late to get on the ship and he put the fence down. Without hesitation, and much like a scene from *Smokey and the Bandit*, Pat backed the truck up and then drove past the German guard, full-speed-ahead and slid on to the ferry leaving less than five inches of space between the back of the trailer and the gate to the ferry.

Once on the ferry, Pat phoned Charly in London on the radio phone and told him that he had gotten on the ship illegally and asked if Charly could get someone down from customs to meet him. Charly tried to talk to him but Pat couldn't hear him. That was unfortunate because Charly was trying to tell him that he couldn't get a customs man down to meet him. It was highly unlikely that a British civil servant, especially in customs, would drive the 50 miles from London to Harridge at two o'clock in the morning to meet an incoming Rock 'n' Roll truck. Fortunately Pat met a friend on the boat who had just come back from a middle east truck run and was good at screwing up papers to make them look like he had gone through all of the borders so there'd be no problems. When Pat arrived at Harridge, he drove straight through without any questions being asked.

(Pat had a way of getting out of tight corners on behalf of the band. Later on, during the American part of the tour, Pat would get stopped for speeding through a small town in the mid-west. He was brought up before a judge and it looked like they were going to lower the boom, lock him up for a few days and forget where they put the key. This would have been a disaster for the band so while he was defending himself in the courthouse he came up with a story that had everybody in the place in tears. He told the judge he was with an Irish folk group that travelled from town to town giving free concerts to kids. To explain the large truck that he was driving he told the judge that during these impromptu concerts, the group gave away instruments to the kids and he was carrying those freebies in the back of his truck. The judge dismissed the case without even bothering to check the story. Once again Pat made it to the concert on time.)

The Royal Albert Hall concert was a very special one for the band and the five thousand tickets sold out in less than three hours. It was going to be a farewell to England because the band was moving to America during the upcoming tour there.

The Albert Hall doesn't have many Rock shows so they hire an independent firm to come in and check the wiring and the metal work and make sure that you don't do anything that will damage the old building.

The show that night was recorded by the Island mobile studio for *The King Biscuit Hour* radio show in America and produced by Ken Scott. Most of the press was there and for the most part they raved.

Robin Denselow writing in the *Guardian* the next day commented: "With no distinctive gimmicks, no great publicity drive, or even much of a distinctive sound - except that their music is excellent and unmistakeably British - Supertramp seem to have sneaked in from nowhere to acquire the status of a respectably successful band. That reputation is well deserved, as they showed with this concert at the Albert Hall, but I confess that it still surprises me slightly. The band played well, sang

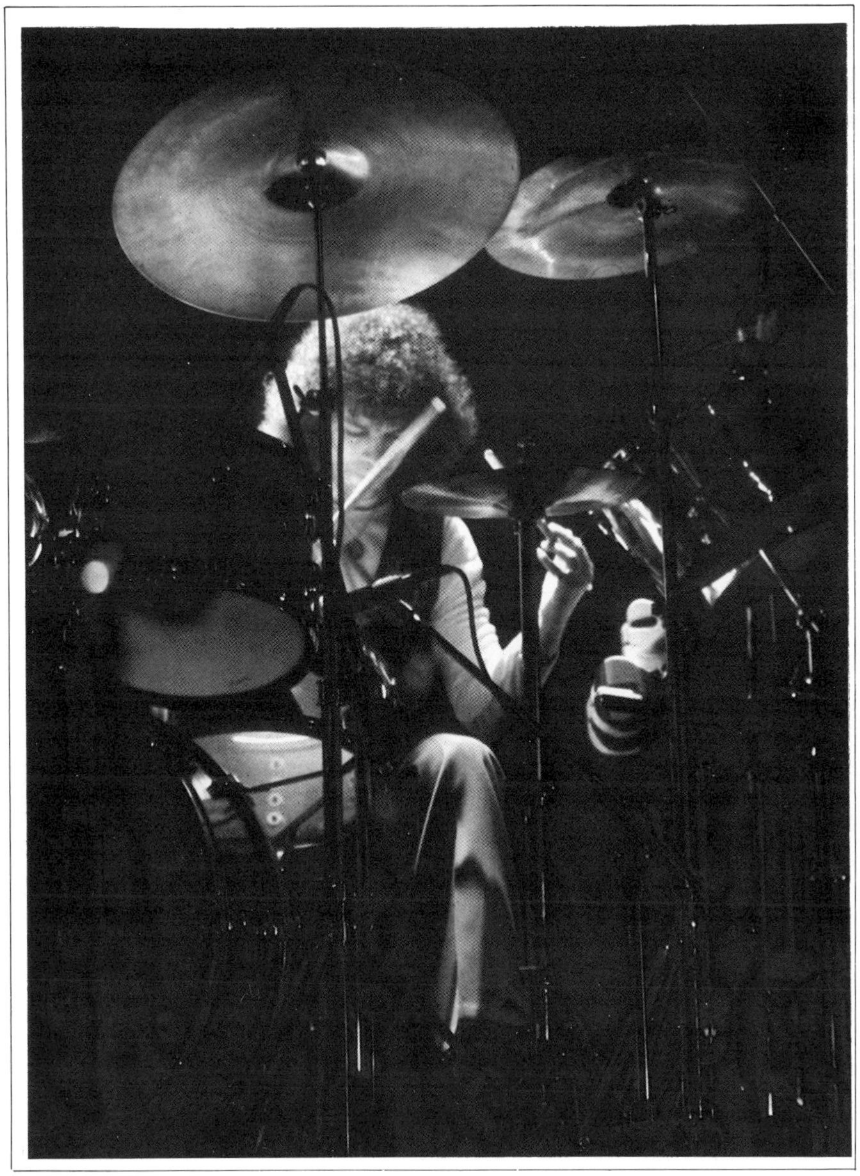

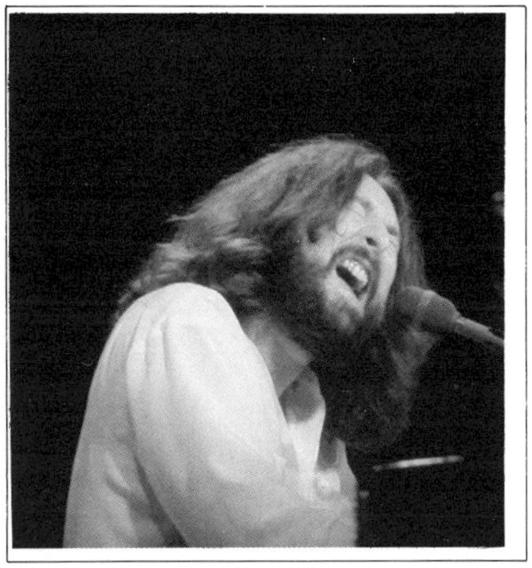

well, and demonstrated a range of excellent songs, certainly. But there was only a narrow margin on all counts that separated them from the countless other good British bands who are doomed to failure.

"Supertramp's main bonus was their sheer professionalism. A versatile five-piece, they were constantly swapping instruments, so on one song they could have three keyboard players and on another two of them could move across to bass and saxophone. They could swap around with their vocals and harmonies too. And with their carefully arranged material - with the songs performed as elaborate set-pieces, rather than the basis for improvisations - they kept a careful balance between their considerable store of pleasing melodies and the occasional patches on instrumental dexterity.

"At times they showed an instrumental and vocal skill, and lightness of touch, that was reminiscent of 10cc - but without their cleverness or wit. Elsewhere, there were echoes of several other British bands, all blended smoothly and professionally together into a style that was far too clever and pleasing for me possibly to attack, but never with quite the originality or edge that marks out a band of truly first-class status. They deserved a good reception, but not quite as good."

"Superlative. Absolutely superlative," was the way that *Melody Maker* writer Esdale Maclean saw the show at the Albert Hall. "Supertramp at the Royal Albert Hall, London played a set which brought to the best aspects of their recorded work with the gusto of a stage show.

"They came across as a warm, vital band and gave such a unified performance that they seemed to be thinking with one brain.

"They played with a precision which never faltered, and, more importantly, put heart and feeling into their material, which rounded out their act.

"On the concert stage, stripped of all the studio gimmickry (there was one blatant use of tapes - on Rudy) strings and grand airs, they offered the audience only their songs, played with a loving care which emphasized the oneness of the band. That they are all into the material is obvious, for the songs are so crafted that an uninterested player would stand out a mile. But here we had heart and skill.

"Onstage, Supertramp's engine room of Bob Benberg on drums and Dougie Thomson on bass, gains more honours than on record. They give the band a hearty kick at the bottom and steam along completely in control of their own power. The only criticism here is that Thomson is a very stylised funk-oriented bassist who thumps his notes out abruptly and would be better advised on the softer passages to make them flow and blend into each other. Roger Hodgson, who played bass on their first album, was far more subtle - but there again he lacked power.

"Hodgson and Rick Davies between them played a number of keyboards with Davies' unique chunky style sounding equally at home on the Steinway or a Moog. Hodgson provided economical accompaniment on electric guitar, but the jack of all trades was John Helliwell, who embellished the sound with flighty pieces from a variety of saxes and also lent a hand on synthesizer. He added a touch of humour by referring to 'his' band and introducing one number, 'This is a song I let them write for me on my last album.'

"The highlights were many: Sister Moonshine, Ain't Nobody But Me, and Lady from Crisis? What Crisis?, while the better songs from Crime - Hide In Your Shell, Rudy and If Everyone Was Listening benefited greatly by the absence of superfluous studio distractions. And for an encore it was good to see Roger Hodgson accompany himself on acoustic guitar for a beautiful throwaway version of Home Again from the first album before the band launched into Crime Of the Century.

"The faults. Well, you tell me. One or two passages seemed rushed, and Dreamer suddenly accelerated halfway through. But that is splitting hairs and finding fault purely for the sake of it in what was a totally superb performance."

Invitations had been sent out to the media and close friends of the band for a party after the concert at the hotel and included was the sanitary ribbon that usually hangs over the toilet at the Holiday Inn. To get into the party, you had to present the invitation and be wearing this ribbon to get in. Lenny had provided coaches to bring people from the hall to the Holiday Inn for a party that turned out to be the social event of the music industry that week in London. All the relatives were there including Rick's mother and aunt and all of Lenny's family.

"I remember after the show, while everybody was in the dressing room and all the family and relatives were there, the very proper manager of the Albert Hall came over to me," remembers Charly. "He was wearing a white tux with a flower and he told me that he'd appreciate it if I could have all of the people leave in about ten minutes because all of the employees at the hall wanted to go home. I invited him into the dressing room to see what was going on. He didn't want to go in at first because he expected to see the type of madness that had often occurred with other acts. All he saw this time was grandmothers and mothers and children. He came in and had a cup of tea. Everybody cheered him and he finally said, 'You can all stay as long as you want and anytime that Supertramp wants to come back to the Albert Hall, they'd be more than welcome.'"

That was February 5 and the group had until February 15 to get themselves to America. Dave and Cass Margereson were already there. For some people that meant selling property, cars and band equipment. The band had a flea market sale over in a church basement to sell all the furniture.

In the next few days the band slept a lot, ate well and said a lot of farewells to friends. On Sunday morning February 15 they were at Heathrow Airport for the British Airways flight to New York. The wives came to say goodbye because the next time they saw them would be in California at the end of the first leg of the U.S. tour. There were 17 people leaving that day and when they got to New York the first thing they did was go to a Mexican restaurant compliments of Pat Luce and A&M Records and then head back to the Mayflower Hotel on Central Park West where they stayed for a few days before they left for Allentown, Pennsylvania on the first date of the American tour.

Steve Rosen of *Sounds Magazine* caught up with the group in the U.S. in May of 1976 during a short break in the touring schedule and reported back: "Supertramp hornman and funnyman John Helliwell gazed longingly out the A&M Records publicity office window at the burgundy Dino Ferrari.

"'I wouldn't mind one of those,' he mused. At which point this reporter said, 'C'mon, you could afford one.' Helliwell's eyes opened and an incredulous smile creased his face. 'We're not rich, man,' he explained, though one might find this situation difficult to believe after, in the U.S. at least, the almost overnight success.

"Though the band is not quite as pleased with Crisis as it was with Crime, it is nonetheless climbing in the American charts. It has been slow going for the band in the States and with the first two albums both doing so well the audience will certainly be growing. Tramp has found American audiences to be receptive to the music and though they dislike the term 'an intellectual band' they do play music 'for people to listen to.'

"'If we're playing and somebody yells out 'Boogie!' it doesn't bother us too much . . . it just bothers the people around that person. It doesn't put us off really because it doesn't happen that much. We don't really get people shouting bad things . . . it's usually people shouting out (Helliwell imitating American accent) 'Supertramp are aaall riiiight.'

"'But then the best one was somewhere in England,' resumed Helliwell, 'and we asked if everyone was listening and we stopped and there was about a five second period of quietness from the audience and then somebody yelled out 'Perfect'. And everybody clapped.'

"Supertramp admiration goes beyond the verbal; at one particular concert when Davies began the intro for Poor Boy, a young lady ran on stage, grabbed hold of him, and almost knocked him off the stool. It's a feeling the band likes but one they're not trying to cultivate. Currently on an 80-stop tour of America and Canada (after which they head to Japan, Australia and New Zealand) they're simply playing the music which has been six years in development. Helliwell, Davies, Bob Benberg, Roger Hodgson and Dougie Thomson are content to produce material of considerable merit and hope it finds an audience. 'And when it does I'm going to buy one of those Ferraris,' chides Helliwell.

"'I know when I go to concerts I just go to listen to the music,' John offers. 'You just want to be able to hear everything and see the band play and to really dig on the music. It's all subconscious . . . we don't try and do anything in a particular style. We're just five diverse influences playing music and if you listen you can really hear quite a bit. All we really want to do is to get across to as many people as possible.'"

From the U.S. and Canada, Supertramp headed for Japan, New Zealand and Australia to "get across to as many people as possible" before heading back across the Pacific to their new base of operations in Los Angeles and the prospect of starting work on a new album. □

Supertramp   Even In The Quietest Moments...

CHAPTER ELEVEN

After eight solid months of touring the world, an exhausted Supertramp filed through customs at the Los Angeles airport after a long flight across the Pacific. (Actually, having left New Zealand, it took Rick about 23 hours to get home because for some reason he went around the world the wrong way. "I had pneumonia at the time," remembers Rick. "It was really bad to get into a plane because of my ears - and we must have landed and taken off at least six times. When I finally arrived in New York, I didn't really have any ears left.")

There would be time for a short break, but the group members were under no illusions that it would be more than a short breather before it came time to ponder the next album. And beyond that, another major concert excursion to meet the growing demand for personal appearances by the band around the world. There had been a number of offers from South America but it didn't look like there was going to be too many holes in the recording and concert schedule to accommodate.

"The Crisis world tour was fantastic," says Dougie, "but not everybody enjoyed it. Those things are so long but it is possible to enjoy certain portions of it. I always like to take advantage of the travel. Tokyo was fantastic and I drove a lot of Australia - the snowy mountains, right up to the tropics. The Crisis tour had been particularly hard, especially the American and European part because we were playing five days a week. We didn't have a lot of money so we couldn't screw around a lot. I'm a real traveler so I don't mind the touring aspect of all this. It's a big thrill for me.

"The American part of the tour we were starting to be accepted by bigger audiences but it was pretty intense. We worked five nights a week, sometimes two shows a night, because we had started to sell out. It was pretty hard work but it was exciting at the same time because at the end we knew that there was Japan, Australia and New Zealand to look forward to. We'd never been there before and it was like new frontiers. I don't remember consciously having the thought that it was happening in a big way for us. We were being successful because we were always planning ahead.

"The press was pretty kind to us on that tour. I always read a bit of good and a bit of bad press. I like to see what people were saying. On the Crisis tour we got a lot of good press which was encouraging because it meant people wanted to know, and more and more people were coming to see us just by word of mouth."

Dougie was not the only one who didn't really mind the long-tour aspect of being in a successful band. "I think it's a lot of fun and as a matter of fact, after the Crisis tour, I could've gone out and done it again after a little rest," admits John. "But various individuals in the group react differently to the situation of being on the road constantly. It blew us out for a little while, so we came back, rested for a bit and then had to think about keeping the momentum going. We had to do another album and we were determined to plan it out before going into the studio. We thought that the Crisis album was a little bit disjointed and the band as a whole at that time didn't really like the album. We wanted to do a more cohesive album this time around so we rented a house in Malibu where Dave Margereson lived and we rehearsed there."

Continues Bob: "Dave had a house that was picked for its out-of-town location. We were all living in Los Angeles at this point and we knew that there was no way that we were going back to the A&M lot to rehearse or record. But more than that, the city itself didn't really appeal to anybody in the band. At the house in Malibu, we just moved the furniture out of the living room and rehearsed there. Dave lived in the guest house in the back of the main house.

"We put together the album in rough demo form learning from our experience with Crisis. Sometimes Rick wouldn't be there, sometimes Dougie wouldn't be there and so on but we got it together in pretty rough form."

After the rehearsals, there were a couple of decisions to be made. First they had to find a suitable recording location and second, they wanted to find a producer. This was no reflection on Ken Scott's ability because the sound he got on the band's third and fourth LPs speaks for itself. There was just a feeling amongst everyone that they wanted a change from the time-consuming perfection that Scott strives for on all his recording projects. The group also wanted a shot at producing the record themselves with a top-notch engineer.

Their first choice was Geoff Emerick who had worked with people like Paul McCartney and had won a Grammy in 1975 for his work on McCartney's *Band On the Run* LP. But at the time the band was due to record, he was working with America in a studio in Hawaii. Instead, Emerick suggested that the band use his protégé Pete Henderson and as he had come highly recommended, the group decided to use him.

They pondered a number of studios but they finally settled on the Caribou Studios in the mountains of Colorado just outside of Boulder. They moved up there for a few months prior to Christmas of 1976 and it soon became obvious that not everybody was happy with the choice of location.

"We started to work there, but personality-wise, the group at that time wasn't really together," remembers John. "People were having different thoughts and going off and doing different things, so the group wasn't cohesive at all."

"We moved the whole kit and kaboodle to Caribou up in the Rocky Mountains," says Bob, "but I think that Dougie and I were the only ones to enjoy it. Rick wasn't very happy there and Roger was the only one up there without his girlfriend, so he was a little bit lonely stuck out there in the middle of nowhere.

"I thought it was fantastic to record where there was pine forests and snow. Everybody had their own little cabin with big brass beds. The place is actually a working cattle ranch and the main studio was like a two-storey barn with the studio upstairs. There was a big main eating place where your meals were scheduled each day. I'd usually ski down to the studio. I'd go up to the top and put on these little cross-country skis and skid my way down to the studio. The recording experience itself I thought was great."

Caribou being at 9,000 feet in the Rockies, the air is a bit thin so they keep oxygen in the studio which Roger made a lot of use of while he was doing his vocals.

Dougie had another perspective. "Going to Caribou was kind of fragmented because initially Roger and I were into going there, but Rick wasn't so keen on it. As it turns out, we went up there for too long. To me that was the beginning of Rick and Roger not being happy in the creative mode. Rick had a lot less influence on the album than what was good for him. I would have been happier if he'd been a lot more into it but the circumstances didn't permit that. That was a real transition period for us in my opinion."

With most of the basic tracks for *Even In the Quietest Moments* finished at Caribou, just before Christmas, the band moved back to Los Angeles and went into The Record Plant there to finish it up.

Pete Henderson had done the recording with the band at Caribou and when the group got back to Los Angeles Geoff Emerick was available. This made it a bit sticky because the band had started to feel comfortable with Pete and were happy to let him continue working with them.

"During the time that we worked with Pete

Rick and Sue - flight from Vancouver to San Fransisco, '77.

Henderson, we thought that he was working out really well," says John. "We had a nice relationship going with him. Geoff came in and did some of the mixing but we'd gotten to know Pete so well by that time that we really felt that we were better off to let him finish with us. That's not to put the knock on Geoff because he's really good but that was the situation we found ourselves in."

During the band's stay at The Record Plant, journalist Matt Mabel dropped by to report back to *Sounds* in England just what was up with Supertramp.

Mabel later wrote: "You work hard and eventually convince your record company to give you an open cheque book to accompany you into the studio. The result is a huge hit spurred on by a nationwide tour.

"A year later, you repeat the cycle and become staple diet of both the album chart and disc jockeys who profess to program 'rock' radio. The second tour goes so well that a 'thank you' gig is arranged at London's Albert Hall. It sells out.

"After the gig, you vanish, leaving the album charts and the playlists behind. Another year later, you sit between colourfully carpeted walls at The Record Plant in Los Angeles and say, 'I hope they haven't forgotten us in Britain.'

"So says Roger Hodgson after ace Record Plant engineer Geoff Emerick gives the Supertramp co-leader permission to leave the control room where the mixing of the new album Even In the Quietest Moments is almost complete.

"In their own minds Supertramp haven't moved to L.A. according to Hodgson, who loyally sports an A&M Records t-shirt and is pretty shagged out, as the Americans would say, after two-thirds of a day of listening to playbacks.

"'We'll live in a Supertramp bubble. We are each other's friends so it's like the English vibe is still there. L.A. is a totally crazy place, none of us like living here particularly. We like the weather and that's about it.'

"Since they'll be touring for nearly a year following the album's release, there is hardly a question of living anywhere in the first place. Bette Midler cleverly dubbed the City Of Angels 'The Home Of Absolutely Nothing' on this year's Grammy Awards telecast, and Supertramp fit comfortably into her definition.

"'We haven't found anywhere we want to live really, although I don't think we want to go back to England. I don't personally miss it but some of the others do. If anything I miss the subtleties of the English.'

"Supertramp have taken a big step on the new LP and decided to produce themselves, jettisoning the services of Ken Scott. That move comes as a reaction to their last release, Crisis? What Crisis? Problems Hodgson sees in Crisis have been solved on Even In the Quietest Moments.

"'Crisis,' he explains with an either-you-laugh-or-you-cry smile, 'came to mean more to us as a title than it did to other people because it was really a crisis album, coming right off the road and going into the studio.'

"'It could have been much better than Crime Of the Century but it wasn't. We had a lot of bad luck in the studio. We really didn't enjoy making it and in the end it was kind of a patch up job. A lot of people liked it but for us it missed.'

"Funny how they don't tell you that before the album comes out. Still, this time around after the 1976 North American tours, they took a three month planning period, similar to their occupation of a Somerset farm house three years ago planning what would become their best seller, Crime.

"With 40 songs in hand, the band worked out arrangements of seven and had the set pretty much in mind before they began recording at Jimmy Guercio's Caribou studio last November.

"Appropriately, working with material that sounds as if it has come more from the heart than ever before, the Tramp have captured a warmer, fuller sound.

"'Working with Ken we became perfectionists in a way and went overboard on Crisis and became perfectionists technically. Now we are concentrating on getting the feel of a song down. That's why it has taken so long. Some days we don't feel like playing. So we don't play. Now the sound is not quite so clinical, it's more live and definitely much better.'

"Hodgson himself, has discovered the Oberheim synthesizer since we heard from him last. 'It's an amazing instrument, we did most of the strings and a lot of other sounds with it. It gets any sound under the sun.'

"Two of the new tracks stand out in his mind, one of which is reckoned to be the band's best, a ten-minute job called Fool's Overture which once had the provisional title of The String Machine Epic. It closes the album.

"If you're wondering why the Overture is reserved for the end, then you'll have to get into the, er, depth, of the message. The album ends with a conductor tapping his baton on his music-stand after a track dealing with The End Of Everything As We Know It.

"With such honest material they are leaving

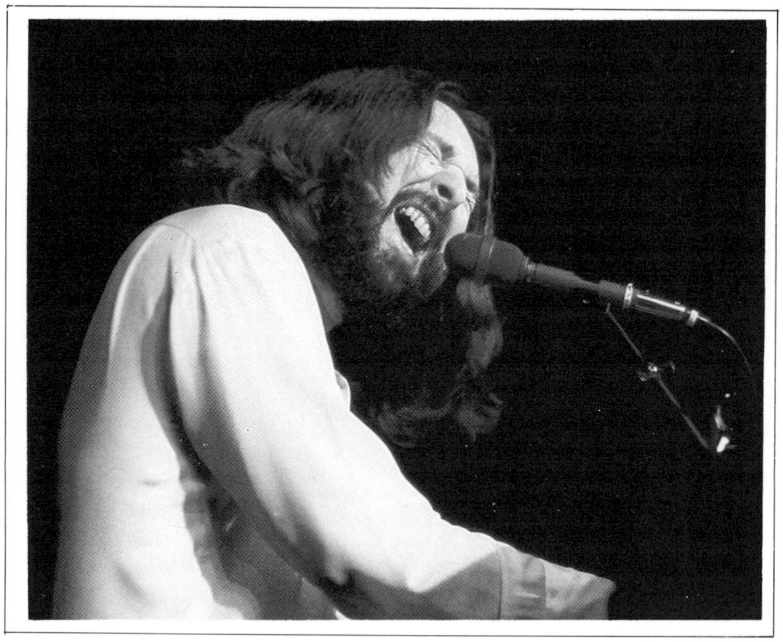

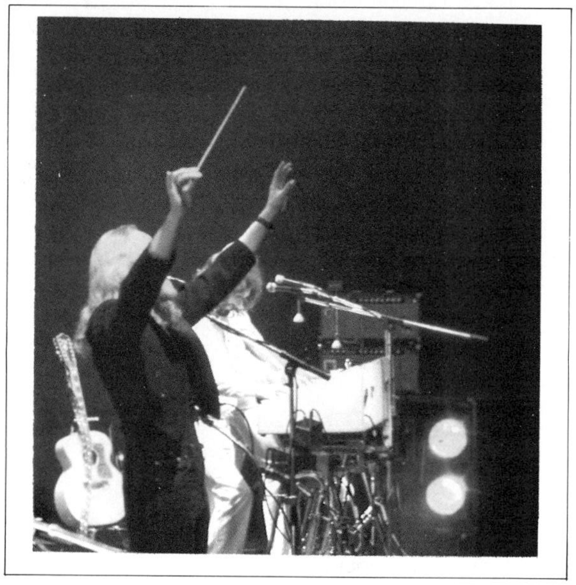

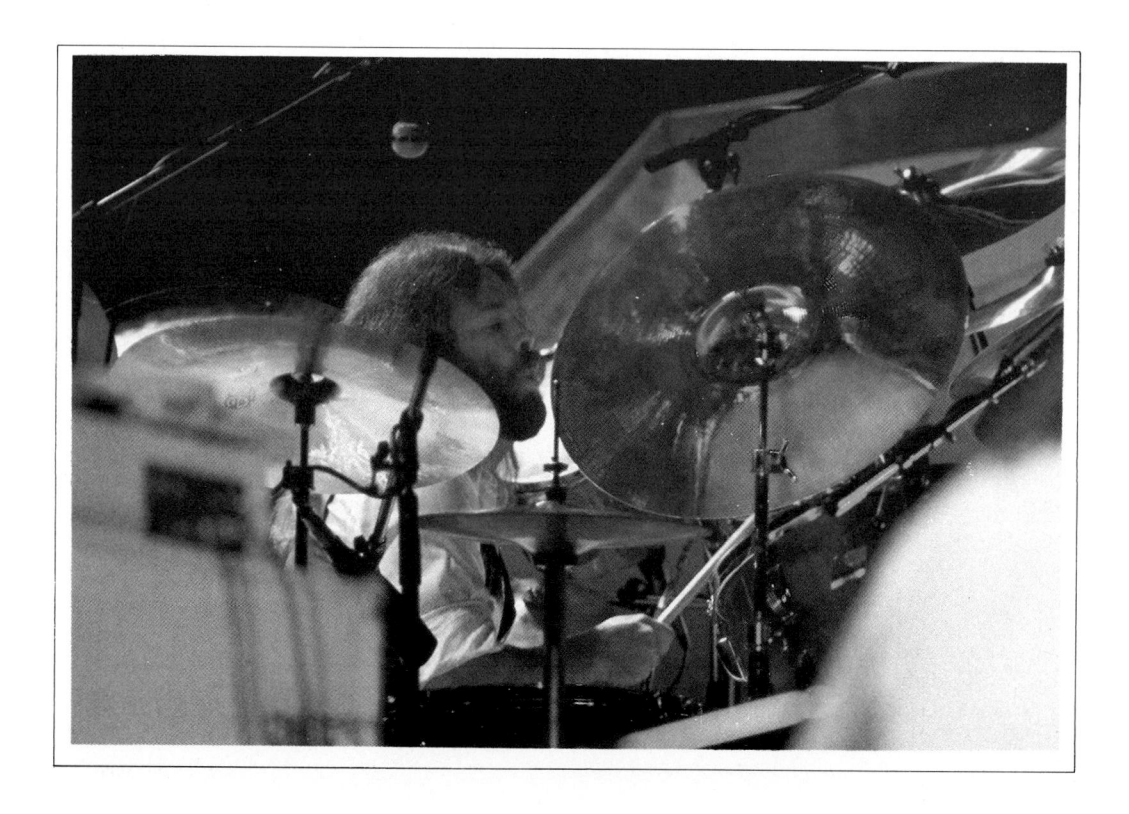

themselves open to plenty of criticism which, no doubt, by presstime has manifested itself.

"The other stand out track for Hodgson is so because he sees it as 'a hit,' in a voice approaching the Queen's English. Not that Supertramp think product-wise, of course, but 'it will help in America because you really can't do anything here without one. You just write and record your songs. Give A Little Bit is one of mine. Obviously if you play the game right it is good if you have a number that is going to be a single. Next year, we'll probably put out singles as singles as well. We've got songs that would make great singles but wouldn't fit so well on an album.'

"The tour, which begins in Canada to coincide with the album's release, took a month's rehearsal. Fans who have already seen the Crime Of the Century Film time and time again will be happy to know that it will be taking a back seat to a new film shot to coincide with Fool's Overture. There'll be slides too.

"'The set is going to be really amazing. For a start it will be much stronger 'cause we've got three albums to pull material from. We can pick the ones we enjoy playing and the ones which are the most popular.

"'It'll be great to play England again. We don't want to lose our English identity. I dread the thought of anyone ever thinking we were an American band. After the American tour we do England, then Europe, some recording, then another American tour, a bit more recording after that, then Japan, Australia, and if we last that long, we'll be happy.'

"So, you spend time on another album, until you are completely satisfied, you aim for the charts and the air waves, and try to remind your audience that your vanishing act can go on forever. Supertramp's quietest moments have temporarily been cancelled."

Late in the recording and mixing process of *Even In the Quietest Moments* - early in 1977 - Ritchie Yorke, a Canadian-based Aussie journalist with a considerable international media profile, spent a most memorable evening at The Record Plant (after dinner at a strange vegetarian restaurant called the Yellow Submarine) and spoke to the individual members of Supertramp about the various tracks on the LP.

"The opening cut, Give A Little Bit, is one of Roger's songs," said Rick. "It's a lightweight opener, a nice daffy song. You might even call it commercial (chuckles)."

Adds Bob: "Roger had been working at Malibu for quite a while on this tune. I'd hear the song in hotel rooms and places like that. He had the song on a little tape when I first joined the band so I was quite familiar with the tune. We tried out various drum things and it seemed right to ride it along on the snare drum . . . giving it something almost like a train beat. So it's all on the snare and bass drum, with no tom-tom fills or anything. It was something to march right through, to keep it really happy."

"Give A Little Bit is very simple," comments Roger. "The album starts out simply and builds in intensity. The song seemed the best opener. As I said, it's a very simple song - give a little bit of your love to me and I'll give a little bit of love to you."

"Rick had been working on Lover Boy for quite a while and finally came up with the long middle section," says Bob. "I just heard that as a really slow, really solid sort of beat, just to give the song dynamics underneath it all, because the song itself is really powerful and it needed something really solid underneath it."

Over to Rick: "Well, now, this is the first time that I've had to provide a description of Lover Boy. Well I really wrote the song so I could tell interviewers what I wrote the song about. I was inspired by advertisements in men's magazines telling you how to pick up women. You know, you send away for it and it's guaranteed not to fail. If you haven't slept with at least five women in two weeks, you can get your money back. It's sort of based around that. I mean, you just can't stop the lover boy! It's really an excuse to get into some big sounds - the big city noises and a big chorus. It's an exercise in doing something with the music. You can't stop the lover boy because he's guaranteed. He's sent away for his thing."

"Downstream is about the sea rather than a stream," continues Rick. "The actual song is old but the lyrics are new. It's just me and the piano. It was done in one take, piano and voice together. We're going to put a lot of harmony vocals creeping up towards the end of the song. It's quite a step for us not to fiddle around with things for months on end."

"It's my favourite song on the entire album because it's so personal and so pure," Bob contends. "I love it when Rick just works with piano. What the song is saying and the way he puts it out really floors me everytime I hear it."

"Downstream is of course a love song by Rick," figures Roger. "He's just got married so the song's probably about his wife Sue."

"The song Even In the Quietest Moments is one of Roger's pet projects I think," says Bob. "It's also been on the way for quite a while. The track gave me a chance to knock out a pretty meaty beat through the middle section while keeping the rest of it rather gentle. I stayed out of the way in the rest of it - just adding little things here and there."

Adds Dougie: "This is a song we first came across in Malibu. It's a pretty simple little acoustic song which gets into a good groove in the end. It gives Bob and I a chance to sit on it. It's one of Roger's nicest melodies."

"It has two basic parts," says Rick. "It starts off in a very standard melody thing and then it notches onto a sort of one chord progression or perhaps we should call it a digression. It's a thing where there's hundreds of sounds coming in and going out, a whole collage thing. You'll have lots of fun trying to figure out what's what."

Roger: "Quietest Moments is another love song. It's kind of a dual love song - it could be to a girl or it could be to God. I've left it ambiguous so everyone can take it how they wish. Basically it's just about a guy who's searching. I'm a seeker. I think I'll always be a seeker."

Everyone seems to have an opinion on Roger's song "Babaji."

John: "Babaji is one of the people who is supposed to help run the earth, to run this planet we're living on. He's one of the big mystics."

Rick: "Babaji is one of the biggest mystics we've ever heard of, isn't he? He's supposed to be six foot three. (Laughs)"

John: "He's immortal. There are accounts of people who've met him but he's supposed to be able to travel in and out of the physical world."

Rick: "You won't ever see him if he doesn't want you to see him. I mean, you should really talk to Roger about this. It sounds highly suspicious to me. But I don't want to get into any controversy about it."

John: "Good lord no!"

Rick: "You can't see him unless he wants you to see him. So if you haven't seen him, it's not because he doesn't exist but because he doesn't want you to see him."

Bob: "Babaji is like Roger's light of life. I don't know exactly how Roger would put it but he's Roger's guiding light sort of guy. Roger came up with the different bits of time I play. That cut took the longest to work the drums out for - it was crucial just where I played what, whether that trip should be on high-hat or on the bell. It all had to be right in the right spots. I had to make the moves in the right place."

Roger: "Babaji is a very high spirit à la Christ and Krishna. He's less known because he didn't have a public or a mission like Christ or Krishna. He's kind of a back room boy. He runs the universe and he runs everything. He's an unbelievable spirit or force on God. He is God really ... a manifestation of God. He's had physical form for hundreds of years. He doesn't have to eat or anything. He inhabits the Himalayas with a small band of disciples. He's a legend in India but he's lesser known in the west. I don't know, talking about him kind of lessens him somehow. It's weird. It really is fascinating."

"I'm just finishing off the lyrics for From Now On," admits Rick. "Words hot from the brainbox. It's turned into a fantasy about a Mr. Average, if there is such a person, who goes off into these weird trips. He plays mental games with himself to get away from the monotony of his work. He pretends he's on TV, like a pirate or running through the desert, and he just opens up a lot of avenues. There's a big chorus at the end saying that he's going to live a fantasy forever, that he's resigned to living in fantasy all the time, that he can't really take the normal life he's leading. He'd sooner be lots of different characters."

"That's another of Rick's old songs," says Bob. "I've always enjoyed it and I just love playing it. It really suits my style and I had a chance to open up a little towards the end of it. I love John's sax trip in the tail end of the song."

"The music to that song is quite old," adds John. "It was one of the very first things I heard Supertramp play when I first went down to have a blow with them, and that was over three years ago. I really liked the number then."

And what of the final track on the LP, the ten-minute "Fools Overture"?

"We've been calling that tune the String Machine Epic for so long now it's hard to get that out of our brains," says John. "It came primarily from a few melodies that Roger had worked out on the string machine thing we use on stage to create string sounds, or sounds thereabouts. The track is a combination of a year's work. We've been putting strings and brass instruments on to pad it out a bit. (Chuckles) It's going to sound really good."

Adds Bob: "On this album, that's the real sort of grand tune for me and for everybody in the band. It's the epic of the album this time out. I tried to get as much of that grand power in there as I could."

The final word to Roger: "Ooooh! (Laughs) Well, I'd like people to make up their own minds about this one really. I like being vague and yet saying enough to set people's imaginations running riot. So there's a lot of suggestions in there about the coming holocaust, the fall of mankind, or whatever you want to call it. It's

Roger and Dougie and a Dutch journalist promoting "Quietest Moments."

another searching song really."

There were a number of changes on *Even In the Quietest Moments*. First, the album was basically produced by the band with the help of Pete Henderson, the engineer. It was the first time that the band had actually taken on that task since the first two albums which Rick jokingly admits "were no adverts for our production skills."

Though they made a lot of use of the Oberheim string machine programmed by Garey Mielke, the band worked with Michel Colombier on a number of the orchestral arrangements for the LP. Richard Hewston had done the string arrangements on Crime and Crisis, but at this point, he was close to 7,000 miles away.

For the album cover concept, there would be another trip made up to the Caribou Ranch in Colorado to drag a grand piano up into the mountains and let the snow settle on it. The lengths an art director, in this case Michael Doud, will go to get the right effect for the design Doud/Hagiwara had devised. But there you have it. The piano sat shivering in the cold mountain air, the snow accumulated on it and photographer Bob Seideman was there at precisely the right moment to catch the scene with the addition of some sheet music headed "Fool's Overture." (Anyone proficient in reading music might note that the actual music is in fact "The Star Spangled Banner." Subtle, lads, very subtle.)

As the album was coming to a close at The Record Plant in Los Angeles, their minds were turning collectively to the prospect of another long tour through North America and Europe. Ritchie Yorke broached the subject when he visited the band in the studio and got some rather comical, albeit misleading, insights into the stage show.

John: "We'll have glitter suits."

Dougie: "Flamethrowers."

Rick: "We'll have a huge statue of Donald Duck at the back. No seriously, as soon as the gong goes for Crime, it will sprout bubbles. We hope this lighter approach will go down well."

John: "Yeah, we're playing two weeks at Disneyland."

Rick: "Which is where we got the duck, incidentally. We couldn't pass it up because it was going to be thrown out. We got a few of the guys to make up the bubble thing. It took a few months but it's going to be all right."

Russel was asked about the secret of Supertramp's sensational live sound. His response? "Money!"

"Really! In the sense that nobody else ever wants to spend that amount of money on a sound. Everybody else rents . . . they rent whatever they can get, whatever the quality is in that particular year. There are only two companies in America which can cover everyone and if you don't get those people you have to go down the ladder to poorer and poorer sound. So it was better for us to buy, because to perform our trip well, they just don't make the right stuff for rental. We've slowly built up a system that's become not only legendary but a bottomless pit in terms of finances. But a motto of ours is that it's always better to buy. The sound on this upcoming tour is going to be infinitely better than other tours. The last one was less than perfect. But it's a costly business. It's painful. They make it, and I spend it."

The sound system that Russel had been talking about was the acknowledged Ferrari of audio systems designed by Martin Audio Limited of London, England. David Martin, who had previously worked with Deep Purple, designed the system and formed the company in England in 1971. Since then he has had his equipment used by most of the top names in the Rock world for touring purposes. It was really Supertramp though that demonstrated what the system could do given their constant striving for perfection in live sound. Anybody that has ever attended a live Supertramp show can attest to the fact that the clarity of sound, whether it be in an arena or in a large open-air stadium, is second to none. But then what would one expect from someone like David Martin who likes to quote Rudyard Kipling when expounding his business philosophy. "They copied all they could, but they couldn't follow my mind, and I left them sweating and stealing, a year and a half behind!" You don't mess with a technician with a poetic bent. Midas mixing boards also played a large part in Supertramp's overall excellence in sound.

Even In the Quietest Moments was completed in mid-March and was released shortly after to coincide with the opening dates of the tour that started on April 6, 1977 in Regina, a city on the Canadian prairies. "Give A Little Bit" was released as a single from the LP and it was obvious almost immediately that it would rapidly climb the charts, especially in Canada where Supertramp's following had reached fanatical proportions.

When the band reached Canada, the excitement in the air said it all really. *Even In the*

Quietest Moments hit the streets as the band took to the road and in every city at Supertramp information-central, in the hotel room manned by Charly Prevost, the phone was never quiet.

Ring! It's the head office of A&M Records in Los Angeles with news that the initial reaction to the new album is unprecedented. San Francisco has discovered Supertramp and they're shipping the album like proverbial hot cakes. Los Angeles is ready. A sold-out Forum date is waiting there with a big party to celebrate the event afterwards.

Ring! It's a call from Bobbi Cowan Associates, the band's Los Angeles-based public relations company. "Great news!" says the excited voice at the other end of the line. "The trades love the album. The reviews are great and *Record World* magazine has you on the front page as Flashmaker Of the Week for being the album that was most added to FM stations across North America."

The trades are the internal bibles of the music industry, the magazines that influence radio stations, record stores and the rest of the media around the world. There are urgent requests from magazines around the world for interviews including one for an upcoming feature in *Melody Maker*, one of Britain's top music papers.

With every news bulletin posted in the dressing room by Prevost at each gig, you can feel the elation within the band although unspoken as though any open cares-to-the-wind optimism might somehow prick the balloon. Dave Margereson allows only a nudge and a smile: "Looks like it might be our year," he says.

"I don't know what it is," Roger says one day in a rare free moment in an airport waiting room. "It feels as though the whole thing was pre-destined in a way, but we're always surprised as each day unfolds. There is always something to give reason for getting up each morning. The whole thing is still an adventure."

Even In the Quietest Moments shipped platinum in Canada which meant that there was a demand for over 100,000 copies of the LP. At the same point in time, *Crime Of the Century* had sold over 380,000 copies and *Crisis? What Crisis?* was nudging the 200,000 sales mark. For a country with a population of slightly over 20 million, those are impressive sales. As the band was to find out later, it was only a humble beginning to the sales plateau that they would eventually reach in Canada.

From the reviews that were coming in on *Even In the Quietest Moments*, it was one of those albums that critics seemed to want to take a middle ground on.

Geoff Barton of *Sounds* in England was one journalist who had his misgivings about the project. "Lazy acoustic guitar playing - strum, strum, strum it goes, rather nicely. And then a voice drifts in, crooning, 'Ooooh yeah. Alright, here we go again,' and the guitar gets strummed some more.

"Soon enough, up crop the lyrics. 'Give a little bit, Give a little bit of your love to me. Give a little bit, Give a little bit of my love to you.'

"And so on, numerous variations on this simple, Framptonesque theme. Slowly, subtly the song gathers impetus. A sax parps. A bass thuds neatly into the scheme of things. Vocals, at once slight and solitary, and double tracked, given a little more weight. And the guitar keeps on strumming.

"After just over four minutes, the song comes to an end. Concise, precisely executed, but on the surface of it, no great shakes - totally harmless, completely innocuous in fact.

"So how come I reckon it's the most stunning song Supertramp have ever put down on vinyl?

"Hard to say really. While Give A Little Bit - for that is its title - is serene, peaceful, romantic even, I'd say it pulled at my heartstrings but I'm afraid of being branded a sentimentalist, it's as basic as basic can be. Simply beautiful could be the phrase.

"And I only wish I could find the rest of Even In the Quietest Moments as captivating as this, its opening track. But sadly, after the towering high of the first cut, matters go slowly but steadily downhill.

"If I can remember correctly, in my largely favourable review of S'tramp's last LP Crisis? What Crisis? I pondered upon the possibility of the band becoming rather too formularized in the future. And in many ways, with this newest, long-awaited platter, this 'possibility' has cemented itself into cold, hard fact.

"The remaining three numbers on side one, Lover Boy, Even In the Quietest Moments and Downstream, do little more than tread over old ground, could be interchanged with any number on Crisis? and you really wouldn't notice the difference. The title track in particular, with its staccato, repetitive chorus-chant of 'Don't you let the sun disappear' brings back recollection of Lady.

"Side two is a little better. Babaji and From Now On continue along less-than-enthralling lines, and the closing number, Fool's Overture brings events down still further.

"A pity, because with this one, a much-touted (in the biography at least) 'twelve-minute tour-de-force,' the band really do try desperately hard to break out of their soft, sensitive musical shell and go off on a new tangent. Unfortunately it doesn't work out.

"Fools Overture is not nearly awesome or dramatic enough to be truly tagged with the label 'magnum opus'. Ostensibly a tale about Britain's current sorry economical state ('The island's sinking, let's take to the sky'), we hear Big Ben chiming, Churchill burbling on about something or other, wind whistling and rain falling, together with numerous other sound effects, all running rather clumsily against a song of very little menace or foreboding at all. Maybe Fool's Overture will come alive in the context of a S'tramp concert. We'll have to wait until August at the earliest to see.

"On the plus side are the band's lyrics, sincere, wholesome but never cringe-inducing; and the musicianship of Messrs. Hodgson, Davies, Thomson, Helliwell and Benberg, sheer perfection, never overstated; also Give A Little Bit itself.

"But one hot track out of seven simply isn't good enough, is it?"

In Canada, even the public got into the critical battle. An irate reader of the *Winnipeg-Tribune* wrote a letter to the editor after Jim Millican had written a rather unfavourable review of the album on April 30, 1977.

"I feel that I am qualified to write about this band," wrote Howard Morry of Winnipeg, "because I have all their records, and have seen them four times in the past year and a half (including once in Vancouver and both concerts in Winnipeg this year). Mr. Millican is of the impression that Supertramp is on an 'artistic decline.' He also stated that the band 'basically produces prefabricated music from the original forms which can be found on Crime Of the Century.'

"First I would like to say that Crime Of the Century was a classic album, and no record could match it for sheer perfection. However, Supertramp's second album Crisis? What Crisis? was also of excellent quality. There was the combination of orchestral arrangements, matched with a rock beat that made Crime Of the Century such a landmark. The lyrics dealt with the universal insanity theme, that had become the group's trademark by this time. While Crisis may not have had the same impact as its predecessor, it was certainly one of the top albums of the year.

"This brings us up to the latest release, Even In the Quietest Moments. Like the two albums before it, this record has more to it than can be ascertained at one listen. The first time I heard it, I felt that Supertramp had come up with an average effort. However, after listening to it a few more times, I realized that the complexity of some of the songs takes a while to get used to, and it soon became one of my favourites. That is the secret to enjoying Supertramp. You must listen to them a few times before you can fully appreciate their music. The songs that particularly stand out on this album are Give A Little Bit and Fool's Overture. They are songs the magnitude of School and Lady. An artistic decline? This is hardly the case. If anything, the group is becoming more tasteful by using John Anthony Helliwell's saxophone more generously. This adds a certain class to their style.

"Mr. Millican's comments about the group playing prefabricated music from Crime Of the Century is a very narrow view of their music. Supertramp is constantly changing their style. Crime Of the Century was basically a record of interwoven orchestral and rock patterns that were built up into amazing crescendos.

"Crisis? What Crisis? on the other hand, was much more subdued as far as a musical 'build up' went. It compensated for this by having a concept more compelling, and instrumentation more powerful than Crime.

"To complete the triumverate, Even In the Quietest Moments is a definite departure from the other two albums. It depends much more on individual solos (guitar, piano and sax), and is more subdued in its crescendos. This puts more emphasis on the songs as a whole. The vision this record conjures up is one of universal insanity, just as the other two records were. This is not, as Mr. Millican suggests, 'a parody of their greatest success.' It is merely consistent with the vision that they have. They genuinely believe in what they write, and deserve the enormous success that has been coming their way recently. If they were to start changing their basic concepts, they would be sacrificing their beliefs and cheating the fans. I was very surprised at Mr. Millican's comments on Supertramp, and I urge him to listen to Even In the Quietest Moments a few more times. I am sure he will change his mind. Even if their perfection is predictable, it is still perfection!!!"

Mario Lefebvre of *Pop Rock*, a French-Canadian Rock paper published in Quebec, the place where Supertramp first picked up its most fanatical following on the North American continent, had this to say about the LP.

"Even In the Quietest Moments est le cinquieme album de Supertramp, celui qui indiscutablement fut le plus attendu. On l'a enregistre aux studios Caribou dans le Colorado pendant plus de deux mois, on a travaille pendant pres de six mois a l'ecriture des chansons, a l'elaboration des arrangements.

"Il est donc superflu de dire qu'on a mis le paquet. On voulait faire de ce cinquieme microsillon, un succes aussi imposant que Crime Of the Century. Au point de vue des ventes, on reussira probablement, musicalement cependant, il faut avouer que Even In the Quietest Moments est legerement infeerieur.

"Ce n'est cependant pas un grave reproche, une lacune irreparable surtout lorsqu'on se souvient de l'intensite, de la beaute de la puissance du microsillon en question. En toute verite, pour bien situer le lecteur, disons que le microsillon est une suite parfaitement logique a Crisis plutot qu'a Crime, il se rapproche beaucoup plus du premier que du second.

"Even In the Quietest Moments n'a peut-etre pas l'impact de Crime Of the Century ou encore le sarcasme de Crisis mais il devient rapidement a lui seul, une entite qu'il faudra considerer comme une autre palier de franchi dans la reluisante carriere de Supertramp. Pour simplifier en quelques mots, ce que j'ai dit en plusiers lignes, disons tout simplement que c'est un disque comme on avait droit de s'attendre de la part d'un grand groupe comme Supertramp."

At the outset of the Canadian leg of the tour, Supertramp, who travelled initially using Gallagher and Lyle as their opening act, had one small problem to contend with: What songs to leave out of the show and still keep everybody happy. In Winnipeg, Manitoba where they drew over 16,600 people over a two-night period, the show ran well over an hour and a half. It was just a little too long for the dynamic effect that they were after. In Lethbridge, Alberta at the Sportsplex a few nights later, the show was pared down and the result was magic.

They opened the show with "School" and the opening few bars of harmonica from Rick never failed to bring the crowd to its feet. From that, they went into "Ain't Nobody But Me" and then Roger's high-pitched vocal performance of "Give A Little Bit."

"Bloody Well Right" - a perennial crowd pleaser - led the way to "Sister Moonshine" and "Poor Boy."

An integral part of the band's show is the lighting and visual effects. Co-ordinated lighting, film and slides are all vital elements of Supertramp's almost mesmerizing stage presentation. In the song "Even In the Quietest Moments," the black curtain at the back of the stage opened to reveal a film of a sunrise over a mountain throughout the opening of the song. The lights are all pervasive through the concert, setting the mood for each song and adding to the dynamics of the overall Supertramp stage presence.

"Hide In Your Shell" followed, and at the end Benny Gallagher and Graham Lyle came on stage to join in on the final chorus. "From Now On" followed, then "Dreamer" and "Rudy," which again saw the use of the back drop screen for a speeded up vintage film of the London to Brighton train ride as seen from the perspective of a camera placed on the front of the steam engine. The effect was spectacular, timed in such a way that the train pulled into the station and the people disembarked just as the middle section of Rudy came to a close.

Next came the concert *piece de resistance* - "Fool's Overture" with its overdub sound effects of Big Ben's chimes and Winston Churchill's voice urging British people never to capitulate to tyranny. Serious stuff with a modern day message. Later in the epic, there is a collage of both famous and infamous celebrities along with various candid shots of the members of Supertramp through various periods in their lives. The crowd was impressed to say the least.

"Another Man's Woman" was the next offering, then into "Lady," which for all intents and purposes was the final song of the show. But, of course, there's the compulsory encore that the band has learned to live with and so they come back on to do "Crime Of the Century," complete with the now familiar film of the prison bars floating through space as the song closes. The crowd appeased, many end up staring at the stage in silence long after the show is over.

The Canadian section of the tour was not without incident and after five nights of concerts in Regina, Saskatoon, Winnipeg and Lethbridge, the band arrived in Edmonton on April 12 with Roger trying to shake off a wicked cold. The Edmonton Coliseum was sold out and Roger tried bravely to make his way through the concert but early in the set, as he attempted to sing "Give A Little Bit," it was obvious that he wouldn't be able to go on. Rick took over on vocals but after a shortened set, Dougie took the mike and announced to the crowd that they would have to stop the concert. "We're working it out with the promoter and he hopes that within the next week or so he'll be able to announce the date and time of a make-up concert. You'll all get in free, so please, everyone, keep your ticket stubs."

Platinum album presentation for *Even In the Quietest Moments* by A&M Canada.

Details were worked out with promoter David Horodezky of Brimstone Productions and another concert was scheduled for July 14. It was agreed that the band would finance their own return concert in Edmonton. Loose figuring indicated that it would cost the band $40,000 to play the date, and without batting an eyelash, they penciled it into their calendar.

The next night's concert in Calgary at the Corral was also cancelled with a return date booked for July 15 and Roger, Rick and Dave Margereson stayed in Edmonton for a while to get some rest and try to fight off the cold bug that had Rick feeling a bit under the weather.

As a parting gesture, Dougie on behalf of the band, presented David Horodezky and his sidekick, known to everyone as The Bear, an all-expenses trip to Las Vegas for a week. The group also presented Horodezky, The Bear and some of the other people in the crew with watches.

From Calgary it was on to the Pacific Northwest where they had a number of concerts booked with Procol Harum. It was a major highlight of the 1977 tour for Bob.

"We joined up with Procol Harum and then did four gigs with them at Pullman University, Seattle, Vancouver and Portland," remembers Bob. "Procol Harum has been my favourite band every since I heard "A Whiter Shade Of Pale." During their set they were doing bits and pieces of everything from their records but for me the opportunity to sit behind the drummer B.J. Wilson and watch him play up close was just terrific. I've tried to emulate some of the things he does in drumming. I'm not saying that I'm like him but I have tried to follow his lead and learn from him. It's his approach more than anything. So there I was with the creator of this style that I love sitting right there playing away. It was a little nerve-wracking meeting him for the first time but after I'd had a couple of drinks with him and played darts, he was just another guy. That was tremendous."

In Vancouver, Jeani Read of the *Vancouver Province* wrote: "The Supertramp concert Friday at the Coliseum was, as might have been expected from this excellent intelligent group, a tour-de-force of musical finesse and technical integrity.

"Supertramp is a very clean capable group of players and singers exhibiting a fine and fresh level of musicianship, changing roles and instruments continually, excelling in almost everything, and producing a variety of texture and dynamics that is sheer pleasure to hear in live performance."

There were a number of U.S. dates including a sell-out in Los Angeles at the Forum before the band returned to Canada at the beginning of June for two sold-out concerts at Toronto's Maple Leaf Gardens that was opened by a Vancouver-based group called the Hometown Band.

After the show, the group members were presented with platinum albums for *Even In the Quietest Moments* by A&M Records of Canada to commemorate the sale of more than 100,000 copies in Canada. Roger, a long time supporter of the Greenpeace organization - actively involved in stopping the annual whale and seal hunts - raffled off his platinum album with the proceeds going to Greenpeace. A&M had flown in several members of the British press for the concerts that drew close to 30,000 fans over the two nights in an attempt to help stimulate some press in Britain where the band had not appeared for close to two years.

A rather humourous sidelight to the band's trip to this area of Canada was an article that appeared in the *Spectator* in Hamilton, a city a few miles from Toronto. Headlined, "Thief with a taste for irony" the article read: "It wasn't quite the crime of the century, since only $1200 worth of goods was stolen. But Jon Robinson, 21, of Hamilton, was the victim of a thief with a cruel sense of irony. Late Tuesday or early yesterday, a thief slipped the lock with a knife at Robinson's Eastbourne Avenue apartment. Two guitars and a stereo along with one long play record were taken by the robber. The lone album reported missing from the victim's collection was Supertramp's Crime Of the Century."

From Toronto, the band headed back into the U.S. and along the way moved into the sleepy university town of Burlington, Vermont where, as usual, they met with a very enthusiastic audience. Enthusiastic, yes, but if one were to go by writer Susan Green who reviewed the show for the *Burlington Free Press*, you might have thought that Black Sabbath had just played in the local arena.

"If only we could harness the raw energy of youth," she wrote, "perhaps there'd be no need to worry about dwindling supplies of fuel to keep America in power.

"The electricity generated Monday night at Memorial Auditorium might have been enough to give Burlington endless kilowatt hours of juice. The kindling for this human chain reaction was Supertramp, a multinational rock quintet, but the fire that raged was the angst of Vermont's teenage population.

"'What you see is just illusion, You're surrounded by confusion . . .' guitarist Roger Hodgson sang on Hide In Your Shell from the band's first album Crime Of the Century. It was an emotional delivery, prompting a frenzied response from the crowd.

"This music speaks to their condition, to borrow an old Quaker notion, and despite the hype, the big bucks and the slick promotional material, Supertramp exists because it answers some basic needs in young people. It could be that the force of 'heavy metal,' as this band's sound is sometimes categorized - though it's more like soft suds compared with some rock groups out there - imbues listeners with a sense of nonlimitation compared to a day-to-day existence that may seem confining."

Supertramp! Heavy metal! Teenage angst! Nonlimitation! Well lads, you can put that one in your portfolio and press it.

As the tour moved back into Canada in late June, a concert in Moncton, New Brunswick at the Coliseum on June 25 turned a bit ugly when no more tickets were available for the sold out concert. In a report carried in papers across Canada through the Canadian Press wire service, it stated that the trouble started when Coliseum officials closed the doors of the arena with a crowd of 9600 already inside.

The report read: "City police said Monday they expect a total of 129 charges against a number of persons following an incident Saturday night in which police confronted a large crowd of young people who were refused admission to a rock concert by the group Supertramp.

"The first seven men, all in their late teens or early 20s, appeared in Provincial Court Monday on charges related to the incident. The charges included drug offences and possession of an unregistered firearm.

"Twenty-five riot-equipped Moncton policemen dispersed the crowd. Some rocks and beer bottles were thrown, smashing the windshield of a Police van. Two policemen were hit by rocks but were not injured. None of the persons charged are being held in jail."

Always a highlight of any trip to Canada by Supertramp is their concert appearances in Montreal. This tour was to be no exception. Both dates on June 28 and 29 at the Montreal Forum were sell outs and the crowds on both nights were rabid.

David Freeston, a music critic at the time for the now defunct Montreal Star newspaper, was there on the first night and under the headline, "Supertramp gutless sophistication" reviewed the show this way:

"Supertramp isn't a personality band. It isn't like their fans could tell one member from another, nor even recognize any of them on the street.

"At most they project - individually and collectively - a lumpy and busy image; one that suggests they do things the hard way, and have neither the inclination nor patience for frivolity.

"Yet for some mystifying reasons, legions are persuaded their music has some personality.

"The British quintet has, during the last year or so, emerged as one of the most popular 'rock' groups, parlaying a carefully stitched together kind of keyboard-based rock (laced with a bit of sing-songy music hall), into three monstrously successful albums.

"They've also become a top concert attraction. Last night they and their $250,000 sound system were on display at the Forum, and they'll be back again tonight in front of another 19,000 fans.

"After a warm-up set by British singing duo Gallagher and Lyle, Supertramp took the stage and swung into their ditties to thunderous roars, a galaxy of lit Bics, and a profound kind of rapture.

"Rodger Hodgson on vocals and keyboards, Bob Benberg on drums, Dougie Thomson on bass, John Helliwell on reeds and keyboards and Richard Davies on vocals and keyboards ran through their collection of songs without missing too many beats.

"They looked earnest as they pounded and blew away at their instruments, seemed versatile as they scuttled back and forth trading them for others, and they sounded like fairly crisp and efficient journeymen. Which is exactly what they are and nothing more.

"They have a knack for the occasionally attractive melody, a facility for lyrics that add up to well-intentioned and ingratiating tripe, and have complete mastery of the style which transfigures cliches into gutless 'sophistication.'"

Critic's angst aside, there was one slight inconsistency in Freeston's review. Gallagher and Lyle, in fact, did not appear on the Supertramp show that night. Chris de Burgh had replaced them as opening act. The upshot was that Freeston was dispatched to places unknown and the second night writer Mark Harding was using Freeston's press credentials. Judging from his review, he seemed to have watched the show.

"Two nights and two sellout crowds of more than 20,000 exhuberant fans at the Montreal Forum," wrote Harding. "For these 40,000-plus admirers and devoted followers of Britain's

John & Bob on ferry to Vancouver, Canada.

Quietest Moments Tour on bus in England.

Charles Helliwell drives the bus.

musical quintet Supertramp, the group's appearances have come and gone all too quickly.

"After an extensive tour of North America, Supertramp came to Montreal where, as they readily admit, they are always received with warm, outstretched arms.

"The audience's appreciation and respect for the group can be felt hours before the piercing sounds of Davies' mouth organ leads the group into their traditional opening number, School from the Crime Of the Century album.

"An air of anticipation lingers throughout the hockey arena. There is a feeling among all who either sit back and watch or take part in pre-concert activities such as toilet paper tossing, frisbee throwing and beachball bouncing. They know why they're at the Forum.

"'Bonsoir et bienvenue a un soir avec Supertramp,' hollers Supertramp reeds player and concert spokesman Helliwell above the roar which follows the group's opening numbers of School and Ain't Nobody But Me.

"In an unmistakably hurried fashion, the group was led by Hodgson's 12-string acoustic guitar into their current single Give A Little Bit. If there was a flaw to be detected in last night's show, it was the band's tendency to rush from one song to another and forego the fireside chats with the audience that usually sets the concert's relaxed atmosphere.

"Also missing was the group's live performance of the title track from their most recent album, Even In the Quietest Moments, which must have been expected from the thousands who jammed every inch of standing room, and sitting room space allotted for the show.

"But despite these and other glaring errors, such as forgotten lyrics and disjointed instrumental solos, the group was repeatedly forgiven by their audience who would have risen to a standing ovation even it if had been Auld Lang Syne.

"Supertramp's forte, however, is a keen sense of knowing what their audience has come to hear and is familiar with. Sixteen numbers were played and only four were taken from Even In the Quietest Moments LP, which was ranked as the number-one selling album in Montreal two weeks ago and number seven last week.

"Songs from the Crime Of the Century album and Crisis? What Crisis? LPs permeated the show. They had all been played last year when the group was here and were given the once over again last night.

"But that's what the people wanted, judging from the ovations given to the group's earlier songs which included Dreamer, Bloody Well Right, Hide In Your Shell and Asylum.

"The highlight of the show was marked by a 15-minute uproar from the crowd following the group's first encore. The Forum's house lights were lit and roadies began tearing down equipment, but again the fans' wishes were granted and the group returned one last time."

From Montreal, the band moved on to Ottawa for two sold-out concerts at the Civic Centre. Then they moved on down the road to London and Kitchener before heading out west to play the two promised make-up concerts in Calgary and Edmonton.

In many cases on the Canadian segment of their North American tour, the press had been very harsh on the band especially in the major media centres of Toronto and Montreal. This fact caught the attention of rock journalist Ritchie Yorke who in turn put some of his colleagues on the spit and turned it slowly over a high flame.

"It was really amazing: the fluorescent caverns of the newspapers were filled with jesters, jokers and plain no-hopers churning out garbage in a remarkable avalanche of ignorance," sniped Yorke. "Once again our time-tainted critics displayed their astonishing lack of understanding, perception or sensitivity. Yet again one had to admit that all the chronic complaints whispered behind their backs were true. Most of our major rock critics suck eggs, and probably doorknobs too.

"During the completion of what has to be one of the most artistically successful tours in Canadian rock history, Supertramp were subjected to a fierce barrage of bullshit reviews guaranteed to raise nausea in the stoutest of stomachs. As anyone who was there will tell you, the reviews were completely out of tune with what actually went down in Toronto and Montreal where they played a total of four SRO concerts, two at the Gardens and two at the Forum (exceedingly well-produced by CPI in association with Donald K. Donald). Judged on their reportorial-accuracy skills, these critics wouldn't rate a job on the Medicine Hat Journal.

"Normally it's not considered ethical or polite for a rock journalist to put down, let alone bury, ones colleagues. It's just not done, old boy. Not to mention the subsequent bitter condemnation which invariably follows any criticisms of the critics ... then, as anyone who's been offed in such fashion can assure you, revenge becomes an obsession. So be it. My alleged 'mellowness' notwithstanding, pure passion prevents me from holding my tongue any longer. It's time for the

Members of the band and crew prior to "Quietest Moments Tour."

lashers to laugh through a few return parries. Gaping ignorance of this proportion cannot remain unanswered, and having been a willing witness to all four Supertramp concerts, I am compelled to rise to their defense. Having done my share of concert reviewing for Toronto dailies, I can well appreciate that concert critiques are by nature highly subjective emotional exercises; what's one man's meat and all that, but true genius cannot be confused or mistaken. It's simply there in front of your eyes and ears. To miss the point is to demonstrate an appalling lack of connection with the course of contemporary music.

"Upon reviewing some of the reviews again, I can only conclude that I've never read so much horseshit in my entire career. The critics have been hung by the noose of their own words. These so-called reviewers were not at the same gig I attended and nor did they hear the same band. Nor did any of them refer to the highly enthusiastic audience reaction.

"As a sometime predictor of forthcoming rock superstar success (I had the good fortune to put the finger on Led Zeppelin and Yes before they broke in America, predictions which apparently established my crystal ball credibility where it most matters), I'd like to venture an opinion that the future of rock music may well be already aloft on the wings of Supertramp. After attending some of the Quietest Moments sessions at the Record Plant in L.A. and after witnessing five separate performances of Supertramp (Toronto, Montreal and the first Kitchener show) and after long and careful consideration of the band's last three albums, I'm convinced that Supertramp is the finest group this music has thus far produced. There are no exceptions and I make no apologies for this flat out statement. I sincerely believe that Supertramp's music surpasses by any yardstick the best of the Beatles, the Stones, Zeppelin, the Byrds or any other group. For me, Supertramp are the creme de la creme, the very pinnacle of the rock pile.

"My convictions run so deep that on being asked to list my ten favourite albums of all time for Paul Gambacinni's forthcoming book on Rock's Top 200 LPs, I had no hesitation in settling on a top three of Even In the Quietest Moments, Astral Weeks and Crime Of the Century. I know I'll never regret the choices.

"I mention this only to demonstrate that my own view of Supertramp differs substantially from the cockeyed comments above. I'd like to think that my opinions of Supertramp are shared by one hell of a lot of people across this country, and that it's not us but the daily rock critics who are out of tune with the times. Certainly a large number of friends and associates insisted to me that Supertramp provided the best concert they'd ever seen anywhere. People don't rip off lines like that lightly. You're either there or you're not. And it's got nothing at all to do with the proposal that so many fans - 80,000 in Toronto and Montreal (and thousands more elsewhere) can't be wrong.

"What I'd really like to know is what's wrong with paving the pathway to the musical future: What's wrong with putting out the best sound possible in a sports stadium, and playing as tightly as any band in memory?

"Smoke bombs and coleslaw have nothing whatsoever to do with great music, which is surely the ultimate achievement of any concert. Is it bland to offer a unique and extraordinary commentary on the state of this crippled planet when so many rock acts have not progressed beyond the 'My baby left me' dogshit syndrome? Is there something gutless about getting to grips with the Predicament, thrusting accusation at those who have raped and ransacked the planet's resources, putting into words the rage and alienation that all of us who feel must feel so painfully in these tortured times? Is there inherent falsehood in taking the counter culture philosophy propagated in the late 60s and restating it in a late 70s setting? Is it bad to care?

"What's wrong with pounding out the finest bass and drum sound ever heard and blending it into the most functional and unfailing sound system owned by any band anywhere? What's wrong with ploughing in excess of $250,000 into providing the best sound it is presently possible to attain within the limitations of giant concrete sports palaces? What's bad about making your live sound at least the equal of your studiously-produced records? What's wrong with being subtle and innovative and so frequently profound?

"There is nothing gutless about their brand of sophisticated art, although writers would be well advised to take the time to understand the real meaning of this adjective before flogging it around so recklessly.

"Since when has the pursuit of self-awareness been such a disease? What's wrong with checking out other philosophies?

"Quite simply, Supertramp music embodies the best of the 60s, enough of the spirit of the 50s and the most difficult to achieve asset of all, the grafting on of despair and disillusionment of the 70s. They have had more to say about the disintegrating human condition over the past

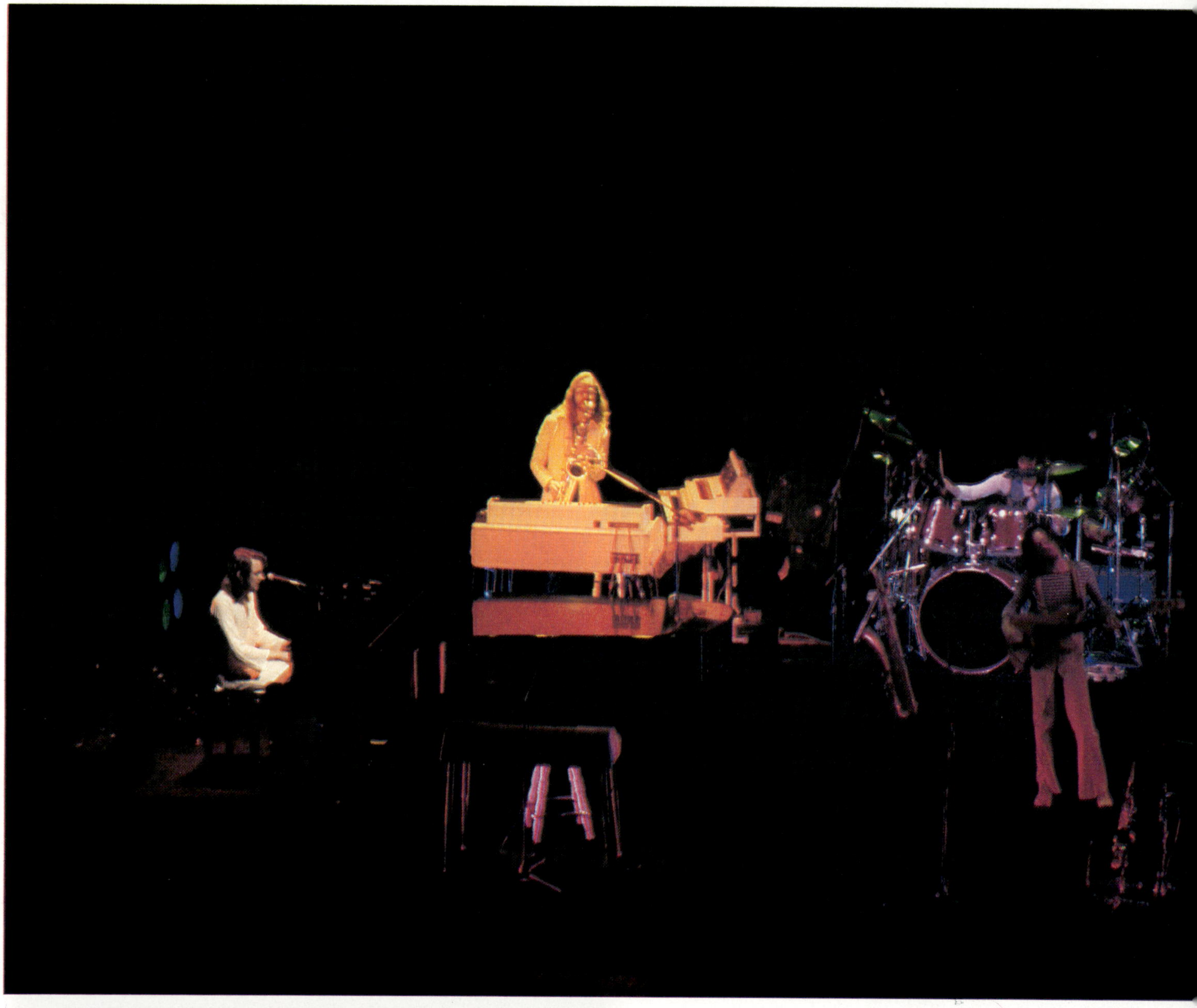

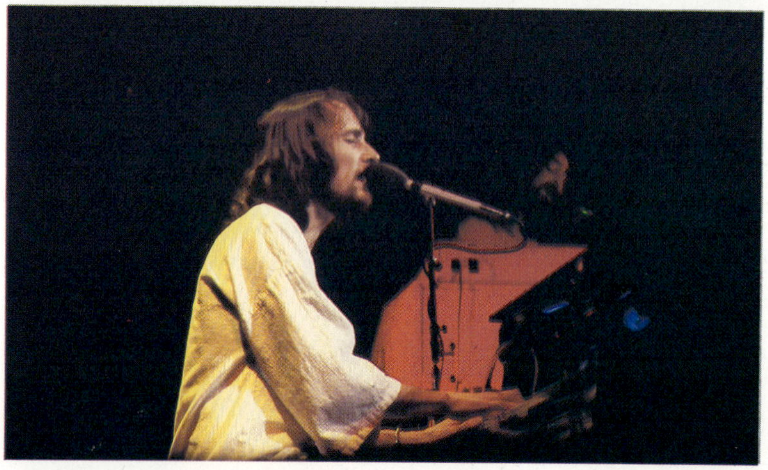

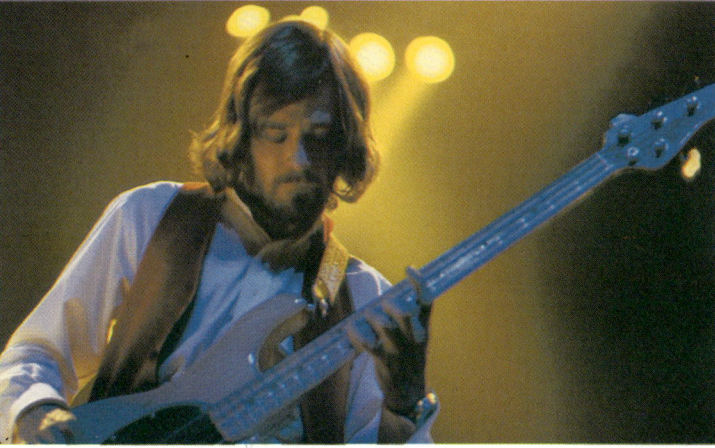

three years than virtually the entire remaining body of their contemporaries."

After the North American leg of the 1977 tour, Supertramp headed for Europe where on August 28 in Copenhagen, they opened their three-month tour through Scandinavia, Britain and Europe. The excursion continued through Denmark, Sweden, Norway, Germany, Switzerland, Spain, France, Holland and Belgium before they arrived in Britain in mid-October.

Writer Garth Pearce caught up with the band in Geneva on September 23, just prior to their concert at the Pavilion des Sports.

"In the 13th century Chateau de Coudree, above Magnet de Canard and Champagne Julep, Supertramp quietly celebrate their success.

"It has crept up on them over seven years with the sort of steady but relentless momentum they have displayed in their music.

"And now the five musicians, who have sold 15 million records, sit here in comfortable anonymity.

"'We have always planned it that way,' says 32-year-old front man John Helliwell. 'No one in the band wants to be a superstar. Our aim is to get good sound, subtle lighting and fine music. We want to give a show without histrionics, leaping around or using flame-throwers. We like to treat the audience as if they are sitting in a giant stereo set.'

"In the last twelve months, the band have moved from Britain to Los Angeles to establish themselves as 1977's new heavy-weights of rock. They return to England on October 15 for concerts which include dates at London's Wembley Empire Pool.

"And here in Switzerland, as throughout America and the rest of Europe, there have been audiences of 10,000 on a massive tour which began six months and 42,000 miles ago.

"'Yet we only sold 15 tickets in Paris three years before,' recalls John. 'Our music takes time to grow on you. Before our first successful album, Crime Of the Century (which has sold nearly one million in Britain alone) there were very lean times. The only gig we did in months was at someone's wedding in Jersey. I can't remember if we even got paid.'

"During the bad years the group took a big gamble by plunging into debt to buy their own sound and lighting equipment. It paid off by adding professionalism and style to the sort of rock act which is so often spoiled by amateurish special effects.

"Says bass player Dougie Thomson: 'When we first started, we would do anything to get people into the halls to see us. We would even go out into the streets to give tickets away.'

"Roger, 26, who co-writes all the songs, said: 'Hundreds of songs are thrown out. We don't go ahead with anything until all five of us agree that it is right.'

"The results are albums like the much-acclaimed Crisis? What Crisis? and Even In the Quietest Moments, which was released on April 1 and is still high in the British and American charts. A single, Give A Little Bit, became their third top 30 hit out of four releases. 'We already have between 50 and 60 songs for our next album,' reveals Rick. 'We regard that as our security for the future.'

"But it is the investment of past years which Supertramp are yielding today. And it is this which makes them the most interesting group of this autumn's packed pop season."

Arriving in England in mid-October, Supertramp played Birmingham, Liverpool, Manchester, Coventry, Newcastle, Glasgow and Leicester before bringing their show to London where they appeared for two nights at the Wembley Empire Pool. It was their first appearance in the British capital in almost two years and was a date eagerly anticipated by both the fans and the band.

"In my record collection Supertramp stack up between 10cc and Pink Floyd, and they stack up well," wrote *Daily Mail* writer Bart Mills following the concerts. "Supertramp are a middle-of-the-road progressive group who have found a vast international audience for their intelligent, sinewy music.

"After a two-year absence, they have brought their immaculate stage show back home, giving two packed houses this week at the Empire Pool, Wembley, a restrained replay of their best album tracks.

"They say it with music and use lighting sparingly - just a few frames of film on the backdrop.

"Their songs are progressive in the proper sense of the word. Key shifts and chord changes aren't mere show-off rhetoric - they really do 'progress' directly out of one phase of a song into another.

"Their current album Even In the Quietest Moments equals its million-selling predecessors in musical inventiveness.

"Rick Davies' keyboards still dominate. After his percussive piano intros, drums are an afterthought.

"Davies and guitarist Roger Hodgson write all the five-man group's songs. Their themes this year appear more mystical than previously.

"If only they wrote about Susie or Gloria, instead of The Lord, they might sell a lot of singles and get their name about a bit more."

The *Daily Telegraph* saw the concerts this way:

"Some time before their second concert at the Empire Pool last night, Supertramp's perfectionist sound engineers no doubt took pains to exorcise a gremlin which helped make their 111th show this year - but the first in London for some while - an unusually flawed affair.

"This admirable group of four Britons and a Californian drummer have generally eschewed the tricksy use of pyrotechnics in favour of precise reproduction of their recordings. In the past, notably at the Albert Hall, they have succeeded magnificently.

"Tuesday night, however, though blessed with the customarily brilliant lighting effects, was marked initially by a chill which could not be blamed wholly upon the elements. In fact the performance only seemed to seize the capacity audience when a monkey cut a quick rug with an outsize banana.

"There were more important moments of pleasure, however, particularly when the plaintive singing of Lady and Hide In Your Shell found Roger Hodgson at his best.

"Likewise in the finale, Fool's Overture, when the band attained a thrilling cohesion and the back-projected film montage seemed reasonably apposite, so the 8,000 had rich musical pickings. And the eagerly demanded encore? - Crime Of the Century, of course, performed with its obligatory power.

"Thanks also to the excellent Chris de Burgh, in a supporting role, the 145 minutes passed swiftly enough."

From London, it was on to Brighton and then Bournemouth where the band played its last concert on the 1977 world tour at the Wintergarden. *Melody Maker* writer David Boothroyd was there at that last show and later reported back that it was a concert not to be missed.

"Any band that plays 114 concerts on a tour of America and Europe spanning several months, deserve full marks for endurance, if nothing else," wrote Boothroyd. "That Supertramp managed to give their audience at Bournemouth last week an example of their best at this, the last gig, speaks volumes - for the band themselves, the road crew and everybody else involved.

"Supertramp have by now reached a stage of technical perfection that few bands ever approach. Their sound system, which they own themselves, makes most others sound like a transistor radio. The lighting is timed to microseconds and they play their music faultlessly.

"Last week they even installed a private generator in case of power cuts after suffering that way the week before at Wembley.

"But at Bournemouth, it was far from a purely technical masterpiece. There were monkeys dancing with bananas (!), schoolgirl Joan attacking sax-player John Helliwell ('a dream come true,' he said), and a male stripper sitting beneath the parasol from the cover of Crisis? What Crisis?

"It was a night of restrained lunacy, which the audience loved, but the stage antics were never allowed to distract attention from the music. The band played many of the songs from their 1977 album, Even In the Quietest Moments including Babaji, their latest single, as well as older material, ending up as they always do with Fool's Overture and Crime Of the Century, still apparently the favourite of most audiences, and certainly Bournemouth's.

"Supertramp's set is not the most spontaneous you will ever see. They stick to one encore, Crime Of the Century, ending in an explosion of noise with the famous album cover of the fists gripping the iron grill filling the screen.

"But if they changed the set all the time, they couldn't achieve the split-second timing and precision that makes their concerts literally breathtaking. Nobody at Bournemouth seemed to think it sounded over-rehearsed or artificial, just fine music played to perfection.

"If you missed them this time around, you missed something special. The band will be back in 1978; don't make the same mistake again." ☐

Libby, the waitress from *Breakfast In America* cover, rocks on.

CHAPTER TWELVE

By the end of the Even In the Quietest Moments tour at the beginning of November, 1977, Supertramp had played to well over 600,000 rabid fans. There had been riots in such diverse places as Burlington, Vermont; Moncton, New Brunswick; Geneva; and Barcelona and they had sold two million records in Europe in six weeks. *Crime Of the Century* went platinum eight times over in Canada (that represents sales of over 800,000 copies) which at this point had become Supertramp mad.

These were eventful times for the band, but when they finally got back to Los Angeles, there was only one thing on everybody's mind - a lengthy break from the wear and tear of the endless cycle of rehearsals, recording and touring. That's not to say that everybody was not well aware that there was another album to be considered and after that, another lengthy tour. But that was tomorrow; today, a little well-earned relaxation was in the cards.

"By the end of the Quietest Moments tour, needless to say, we were all in need of a rest," recollects John. "Perhaps a little different than some of the other guys, I actually like touring and seeing all the different places - walking around the streets, going to museums, art galleries and clubs. It's what you make of it really. If you stay in your hotel room all day and sleep because you've been drinking the night before, everywhere is going to be the same.

"The band parties occasionally, but on the whole, we realize that our music is so demanding to us. We're also such perfectionists and have to get it absolutely right, so we can't afford to get really out of it. We're professional and we want to give the audience the best possible show. I think it's when you get bands that aren't quite up to par, and they know they aren't, that they can go out and fart around. They don't care as much. We also weren't spring chickens when we were starting to become successful."

"We took a long break after the tour because we were all pretty fatigued," says Dougie. "When we got back to Los Angeles, we had an office complex in Burbank on West Magnolia and we decided to build a little rehearsal and demo studio there that we called Southcombe in memory of the house in which we rehearsed the *Crime Of the Century* album in England. It didn't quite turn out because nobody was happy there. The atmosphere didn't work for the band as a whole."

Even so, Supertramp would rehearse the new album there and even attempt some recording with a mobile studio but it just didn't click.

Rick lost in the backstage crowd at the L.A. Forum. April/79

The break saw the group members go off in their separate directions. Roger headed for Northern California to a retreat called Ananda, that he had visited a number of times in the past, for some rare time alone with his lady Karuna.

After the Crisis tour in 1976, Roger had had a place in Topanga. After a few visits, John had liked the area so much that he had decided it was the place he would like to settle with his wife Christine and son Charles.

"After the '77 tour, we were able to buy our first house," says John. "We thought about Topanga right away and that's where we bought. Dougie and his wife Christine were here for a while as well as a few members of the crew. What I'm into is bicycle riding, running and motorbike riding and it's perfect for that around here. I started bicycling when I lived on the beach and was commuting backwards and forwards to Hollywood for the start of the Crisis recording at A&M and I continued when I moved to Topanga. With the steep hills in the area, it's a tremendous way to keep fit."

With Roger becoming increasingly disenchanted with city life and finding himself drawn to the more rustic setting of Northern California, this period marked the beginnings of a rift between Roger and Rick, Dougie, John and Bob, who had chosen to live in and around Los Angeles. Roger had made up his mind to leave the pressures he found in L.A. and put his roots down in an area that was more suited to his lifestyle.

In the past, the group had lived in each other's pockets, whether it be in one house, in digs that were located in close proximity to each other or on the road. With the success of Supertramp, the individuals in the band found themselves more financially independent. They all had families and it wasn't surprising to find that they were beginning to pursue their own private lifestyles outside of the group context.

In retrospect, this period of separation, in which the individual members of Supertramp found the time and space to assess their own lives and creative goals, was the most auspicious period of the band's career. Rick, who had never been the most prolific of songwriters, found a new creative energy. And as the two expatriate Englishmen, Hodgson and Davies, had a chance to look around and assess their relationship as well as their current living environment in America, the foundation for the music on the upcoming album had been laid.

When Supertramp did reconvene in Los Angeles after the break in April of 1978, they worked for a while in Rick's guest house in Los Angeles to sort out the basic concept of the new album before moving into the little rehearsal studio in their management offices in Burbank. Pete Henderson, the recording engineer that the band had worked with on *Even In the Quietest Moments* was summoned from England and, in a rare display of dedication, flew into Los Angeles from London the day after he was married.

The band initially attempted to record at the Southcombe studio in their management office complex but when it proved fruitless, they moved over to the Village Recorder studio in Los Angeles. It was there that the long process of recording a Supertramp album, which at this point was provisionally called Working Title, was started.

"We put together a lot of the album at our little studio in the management offices," remembers Bob. "I remember playing "Nervous Wreck" over there for the first time before we moved over to the Village Recorder studio. The album went pretty smoothly until we got into mixing and then we ran into the problem of who was going to decide when we had *the* final mix of the LP. It was just a case of too many cooks. It got to the point that we were taking mixes of the songs and checking them out on the tape deck in my car. Then we would take the tape over to Rick's place and listen to them on his stereo in his living room that had speakers suspended from the ceiling. It didn't sound very good so Roger would take it somewhere else. We were pulling our hair out because we just couldn't decide. We were working with Pete Henderson again, who we really liked and was quite brilliant, but he just wasn't in a position to enforce anything or make a final decision. Roger was very much in control at the time and Rick would come in and take control when he thought he needed to. Roger slugged it out day by day though. That's part of the trouble with this band. It's a democracy. The first stumbling block you run into is deciding when you're going to meet to talk about something.

"But beyond all that, Breakfast came pretty easy for me anyway. I remember struggling through some songs. "Gone Hollywood" was a hard one because it was basically down to me to get good power licks in the breaks which eventually came out pretty well. We struggled for two or three days with "Child Of Vision," for instance, trying to get the backing track. We tried on a Monday and Tuesday to get it right with disastrous results but when we came in the next day, we got it in the first take."

The band had planned to take two months to record the album and by September, six months later, they were still hard at it.

"We figured okay, let's set the tour dates and we'll have plenty of time to finish the record and rehearse for the tour," says Dougie. "That was pretty optimistic because the album ran way over time and so did the remixing process."

Doug Pringle, who visited Roger in Los Angeles in September of 1978 for an interview for his Canadian syndicated radio show *The Pringle Program*, asked him why the LP was taking so long.

"Well, it always does," laughed Roger. "You always think this is going to be a quick one and it never is. We are not too good at putting our heads down to getting it done. We are much more of a band that waits for an inspiration. Sometimes, when you feel like playing, the sound is not right. On the other hand, when the sound is right, you don't feel like playing so you have to wait until both are right and that can take a few days. So it goes on and on and for this album we are really putting out our best effort to do something special. Ten songs are a lot to keep track of. There were only seven on the last album so it was a lot easier to keep in your mind. Ten is quite a lot and there is a lot of meat on the album which we have to get through.

"I am enjoying the music but the actual recording process really wears us all down, I think. It just takes it all out of you. There are so many obstacles that can beat you down. When you have that many people working together, the energy level has to be right. It only takes one person to be off and it spreads to everyone else quickly because we feed off each other so much. If you have been trying something and it hasn't been working out, that's when the pressure really starts to build up. You just get totally wiped out. I think it is taking a long time because we really want it to be the best and we want every single song to move us, let alone everyone else. If it doesn't move us, then we keep hammering away until it does.

"This is not all that new. With every single album, we've been through the same thing. There are two ways of doing an album. There's the way that Bob Dylan did some of his albums where he just goes in for four days and plays everything live onto the tape. The sound is terrible but it doesn't matter because he captures the feeling. Then there's our approach where you take your time over it. Luckily we have a very patient record company that allows us to do it. It's just like doing a painting but here we are painting with sound. If you put a guitar on a track, it has to find its own little space and cannot clutter anything else that is on the track. That really takes a long time. You might have only twenty guitar sounds and one sound is right but by the time you find it, you are so sick of playing the thing, you have to leave it for a few days."

When the album was close to the final stages, the LP moved over to Crystal Sound studios for a final mix before it was delivered to A&M Records for release. As the album, officially entitled *Breakfast In America*, was being completed, the concept for the album cover was being developed. It turned out to be another interminable process.

"The design of the cover seemed to go on forever," says Dougie. "Mike Doud, the designer, brought us a napkin one day that he'd had in a restaurant. There was a sketch on it of the Statue of Liberty as a waitress. When we looked at it we all said, 'That's it!' That was quite early on but even though we knew we had a good idea, we couldn't quite figure out exactly how we were physically going to do it. That took months to figure out."

Mike Doud and his company Album Graphics Inc., besides being involved in the creation of the cover art for Supertramp's *Crime Of the Century* and *Even In the Quietest Moments* LPs, has also worked on the design of albums for TKO, The Gap Band, Dave Lambert, the *Dog and Butterfly* LP by Heart and Led Zeppelin's *Physical Graffiti*. Shortly after the release of *Breakfast In America* in February of 1979, Doud explained the creative process by which the final design of the Breakfast album evolved.

"I had the concept and I scribbled it out ever so roughly and I was almost reluctant to show it to the band," Doud told *Walrus Magazine* writer Dean Sciappa. "It was a scribble but it was all there - the city of New York and the Statue of Liberty waitress. As rough as my idea was the band saw the strength in it.

"So, I enlisted Mick Haggerty to help me through it. We had to do two photo sessions with the tableau of breakfast foods as Manhattan. Rigging it all up and getting it all to work took days. The orange juice was taped to a rod with weights on it so the lady wouldn't have to actually hold it up. That was all stripped into the photos - artistic licence.

"The cover itself was done in three different shots. The shape of the picture, of course, is the window of a plane. Then there is the shot of the waitress and then the shot of the city. All stripped together into one. For the city, we built an entire polythene structure around it and we ran dry ice and smoke into it with a cloud backdrop - very surreal. In the city you can see Mrs. Butterworth, egg cartons, toast and waffles coming out of toasters and the plate represents Battery Park. Of course, the OJ is symbolic of the torch.

"Then we shot two models previous to Kate Murdock, a character actress. But we had a growing fear of going too grotesque - too cartoony. In the end, the band pushed for the cartoon quality and they were most definitely right.

"We had different ideas of presenting them on the back cover but, they liked Burt's Mad House on La Brea Avenue in L.A. Burt is in the shot too. We got all of their home town newspapers sent over from London to do the session - except for Bob Benberg who is reading the *L.A. Times* because he's from Glendale. Mick Haggerty designed the menu concept for the inside sleeve and we put it all together."

The *Breakfast In America* cover graphics would go on to win a Grammy Award at that year's award ceremonies in Los Angeles.

Breakfast In America was finally released in March of 1979 after the band had spent more time on its creation than on any previous album. Although Supertramp was hardly a household name in the U.S. at that point, in Canada, they were fast becoming one of the biggest selling recording groups in that country's history. In Europe, the group had received eight gold albums for outstanding record sales the previous year and at the time of the release of the Breakfast LP, *Even In the Quietest Moments* was still high on the record charts in countries as far afield as Argentina, Australia, New Zealand and Spain.

"With Breakfast, this is the first album on which we have captured the group energy that we get when we are playing live," Roger commented. "I know a lot of people have told us that when we play live, a lot of songs really come to life and I know we have always felt that the albums have been held back or a little too clinical because of the approach we have taken to recording. This album has really captured the group energy much more, partly due to the choice of songs. Dougie and Bob were really able to get their teeth into these songs and play their hearts out and it really shows. It is a much more fun album. It has its deeper aspects but it is

SUPERTRAMP

Breakfast in America

Roger with his daughter Heidi at Kensington Hilton, London. Nov/79

much more enjoyable."

Both Rick and Roger were keenly aware of the differences in their personalities and musical approach at this point and one of the "deeper aspects" of the music on *Breakfast In America* is the subject of the relationship of the two songwriters for Supertramp. The musical dialogue on "Child Of Vision," the closing track of Breakfast, is a revealing comment on their differing perspectives. Perhaps Rick's song "Casual Conversations," originally to be called "You Never Listen Anyway," could be similarly interpreted.

"There was a theme for this album before we got into Breakfast In America," says Roger. "We thought at one point that the theme might reflect the difference between Rick and myself and the way we saw life. We realized that a few of the songs really lent themselves to two people talking to each other and at each other. I could be putting down his way of thinking and he could be challenging my way of seeing life. We were thinking of making that the theme of the album and possibly calling the LP Hello Stranger. Our ways of life are so different, but I love him. That contrast is what makes the world go 'round and what makes Supertramp go 'round. His beliefs are a challenge to mine and my beliefs are a challenge to his. You really need that."

"Logical Song" was the first single from the LP and another of Roger's pensive statements with a musical sugar coating.

"You can't preach to people but you can stimulate their thoughts and I think that this song does that," explains Roger. "I hate to use the word 'message' but the thought here is that throughout childhood you are told so many things and yet you are never told who you really are; you are not told anything about your real self. Very rarely anyway. We are taught how to function outwardly but not told who we are inwardly, and no one explains it to us."

It was not long after "Logical Song's" release that it turned into one of the fastest breaking singles that A&M records had ever had and with *Breakfast In America* soaring up the charts, it was obvious that in the U.S., where the band had previously only maintained a cult following, it was to be Supertramp's finest hour.

Another major tour was mounted and the mood of the band was ebullient as they kicked off the North American leg of a world excursion that would stretch from March to December of 1979, wrapping up in Europe.

Talking about Supertramp's new found success in the U.S., Dougie told *Walrus Magazine*: "Everyone's really knocked out by it. Rick and Roger have been together nearly ten years. This whole thing's been a long slow building process. We've seen different areas react like this before, but we've never seen an entire country go like this. It's a real lift for everybody. It's gratifying not just for the band but for everyone around us because for years they've believed in the band an awful lot. Now, it's coming home.

"It's funny, when we first came to America people expected us to be like the New York Dolls or something because they took the word 'Tramp' to imply loose women or something. To us it means a hobo or wanderer. Now our name is almost second nature to most people.

"We were never an opening act for anybody. Right from the very first tour we've headlined. At first it was really difficult to get people to come to see us. We had to give tickets away. We've always had the same type of feeling about what we're doing and we felt we couldn't get that across without doing it our way - headlining. We'd play places and it would be slow, getting people out to see us. But when we would go back to those cities we'd do really well. Each time it was the same process. In some towns we'd draw 800. The next time we'd go there we'd draw 10,000. This time out, we're doing two nghts in some cities with 15 to 20,000 people each night."

As well as another world tour, Roger along with his wife Karuna had something else to look forward to - the birth of their first child.

"I feel great about it actually," remarked Roger shortly before the tour. "I sometimes get the feeling that the baby will teach us more than we teach the baby. It is just like inviting another friend along. Instead of two of us, there will be three to do whatever we do. It is difficult to know how it is going to change us until it comes but it is an unbelievable thing, bringing another soul into the world, and I feel really good about it."

Of course, the baby was likely to be born smack dab in the middle of the band's tour of America. "I know, we planned that one well didn't we," he laughed. "I don't really fancy having a kid in the Holiday Inn in downtown Philadelphia or something so I am going to try and swing it so that I can get some time off to see the baby delivered myself."

As things turned out, the tour began, and at 7:45 p.m. on the night of April 11 just 15 minutes before Supertramp took the stage in San Diego, Heidi Hodgson was born. "The people in San Diego will never know how close it came to that concert being cancelled that night," Roger would later comment.

It had been a long time since Supertramp had been seen or heard from in England and during the American portion of the band's tour, *Melody Maker* writer Harry Doherty flew over for an update. In a lengthy article, which has to be the most definitive and insightful look at the state of Supertramp during this period, he suggested that the band's success in America had widened the division between Rick and Roger that might ultimately lead to a parting of the ways. This was not a new viewpoint. From the beginning both Rick and Roger had indicated that they would stay together as long as it was fun and the creative energy was still flowing. During the period of *Breakfast In America*, while Rick and Roger's musical energies were high, their personal relationship was being strained by the many differences in their personal and musical philosophies.

"It's 2 a.m. in the car-park of the Cleveland Coliseum, and the fan belt on Roger Hodgson's motor home has just snapped," wrote Doherty. "We're stranded. And the baby's crying. And Roger wants to talk about the psychic powers of music. He has a captive audience.

"'Rock 'n' roll is just touching upon what's possible with music,' he confidently begins. 'I really think of rock 'n' roll as being very primitive. I think of what we're doing as being very primitive. We haven't even begun to explore. The power of music has been forgotten. The ancients knew it, and we're rediscovering it very slowly. Music has the power to heal, to hypnotise, to make people totally sad, happy, joyous. I'd like to find out how to do all those things.'

"Rick Davies would probably say that that's a load of rubbish.

"Roger Hodgson and Rick Davies are the contrasting personalities - the philosopher and the realist - who write, sing and play with Supertramp. Supertramp are big business in America right now. They have the rare distinction in the U.S. of making an album that dropped from number one to two with a bullet. It's back to number one this week. Their current North American tour, a massive 50-concert jaunt has attracted audiences in excess of 10,000 nightly.

"Supertramp are British, have released six albums (four with today's personnel) and now reside in Los Angeles. Breakfast In America, the latest in the saga, has been widely interpreted as a cynical overview of the American lifestyle.

Supertramp themselves have conflicting views on the matter, one half admitting that it is an opinion on the U.S. while the other denies all guilt.

"It's a mistake, says John Anthony Helliwell, the band's mildly eccentric sax-player, to read too deeply into the lyrics. Sure, he admits, the tone does poke a finger at certain elements of the American lifestyle, but no more than that. Nevertheless, lines that there are 'so many creeps in Hollywood' and 'you watch the television, it tells you what you should' make it hard to swallow the diplomacy.

"Bob Benberg, their affable California-born drummer, is genuinely surprised at the interpretation. The thought had never struck him. 'I don't think it was meant as a big social comment,' he offers tentatively.

"Bass-player Dougie Thomson, a Scot, doesn't mind California at all. Dougie, in fact, loves it. The good weather allows him to pursue activities - deep sea diving, for example - that it's impossible to explore consistently in dear old Blighty.

"So it's down to the writers, Hodgson and Davies, to clarify the matter. Here we witness, for the first time, the deep differences between the two.

"The droll Davies, looking the worse for wear as the tour nears its end, readily confesses his dislike for the West Coast in particular. So why settle down there?

"'Well,' he explains slowly, 'as we live in L.A., it's very hard to say whether or not we've settled down in America. I don't think that's a place where anybody wants to settle down, not even Americans. It's a kind of limbo place. It's a love-hate thing with me. I tend to breathe a sigh of relief when I get back there. The TV over here is horrible.'

"Hodgson makes light of the Breakfast In America interpretation, though some of the pertinent observations contained in the album were his, but he doesn't disguise the fact that the social freedom California affords suits his religious beliefs much more.

"'I started getting into yoga and spiritual things in England, but you could say it found fertile soil in California. Yoga is considered weird in England but in California, it's not. It's an everyday word that people have a lot of respect for and it's what a lot of people are into. The same as being a vegetarian. In England, you're a weirdie. So there's that and the climate. In California, you feel that you want to be healthy, because you feel good. In England, unfortunately, you almost live your life in a

Rolling Stone

July 12th, 1979 · Issue No. 295

Supertramp's logical mystery tour

By Jon Pareles

BOSTON

RICK DAVIES IS A LITTLE miffed. Before he arrived at the Music Hall for tonight's show, Supertramp's thirty-four-year-old cofounder had been browsing through the jazz and blues bins of a local record store. He was just settling in when Supertramp's *Breakfast in America* began to play over the store's PA system. "So I had to leave," he says dourly, without offering an explanation.

Dark, paunchy, with a birdlike nose that makes his face look different from every angle, Davies has an unassuming demeanor. Had he left because he'd been recognized?

"No, nothing like that," he says gruffly. "I simply didn't want to hear the album again."

I don't pursue the question; Davies retires to his ritual preconcert game of darts. In the next dressing room, reedman John Anthony Helliwell, 34, has just been handed next week's chart positions for *Breakfast* and its hit single, "The Logical Song." Addressing a roomful of roadies, band members and wives, the blond, bespectacled Helliwell assumes his mock-formal onstage persona and recites carefully: "England, Number One; Holland, Number One; Israel, Number Two; France, Number One; Australia, Number One...." Conversations resume, people drift out. By the time Helliwell reaches "U.S.A., Number One," his audience has shrunk to a polite handful. Not much change from last week, after all. Helliwell heads for the dart room.

Calm pervades backstage. I join bassist Dougie Thomson, 28, as he strolls upstairs toward the hall. Since the 4200-seat theater is the only venue smaller than an arena on Supertramp's U.S. itinerary, the wiry, bearded Scotsman is eager to explore it. We walk up the center aisle past hundreds of Supertramp fans, and nobody gives Thomson a second glance. "I'd hate to lose [*Cont. on 14*]

From left: Bob C. Benberg, Roger Hodgson, John A. Helliwell, Rick Davies and Dougie Thomson

PHOTOGRAPHS BY MARK HANAUER

raincoat. That was my biggest reason for living in California.'

"So, for emphasis, there was no deliberate concept. The fact that listeners searched for one was, he claimed, a hangover from the days of Crime Of the Century, the album which brought them back into the spotlight in 1974.

"'It's just a collection of songs. We chose the title because it was a fun title. It suited the fun feeling of the album. There are a few comments on America, but it wasn't premeditated.'

"It would be best, Rick Davies sensibly suggested, if listeners made up their own minds."

Rick Davies also talked about the recording process involved in Supertramp albums.

"'There's no real powerhouse musician in the band,' Davies explains. 'Because of that, I think that we need to be fussy in the production.' But he seems particularly aggrieved that Breakfast In America took eight months to record - 'a ridiculous amount of time really.'

"Roger he says is dominant in the production - 'and he's welcome to it. If I ever did a solo album, I'd just get the best producer I could think of and leave it to him. I skived a lot when we did Breakfast In America. It just gets boring, beyond being any fun at all. You'll walk in and they're playing a certain section and five hours later, they're still on it . . . but I'm certainly grateful for the results. I would just add to the confusion if I hung around.'

"Hodgson maintains that Ken Scott is responsible for their hi-fi status. 'We have a reputation now for high quality, so we can't release bad sound quality. It's worthwhile but if you left me to my own devices, I'd go home with my eight-track stereo recorder and probably put an album out on that.

"'The albums that I like aren't of very high recording quality. If you listen to all the Beatles' stuff, it's terrible. It was recorded abominably but, because the vibe in it is so nice, you don't even think about it. We're doing that slowly. There's more of a band vibe on Breakfast In America than ever before. In a way that's what took us so long. We almost lost that and we spent three months finding it again.'

"Another essential ingredient in the arrival of Supertramp was and is undoubtedly the gruelling touring pattern to which the band has adhered ever since its inception.

"When they record, the band sinks into studio life for months. As a result, they're left with huge world tours to undertake. When they go out on the road, it's never a half measure. This is not the first nine-month tour on which

Charles Helliwell (left) and Jesse Siebenberg backstage at Wembley's Empire Pool. Nov/79

Supertramp have embarked but the weight of the endless one-nighters has taken its toll.

"This will in fact be Supertramp's last major tour - one of the few areas where Rick Davies and Roger Hodgson find themselves in total agreement. The decision it seems has already been taken.

"Both writers are acutely aware of the need to slow down so that their joint and separate creativity may develop to its full potential. When the subject of touring is raised, Davies wears a decidedly painful expression. 'I think we're going to have to use the time a little more creatively than just endless tours because that will kill us in the end. We have to figure that one out.'

"Dougie Thomson strategically points out that Supertramp are caught up in the commercial circle of touring-recording-touring and acknowledges with regret that it is a tight grip to break.

"Actually, it might seem surprising that Supertramp should have such a strong reputation as a touring band. By rights, they should be considered primarily a studio band with secondary touring interests, which would allow them the space to breathe creatively. But that's not the case and Davies is particularly desperate to crack the system, hoping that they might do condensed tours in the future.

"His writing, he says, has suffered more than anything else. 'The five songs that I did on Breakfast are the only things that I've done in three years. I can't think straight when we're on the road. I'm just thinking about where we're going next.

"'The problem is that three of the band are not writers. It's up to them to find their little niches for when the band aren't touring. It's down to 'can we survive without being around each other so much?' Can we all exist within our own little worlds and then come back together as Supertramp? It's difficult, because John loves to tour. He loves to play more than anything else, whereas I'm ready to go home. I feel bad for him. It's a question of being able to handle that.'

"Roger, more pragmatic in some areas than the ultra-sensitive Davies, doesn't have such crises of conscience. He's already made his mind up: he's determined to get touring before touring gets him.

"'Touring agrees with me less and less now. I think this is the last one for me. It's probably the last one for all of us. There's more things to life. I still want to play to people, because that's in a musician's blood, but in a way I get as much, probably even more, playing an acoustic guitar in front of a room full of people than I do getting up there in front of 15,000 people. I get much more reward within myself. It's totally different but I prefer the intimacy which you just totally lose when you play these places.

"'It's a show. I feel like I'm part of a show. I don't feel I'm me. But in a room full of people you know that every single subtlety will be picked up. Artistically our show is like a play. We go out and do the same play every night, maybe slightly different depending on how you feel and how you vibe with the actors. That's how I see us now. It's like an experience that people come and see. That's the biggest motivation, that people do want to see it, and I really believe that it's one of the best rock shows that's ever been.

"'But as far as my life goes, I don't feel that it's expanding me musically or artistically. It's my job, basically, at the moment. It's something that we've got to do in order to earn ourselves the freedom to develop artistically, which means coming off the road.

"'I'm feeling very clear about this in my mind. I don't think we can do much more with the songs. We've done it. The show is as good as it can be. All we could do now with the music we've got and the songs and the lighting is get bigger and better - and there's no point, really, because we don't want to get any bigger than this. By the end of this tour, it'll be time to move on.

"'Rick said something once about the Beatles; that their most creative period came when they stopped touring. That might have been coincidence. It might have been LSD. But I think there's a great truth in that. Touring is a very unreal world. You haven't got your feet on the ground. It's funny, but although I have a great belief in the show, I won't miss it when we stop.'

"I saw Supertramp play twice in America, once in front of 15,000 partisans in Buffalo, New York State (a city which lays claim to being the first U.S. centre to adopt the band, and where the local radio station was first to champion Crime Of the Century and its single, Dreamer), and before a more critical audience of 10,000 in Cleveland, Ohio, an area never before visited by the band. I came away impressed, if not totally converted to their cause.

"The band certainly place demands on their audience, playing a tiring two-and-a-half hour set which might be less than enough for the average Supertramp freak but which I found a little on the long side. They maintain that it couldn't be trimmed down any further, and that songs had already been left out.

"I found it interesting and puzzling that, for all their reputation as studio aces, Supertramp should be a much more powerful proposition live. Songs that aren't exactly bouncing with vitality on vinyl are miraculously brought to life in concert. I'm thinking particularly of Davies' superbly soulful ballad From Now On and Hodgson's forceful epic, Fool's Overture, both of which were monumental on stage.

"The soulful facet of Supertramp is not usually given prominence when the band's music is examined, but I found it there in abundance, although it lurked sometimes embarrassingly (don't ask me why) behind a couple of heavy-handed arrangements. Mostly it emanates from Rick Davies' moody, sombre personality, but John Helliwell's sexy saxophone burts helped emphasize it.

"Helliwell, too, tries hard to give the band an image other than that of dedicated musos, conscious of the weight of the musical arrangements and the need to project more than that. His charming English cheekiness finds favour with American audiences. ('My backing band and I will now play . . .' 'Roger Hodgson will now accompany me for the next song'.)

"A veteran of the early-Sixties trad jazz boom (well, he was 14 then), Helliwell's sax playing has taken him through spells backing Jimmy Ruffin, Johnny Johnson and Arthur Conley and a period in the Alan Bown Set. Now you know where his soul style, which fits perfectly into Logical Song, comes from.

"That soul may be one major reason why Supertramp have taken off with such a vengeance in the States. The band were confident that the market was there, reflected in their decision to leave England after breaking through at home with Crime Of the Century, going to live in Los Angeles and placing themselves entirely at the disposal of A&M, virtually begging to be 'exploited.'

"But few people anticipated the kind of impact that Breakfast In America would make across the Atlantic. Benberg bet Rick Davies a hundred dollars that it would make top five. Davies was never happier to lose a bet.

"Roger Hodgson, on the other hand, was convinced of its destiny.

"'I always knew it was going to be a huge album. I knew our time had come and if it hadn't happened, the big man in the sky was playing a trick on us. I felt that it had to happen, the mere fact that we had to struggle so long for it.'

"Breakfast was a very different album from its predecessors and the band were aware of that. They had become wary of their reputation for turning out conceptual epics, and had decided to turn the tables by releasing a pop album - hence the inclusion of the title track, which had been written eight years previously by Hodgson.

"'If Rick had had his way,' Roger slyly digs, 'it wouldn't have been on this album either. He never liked the lyric to Breakfast. It's so trite: 'Take a look at my girlfriend.' He's much more into crafting a song. He would have been happier if I'd changed the lyric to either something funnier or more relevant. I tried, but it didn't work out, so I was stuck with the original.

"'The songs on this album were chosen because we really wanted to get a feeling of fun and warmth across. I think we felt that we had done three pretty serious albums - Crime Of the Century, Crisis? What Crisis and Even In the Quietest Moments - and it was about time we showed the lighter side of ourselves.'

"Davies does admit that he wasn't keen on either the song or the title Breakfast In America, but came around to Roger's way of thinking after viewing the album in a wider context.

"'That title almost allows for pop songs. The actual song, Breakfast In America, doesn't mean much. Neither do Oh Darling or Goodbye Stranger, so I saw a shape and it fitted.

"'The pop side has always been a part of the group's character. Maybe it's been swamped a bit by the Genesis comparison, but it's always been there. In a way, it's easier to write minor-key opuses than a really good catchy pop song. That's not easy at all. Roger has a stack of them a mile high, you know.'

"Rick Davies and Roger Hodgson rule Supertramp with a velvet fist. Their influence is unobtrusive but firm. There is an unspoken rule that the privacy of the individual must not be infringed. Supertramp is a very exclusive family.

"In three days with the band, I don't think I saw Davies and Hodgson converse once, other than to exchange courteous greetings. They're vastly different personalities but they both write interestingly pertinent songs, with a depth of content that's often overlooked in the rush to applaud (or criticise) the delicacy and prettiness of their music. Who can deny, though, a sympathy with the tone of Logical Song? The accuracy of that lyric is not a fluke; it is the mark of most songs by Davies and Hodgson. As far back as Crime Of the Century, Logical Song finds a predecessor in School.

"It was after Crime Of the Century though that Hodgson and Davies drifted apart. The

Road Manager Charly Prevost at Minneapolis/St. Paul Airport. March/79

Roger tuning backstage at L.A. Forum. At that moment his wife was at the hospital expecting their first child. April/79

One of the many versions of the Trampettes!

"Who'll be the last clown, to bring the house down?" Backstage, Empire Pool, Wembley. Nov/79

philosopher found God. The realist found reality.

"Rick Davies shuffles around the dressing room, mumbling incoherently. Dougie Thomson had whispered that he'd been like a brooding bear for a couple of days now. He had an ear-ache. The tour had caught up with him.

"Davies is an introvert, and jealously protects his seclusion. He doesn't talk much to anybody. Occasionally a dry humour will surface, as it did when we arrived at the Holiday Inn, Cleveland to find that they were still building the front: 'This is a new concept. They wreck the hotels for us before we even arrive.' But his guard is constantly up.

"'We have a strange relationship,' Hodgson comments. 'It's always been a strange one. We're both oddballs, and we've never been able to communicate too much on a verbal level. There's a very deep bond, but it's definitely mostly on a musical level. When there's just the two of us playing together, there's an incredible empathy. His down-to-earth way of writing, which is very rock 'n' roll, balances out my lighter, melodic style.

"'He's never been the easiest guy to communicate with, anyway. I know very few people who're able to get through to him. He doesn't open himself up to people at all. He wants to. But he really cares. He cares too much. That's the trouble. He's over-sensitive.'

"Davies is aware of the air of desperation, paranoia and cynicism that characterises his songs, but is unwilling to give too much away about that outside the content of his lyrics.

"'It's just feelings that you have from time to time,' he notes casually. 'The Crime album certainly had that aspect of cynicism to it. That was a little more calculatedly cynical than perhaps from the heart.'

"I refer to the connections between School, the opening track on Crime and Logical Song. Davies wrote School and Hodgson wrote Logical Song.

"'School was a device, in some ways. I don't know whether Roger would be able to associate too much with that, although I can see the connection with Logical Song. He smiles devilishly, 'Roger went straight from public school to a rock group, so his personal experience is a bit limited in that area. He's very public school.'

"Pressed on the paranoid element in his songs, Davies reveals more. He makes it obvious that the decay of his relationship with Hodgson is a significant reason for his lyrical tone.

"'It gets to be a very personal thing,' he starts

You never knew who was going to show up on stage at some of the Supertramp gigs.

nervously. 'I don't think that half of the frustrations that I feel sometimes has ever come out as much as it can. Maybe it did on Nervous Wreck, but that's not as true as Casual Conversations. That song for me is deeply personal. It can obviously relate to people, as well as boy-girl. I suppose it's me and Roger to a degree; me not being able to communicate with him, wanting to get out at times.'

"A sample of Casual Conversations: 'It doesn't matter what I say/You never listen anyway/Just don't know what your looking for.

"There have it seems been many crisis points: 'Oh yeah. That's the thing about this group. It does reach a lot of crisis points, but it never quite blows up. The characters never quite get to that point. I guess that's what has kept us together.'

"A passionate area of contention with Davies is the lyrics. He cares a great deal about them, and is concerned that perhaps his other half does not share his commitment in that area.

"'I probably get more annoyed about the words than anybody else,' he says, 'I think Logical is nice. I like Casual Conversations but I think for example that Goodbye Stranger and Oh Darling could go a bit deeper than they do. I feel a lack of somebody pushing me in the lyrical area. In all the other areas - singing, playing, arranging - there's always somebody on top of you, drawing out the best.'

"There have been times when specific lyrics have been vigorously opposed by Davies. For instance, he doesn't like to see Hodgson dabbling with religion in Supertramp's songs.

"'I gave Roger quite a hard time with Lord Is It Mine, but he still got his way.' He's silent for a second. 'He usually does. I want to try and steer him out of that area a bit, if he's not already steering himself out of it, because it's getting into a rut. Despite what he believes in, it will get limiting.'

"But surely as an artist, he has the right to write what he feels? Davies disagrees.

"'In a group situation, you have to bend a bit. Fine if either of us is doing our own thing for a solo album, then you're the artist, but in this context the strongest thing must be the group, and I think that that's been proved quite a few times.'

"The move to America, although it boosted Supertramp's career, emphasised the growing differences in background and philosophies between Davies and Hodgson. Davies, for example, thinks it significant that he married a girl from New York - 'a whole different thing' - while Hodgson married a Californian. With a large dose of sarcasm, he enlarges: 'Roger, especially in California, has found a lot of people of like mind, searching souls, and he goes up to his commune and all that . . . whatever it is up there.'

"Roger Hodgson floats around like the Holy Ghost. Dressed in white, an angelic picture, he could easily pass as Robert Powell's understudy in Jesus of Nazareth.

"He is Rick Davies' diametric opposite, more willing to share his feelings, less morose while engaged in his search for The Light. While Davies looks as if he's carrying the worries of the world on his shoulders, Hodgson's carefree outlook creates a striking contrast.

"Hodgson's unorthodox approach to touring is one reason why he isn't as hung-up as his counterpart. While the rest of the band flit around America by jet, Hodgson and his wife and eight-week-old baby girl follow them in his motorhome.

"'One of the reasons touring is so wearing is that there's no grounding influence,' he explains. 'The great thing about a motorhome is that you can keep your own space. A motorhome is a hotel room on wheels, but at least it's your own hotel room.'

"He's aware of the differences that exist between Davies and himself, and feels that it basically originates from their backgrounds. Hodgson joined Supertramp straight from public school (Stowe) - 'I was a very naive public schoolboy.'

"The first wedge between the pair was, Roger recalls, planted in 1972. Class differences were accentuated when Hodgson decided to take acid. Davies, insistent on keeping his feet firmly on the ground, declined the invitation to participate.

"'The result of me tripping was that I had my mind open to all kinds of stuff that he didn't. That created a barrier, because we couldn't share the experience. LSD is a very strange drug. It started my education again . . . totally. It lets you see life in a totally different aspect, and allows you to free yourself of everything you've been conditioned to for your entire life. It really showed me my potential for growth, which was totally contrary to everything I was taught at public school and through my life.'

"Davies and Hodgson haven't written together since Crime Of the Century, and as time passes Hodgson acknowledges that it will be even harder for them to write together again. Various differences continue to emerge: 'We write about totally different things now so it's difficult to

Roger Gross and Tam Smith of the road crew backstage, L.A. Forum. April/79

Sell-out crowd in Fresno, California.

Bob signs autographs before getting back to his game of darts with Rick. Empire Pool, Wembley Nov/79

unify the songs.'

"When I suggest that it must be difficult to work within a band with such contrasting personalities, Roger smiles. 'If that was the only difference, we'd be laughing,' he remarks. I remind him of the contention his religious beliefs have caused.

"'Yeah, but that's good for me, because Rick keeps a rein on me getting too way out in that direction, which is a dangerous direction to go anyway. I had to learn that painfully. No one wants to be preached to, least of all me. So any spiritual songs that I had should preferably be born out of experience.

"'It's been a good test to my faith all along, anyway. It's good having jokes made about you. I mean, we're all weird in our own ways. Every single one of us. The basic thing we've all got is tolerance and that's why we've all kept together. Socially, we haven't got that much in common, but we all respect one another's beliefs and lifestyles. There's a very easy-going element which makes it all possible.'

"The arrival of his baby has further loosened Hodgson's dependence on Supertramp. He is dedicated to his family and to his spiritual growth. 'I'm in the process of trying to de-condition myself. I'm going to try and not lay my trips on this child. It's almost a reverse role. This child has come into the world to teach me how to be a child again, rather than me teach her how to be an adult. I don't want to teach her to be an adult. I just want to rediscover the fun and joy that little kids have naturally, and that we all have really. There should be fun in everything.'

"Quite where that leaves Hodgson in relationship to Davies and Supertramp is not clear, but there is a desire to attempt to cement a writing partnership once more.

"'I think we both really need to have a break, just to step back from everything and look at it. I think we both feel that we want to work closer together again, because that's really where the magic happens. We haven't had the opportunity to write together or jam together in a room for five years.

"'I guess it's our own fault. For a start you have to want to, and I guess there's been so much other stuff filling our heads and minds that we just haven't had the time. Hopefully, the success of this album has given us the time to do that.

"'Rick and I are really starved of musical growth. We've climbed to the top of the mountain. Now what do we do? Most bands just stay at the top and sing the same old songs, but that means nothing to us. We really feel like we've got to grow. The band will stay together as long as it's growing. If it's reached a peak, we might as well find other musicians and do something else.'"

The tour pushed on through the U.S. and then moved into Canada in late July, where they would break all concert attendance records as they moved across the country. In Montreal, at two concerts, they drew over 80,000 people to Jarry Park. In Toronto over three nights (July 19, 20 and 21) at Exhibition Stadium, the group drew well over 100,000 people. *Globe and Mail* music writer Al Niester attended the opening night concert and summed up the impact that Supertramp made on the city during their stay.

"Consider for a moment, if the prospect is not altogether too mind-boggling, all the rock music acts who have ever played in this city," wrote Niester. "Hark back to those early visits by the Beatles and the Rolling Stones, ruminate on the historical moments like Live/Peace in Toronto in 1969, or even Electric Light Orchestra's giant space ship caper of just last summer.

"Now consider also, that by the time Supertramp has finished its three-night stay at Exhibition Stadium, the band will have played to about 135,000 people and taken in more than $1.2-million, both records for the town.

"These facts and figures may not be totally conclusive, but they do offer a great deal of evidence that Supertramp's Toronto stopover may be the biggest thing to hit this town since Hurricane Hazel.

"There are lots of reasons for Supertramp's amazing popularity, but perhaps the most obvious, as one could attest by scanning last night's capacity crowd, is the band's universal appeal. This appeal spans every age from 12 to 35, and there were equal parts of all of these age groups on hand. Supertramp is probably the most universally accepted rock act since the Beatles.

"Last night the band gave a more than two-hour concert that was, as a 16-year-old sitting behind me offered, just like the record. But if this young spectator had seen Supertramp at Massey Hall in 1976, he may have realized that the band is certainly just like the record, alright, but that its added touring experience and popular success has resulted in a show that is now much more than that. Although the members of the band still don't cavort on stage very much, the over-all sound they produce is better then ever.

"The rhythm section of Bob Benberg and Dougie Thomson aims for a deeper part of the

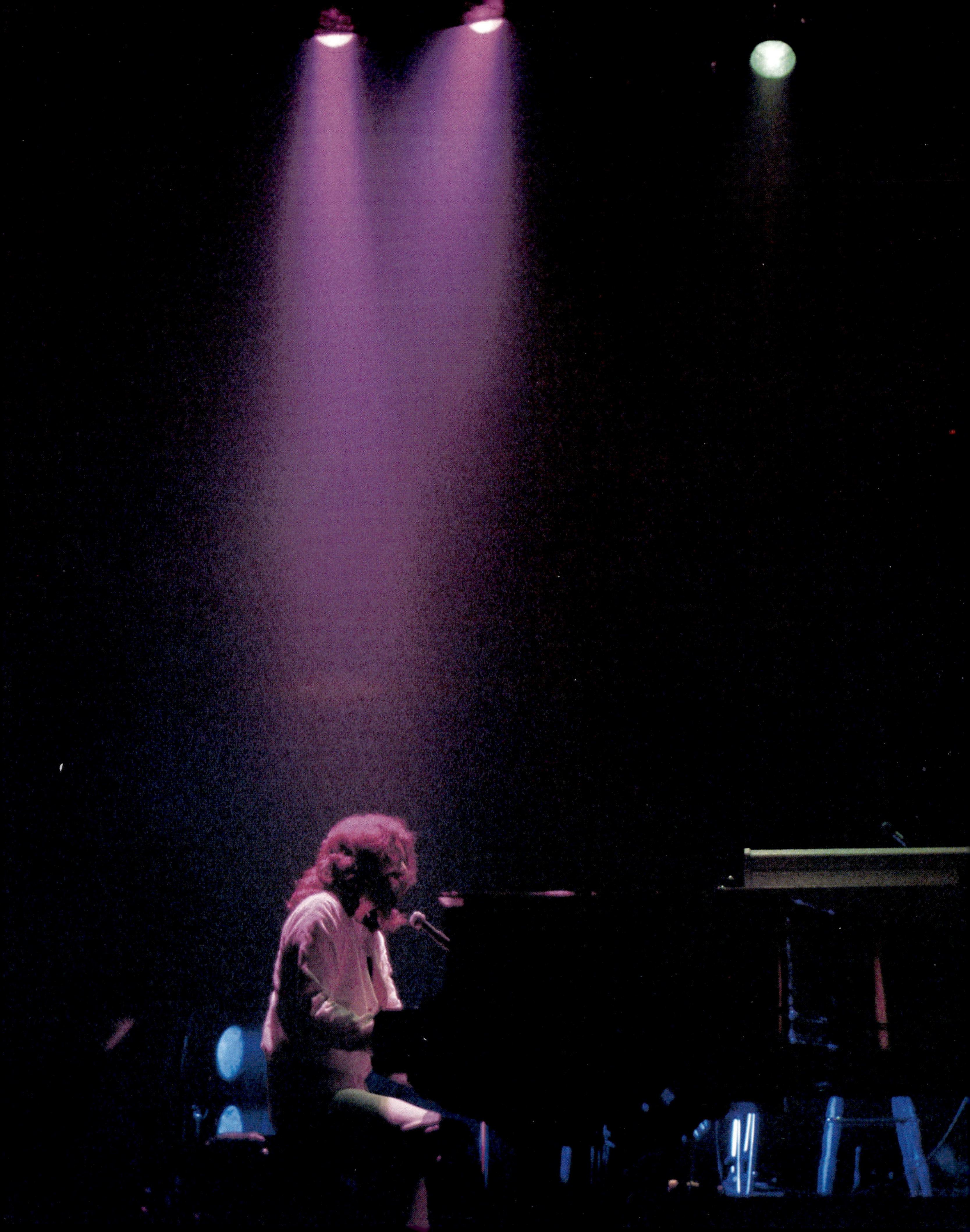

gut. John Helliwell's reeds show more flourish. Roger Hodgson's vocals soar into thinner air. And it's all helped immeasurably by their incredible sound system, eleven transport trucks worth of eighties sound technology that last night provided far and away the clearest sound for an outdoors concert that I have ever heard...

"Because of limited stage movement, Supertramp did pack along some mildly diverting visual flourishes, including a couple of overhead snowflake-like arrangements that gave off such incredible brightness that I'm amazed one of the small planes landing at the nearby Toronto Island Airport didn't do a Black Sunday right in the middle of the infield. But perhaps the most interesting sight of the night was a young man in a T-shirt declaring "Punk Ballet" who modern-danced from one side of the infield to the other.

"The big appeal of course was the music itself. Supertramp combines the best progressive rock elements of the seventies with the flair for melody of the sixties, and I would guess that if the power had cut out at any minute in the concert, enough voices in the audience would have been singing along to carry the interrupted song to its conclusion. They played them all (as you might guess from a concert of this length) starting off with a haunting version of School from the Crime Of the Century album, then progressing through such FM hits as Fool's Overture, Breakfast In America, The Logical Song and all the rest.

"It was the kind of concert that you left singing. The combination of great songs, stellar performances and immaculate sound reproduction made this a concert that, when they list all the finest rock moments of the year, will probably be surpassed only by today's and tomorrow's concluding concerts."

During a portion of the tour, *Maclean's Magazine* writer Judith Timson, spent some time with the band and was surprised to find relative calm in the centre of this musical cyclone that was sweeping the country.

"Outside the Holiday Inn on a typically muggy Winnipeg afternoon, three limousines, shiny, black and empty, snake up the drive and come to a halt, their doors springing open. Out of the hotel come three members of Supertramp, at this moment, one of the world's hottest rock bands. It seems the rock 'n' roll fantasy is about to unfold:

"Hounded by reporters, surrounded by photographers, barely visible in the seeting mob of screaming fans, flesh pressing against flesh, hand tearing at their clothes, the three spring to the safety of the limousines and flop exhausted into the backseat. One of them, pale and shaking from a night of debaucherie, stares glassy-eyed at the crowd: 'Animals,' he murmurs, 'they're all animals.'

"On this day, the fantasy gets deflated. Ignoring the fancy fleet, the three head for a mud-brown Chevrolet Impala. 'Who're the limos for?' lead guitarist and vocalist Roger Hodgson wonders out loud. 'For the road crew. No buses today,' replies one of their managers. Hodgson smiles, delighted at the idea of Supertramp's 'roadies' arriving in high style at the airport to catch a flight to Toronto. As the Impala moves off into the traffic, saxophonist John Anthony Helliwell, with shoulder-length blonde hair, spectacles and a manner so dry it crackles, stares out the window. 'Move along now,' he commands the driver. 'I might get recognized.' He spots an old drunk slumped at a bus stop bench. 'There I think that guy's seen us.' Everyone in the car laughs.

"When you are very successful, with platinum records and sellout concerts to prove it, and when you are intelligent enough not to take yourself too seriously, 'remaining anonymous' can become a bit of a running gag. At any rate, the gag has been the reality for Supertramp. With neither the outrageous charm of the Beatles, nor the animal magnetism of the Rolling Stones, the five members of the band could walk down any street in the world unnoticed. Rejecting image, deflecting hype - they recently said no to People magazine - they are so nondescript that even their own record company, A&M, has trouble recognizing them, turning them away at the door, 'like any scruffy kid looking for work,' says their Canadian manager Charly Prevost.

"But Supertramp does not need to look for work. The group's latest album, Breakfast In America, with its hit single, Logical Song, has since its release last March, climbed swiftly to the No. 1 position on the pop charts in Germany, Switzerland, France, Holland, Norway, Australia, the United States and Canada. And while another A&M recording star, Peter Frampton, once the darling of the under-20 set, has had to cancel shows in Montreal and Toronto because of lousy tickets sales, Supertramp, which has always been wildly popular in Canada, embarked on a mid-summer 17-show tour that has been packing in the largest audiences ever to attend rock concerts in this country - and will continue to do so until the tour ends in Vancouver on August 11.

John beside the private plane.

John gives onstage congratulations to Roger on the birth of baby during Breakfast tour.

"While the groovers at either extreme go mindless with disco or celebrate the banal with New Wave, the vast chunk of audience in the middle has settled down to listen with Supertramp. First night out for the band in Winnipeg, 7000 sat almost impassively in the Convention Centre, behaving as though they all had imaginary headphones pumping the Supertramp sound to them. The first show was mediocre: making that onstage connection again was hard for the band after a three-week break to recover from an exhausting 53-show American tour. But what did the fans care: their average age was 17, they wore blue jeans, T-shirts, even jogging shorts, they looked on the whole, a clean-cut lot - and they were clearly The Converted.

"The band laid out its impeccable 'sophisto-rock,' a carefully orchestrated, symphonic blend of melodious music with lyrics that are sometimes compelling (History recalls how great the fall can be/While everybody's sleeping, the boats put out to sea) and sometimes obscure (You're nothing but a dreamer . . . can you put your hands in your head, oh no!) The trappings were fancy: a superlative light show featuring two technicolor mandalas suspended from the stage; touches of drama - several movie clips as visual backdrops, including one of Churchill muttering 'We shall never surrender'; touches of fun - a dancing costumed banana, a prancing gorilla and the Trampettes, a chorus of roadies dressed in tuxes.

"At the end of an intensive 2½-hour show, a slender, frizzy-haired little blonde six rows from the front leaped to her feet, calling for more. 'They're classical,' she sought to explain. 'They're poetic. They're so . . . artistic.' The artistry has much to do with the clarity of Supertramp's sound, arguably less a matter of art than a triumph of high technology. Their equipment - 50 tons of it, shunted from city to city on five semitrailers - almost has a personality of its own. Worth about $1 million, it is all owned by the band and some of it was lovingly built from scratch. Through it, mellow sax, wonderfully bluesy keyboard work, upbeat tempos and smooth harmonies are translated into superlative sound.

"It is very polished music, with nothing primitive or visceral (or even sexual) about it. Maybe a little bit of angst (I know it sounds absurd/But please tell me who I am) and a glimpse at the breakdown of society, but nothing you couldn't comfortably hum while, say, jogging - the whip does not come down. Supertramp is for people who do not like their rock 'n' roll scary.

"They're just not your average heavy-duty rock band, nor do they come on like one: on the Air Canada flight from Winnipeg to Toronto, the scene was too subdued to qualify even as the British Museum version of Animal House, let alone the stereotyped horror vision of Rock Band on the Road. Most of the entourage - about 30 of them, band and crew - sat together in the economy section, trading quips and a squirt or two from a rogue water pistol. John Helliwell was quietly reading an Isaac Asimov paperback until his eye was caught by a promo on the back cover for a book with the questionable title of All Night Stand. It promised a seamy, inside look at 'the glamour, sex and excitement of a pop group on its way to the top.' Not Supertramp, which has gained the reputation of being a family, or at least an institution, on the road.

"The band's closeness stems from the fact that in the early days the members all lived together in various establishments, one a 17th-century Somerset farmhouse where, with outside financial assistance, they put together their music. Some of the road crew (one is an Oxford graduate) have been with Supertramp for more than five years, an unusual occurrence in the highly transient music business. 'We consider ourselves a bit beyond your average rock 'n' roll syndrome,' says one of them. Outsiders, especially anyone who wants to cruise on the band's energy or status are firmly resisted. And insiders are constantly on 'ego alert': 'We have an expression for anyone who lets the whole thing go to his head,' says Helliwell. 'We say, you're coming on a bit big time, aren't you?'

"From Crime to Breakfast, the band has spanned an ocean, and its move to California two years ago is reflected in its music. In the enigmatic title cut from Crime Of the Century, it savaged 'men of lust and greed and glory.' Now, it simply complains about 'creeps in Hollywood.' Boarding-school boy Hodgson and factory lad Davies have succumbed to the American influence in strikingly different ways. Davies, 35, wears Calvin Klein designer jeans and is thinking of moving to Beverly Hills. He married a New York woman, Sue, who handles the band's merchandising and fan club and is therefore as busy as he is on the road. Sometimes the two stay away from the band at a separate hotel where, says Sue, 'we like to get dressed up and go out for dinner.'

"Hodgson, 28, has found a more mystical calling, marrying a woman from a California commune and settling down into a way of life

Dart board and score sheet, backstage.

Dougie watching soccer game.

Supertramp tour manager "Spy" with the band's press notices backstage in Vancouver. July/79

John eyes the bull during a backstage dart game.

Vicki Siebenberg reads the part about Jack meeting the giant to an enthralled Jesse Siebenberg and Charles Helliwell backstage, Empire Pool, Wembley. Nov/79

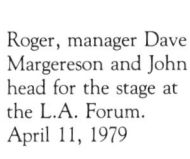

Roger, manager Dave Margereson and John head for the stage at the L.A. Forum. April 11, 1979

that includes meditation, health food and, when on the road, travelling with Karuna (formerly Karen) and their newborn daughter in a camper. He is given to such spiritual declarations as, 'I don't think the music comes from me; it flows through me.'

"Over the years, their disparate personalities, temperaments and beliefs have become less a catalyst for creative tension and more a source of just plain tension. Davies, bearded and brooding, is known as the capital-S Sensitive one, as well as the cynic. His class-hardened approach is perfectly reflected in his feisty (and crowd-pleasing) song, Bloody Well Right: 'So you think your schooling's phoney . . .' Hodgson's counterpoint, from the Logical Song - 'When I was young it seemed that life was so wonderful, a miracle . . .' - gets equal response. The two have not actually written together for years and both doubt whether they could do so again.

"Davies' only expressed vision of the future is a terse, 'Well, I won't be playing with Supertramp for the rest of my life. Thank God I can play a grand piano. There are plenty of old people around doing that.' Hodgson, meanwhile, has become obsessed with larger themes. Unable to read a newsmagazine without shuddering at the self-destructive tendencies of modern man, he is convinced that present-day society is in the final stages of a breakdown. So he's scouting around for 'safe' land to buy and share and thinking of hoarding silver to get him through the coming depression. 'But there'll be a rebirth,' he says hopefully.

"Hodgson thinks sadly that most music today is 'selfish music' that offers little joy: 'Of course, the Beatles had it all - music that touched the head, heart and body. I hope we do a little of that as well.' Davies, characteristically, is far more pessimistic. 'Don't forget we're a very manufactured group,' he says. 'I don't see us as that big.' The fans thronging to see them would probably have their own thoughts about the cultural impact of Supertramp - after all, they appear to be more cerebral than most rock audiences. There is not much 'getting down' with the music; it's more a matter of being uplifted by the polish and perfection of the sound. Still, it would be a supreme irony if the result of all this alchemy, this blending of high-tech hardware and generous talent, resulted in a sound so smooth it disappeared without a trace."

During the eastern portion of their cross-Canada tour, the band became involved in a rather bizarre incident that saw the cancellation of their planned concert in Halifax, a 9000-seat sell-out.

For a few weeks prior to the gig, the head offices of A&M Records of Canada had been receiving phone calls from a man who identified himself as Benny Superscam from Halifax asking to speak to Dave Margereson, Supertramp's manager. Margereson attempted to call him back a number of times, but the numbers that were left were found to be misleading.

A few days after the calls began, a number of letters began to arrive at the A&M offices that made some rather pointed and derogatory statements directed at Dave.

As the date for the Halifax concert approached, the switchboard operator at A&M Records received one last call from the same man who said such things as "we'll blow you away" and "the only true artists are dead." Margereson had a discussion with the band and they decided that because of their vulnerability on stage, it would be safer this time to cancel the Halifax concert. "It was the first time we've ever run into threats," Dave would later comment. "It freaked us out somewhat."

Shortly before Supertramp left for Europe to start the last leg of the Breakfast tour, Roger talked about the overwhelming reaction that the band had received in Canada throughout the cross-country tour.

Well Roger, how did it feel?
It was quite an experience. Those were the largest crowds that we ever played to. I don't know whether we're totally in love with outdoor venues and I'm not sure we'll be doing many of them ever again because there seems to be an atmosphere that you capture inside that's more controllable somehow. I have to admit though that this time around we had a lot of luck with the weather and outside elements. There was just something that was out of our control outside. We lost a bit trying to get through to that many people but I think that we had a good try at it. In many people's eyes we succeeded. We feel more comfortable with 16,000-seaters. The 40,000 ones are a bit large.

The obvious question then is why did you try?
Well we have a choice. Either we're going to be touring for life or we do those places. We do have the means to make them work. The sound system, I think, blossoms outside. It sounds absolutely incredible thanks to our sound engineer Russell Pope. It's the other factors that

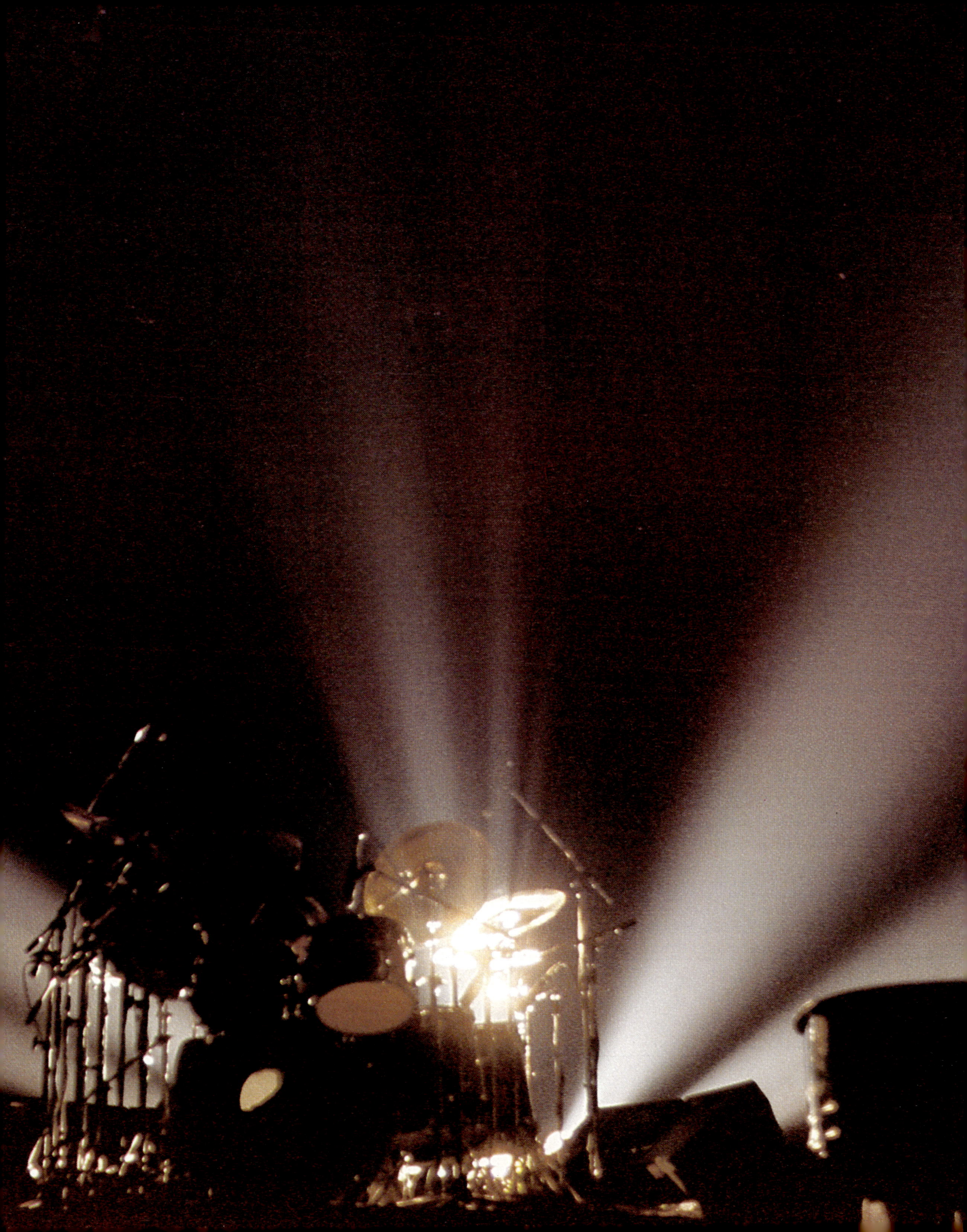

Butler & Chocolate Tribute, Antlantic Hotel after end of European Tour '79.

John and Christine, San Diego '79.

make it difficult. It really feels like hard work on stage most of the time. The sound you're getting on stage is not as powerful or as good as it is when you play an indoor venue. We were kind of disappointed, especially earlier on in Toronto and Montreal, with a few gigs because we couldn't give our best because the sound was against us. That makes us feel unfulfilled.

In both Toronto and Montreal you played to huge audiences each night. Do you feel that you can honestly communicate from on stage to that number of people?

The show takes on a different meaning and it's an experience in sound and colour. Although there were about 40,000 people each night for those shows, it didn't feel like 40,000. It felt the same as 15,000 or 20,000. It didn't feel that much bigger. It felt quite cosy as a matter of fact. They were good places to play. I don't think anybody was disappointed. I know outdoor events have a bad reputation because I don't think many bands explore the ultimate that they can get in sound systems and lights. You really need to take the event to the people in a large place. You need to make the show bigger somehow which is different from the theatre where everything is cosy and intimate. You really have to create visuals that reach out to people and suit the place.

It's easy to fall short technically outside, isn't it?

You've got the wind against you. That's one thing. A gust of wind can change your sound totally so people are hearing a blotchy sound. But one of the positive things is that you don't have to deal with the barn style forums where you play with sounds bouncing around in all directions. The bass end is much tighter outside and on the whole, our sound engineer said that the PA just shone on the whole tour. He was very happy with the sound. The tour was almost the summit of everything that we had learned and there was a real feeling of belief in the show. Canada is very special for us, there's no doubt about that. It's the first place, really, in the whole world, that picked up on us and supported us. We really wanted to give as much as we could this time around.

Do you get a different feeling from each country that you play?

Yes, they are different. In Spain, for instance, they're absolutely nuts. The last time we played there, there was a riot going on outside and the people were bashing the doors down to get into the hall. Germans are very fanatical as well. The English, on the other hand are very reserved. You really have to work hard to get them.

Why do you think that the album Breakfast In America had the major impact that it did?

I think that the songs are very accessible and commercial. They have a long life span. I'm listening to them now like anyone else would and I'm still really enjoying them which says a lot. Even after eight months in the studio with them I was still enjoying listening to them. I think the album as a whole really has an energy that suits the mood of our times. There's a lot of fun in that energy and a lot of joy comes through. I think it's something people need at this time. There's very little music around any more that has that kind of fun in it. No one today has the joy in their music that the Beatles had.

Do you have any qualms about following up Breakfast In America?

I'm really excited about the next one or the thought of the next one. It's a real challenge. I have no worries about it. I have a store house of about forty songs waiting to get onto vinyl. Ridiculously enough, the choice of songs on Breakfast In America weren't my favourites. They were just the ones that suited the band at this time. In a way, I'm holding my best for a later date. That may sound crazy, but it's true. Breakfast to us feels like a light album although concept-wise it isn't lightweight in many ways. We'll probably dive deeper on the next one but I think it would be nice if we could keep the fun aspect of Breakfast. It helps us get into the songs when we play them.

From Canada, Supertramp moved on to Europe and according to Dougie, it was all getting to be a little too much. "It was a really amazing tour," says Dougie. "It was huge. The record was number one everywhere in the world and we were steaming as a group. Everything was happening. The places were all sold out before we got there but the pressure just grew and grew until you just wanted to hide. A lot of funny things started to happen in Europe that put us on edge as well."

Late one night, as the band was coming across France on their way to a concert, a car came down the motorway the wrong way and crashed head on into one of the trucks. The truck driver was alright but the guy in the car was in a pretty bad way. The crew bus had been travelling directly behind the truck and as it pulled up, Tam Smith, one of the guys in the lighting crew

Ian "Biggles" Lloyd
Bisley - '79

Bob leaving stage at
L.A. Forum.
April/79

jumped out and went to the car driver's assistance. He got right into the car and pulled the guy's face open, which was in quite a state, and gave him mouth-to-mouth resuscitation which finally got him breathing until some emergency vehicles arrived and took him to hospital.

The crew went on to the next gig and when the band arrived the next night they heard the story. Tam was setting up the lights and later, at meal time, Tam told them the story. Apparently it still hadn't sunk into him exactly what had happened but, before going back to work, he told Dougie, "I just hope that if anything like that ever happened to me, somebody would be around to do the same thing for me."

The band did the show and at the end of it the crew went back to their regular grind of taking down the lights and sound system. There were no dressing rooms in the place and the band was given a bunch of motor homes that acted as the backstage area. Shortly after the show, they were standing around talking and winding down, when all of a sudden there was a bright flash from the stage area. When they turned around to look, Tam was in mid-air.

Tam had been disconnecting the light socket and apparently there had been a misunderstanding between him and the French electrician as to whether the main power supply had been turned off. Tam had been taking apart the system and had touched the live wire which sent him hurtling through the air and crashing to the ground. His heart had stopped and there was a panic backstage. All of the paramedics had gone home and there was nothing anybody could do.

Suddenly one of the French guys who had been working on the stage jumped down, pushed people out of the way and started pounding Tam's chest. He finally revived him and Tam was wheeled off to hospital where he finally recovered. (In a further bizarre turn of events, Tam later committed suicide for no apparent reason.)

The mood through the band at this point was rather tense as they headed back to the hotel. The events of the past 24 hours had shaken them to the point of exhaustion but, as it turned out, the day had another untoward incident in store.

Throughout the French part of the tour, there had been some shenanigans going on between the French promoter and Charly Prevost which had led to Charly hitting the guy in the face with a cake one night. Charly, on this particular night had gone off to his room in the hotel like everyone else, and later on he had heard an urgent knock on his door and somebody outside yelling, "Fire! Fire!" Charly figured it was just a made-to-order prank by the promoter so he decided not to answer. The knock came again. "Fire! Open up!" Charly refused for a little while and then eventually he went over to the door and opened it just a crack. The hallway was full of firemen and there was smoke everywhere. It hadn't been a hoax. Dave Margereson's room, adjacent to Charly's, had caught fire when one of the wires in the light console had shorted. Dave was out with the promoter Pascal and had a bit of a shock in store when he got back to his room.

It wasn't the first fire incident the band had run into in a hotel on this particular tour. Tony Shepherd, Supertramp's light technician and designer, was partial to rearranging his room whenever he checked into a hotel and as part of the redecoration he would often dim the lights by placing a T-shirt or piece of cloth over the light fixture. In this particular hotel, this came to the attention of the hotel manager, who raised all sorts of hell about the fire hazard it presented and demanded that Tony remove the T-shirt from the light.

Tony, in one of his ornery moods, wrote the manager a stinging but tongue-in-cheek note. "Sir, do you realize who I am? I am considered one of the world's foremost authorities on lighting and have worked in light design for most of my life. I feel that I am well qualified to know whether my method of dimming the lights in my room is a fire hazard or not!"

I hardly need to mention that shortly after the note arrived in the manager's hands, one of the T-shirts caught fire and caused general panic and retribution at the hotel.

"The last month of the Breakfast tour was the hardest we can remember," recollects Dougie. "Usually you want the beginning to be the hardest and all the difficulties to be overcome at that point but this time, just when we needed a break the most, it got really, really difficult.

The band had been recording many of the shows through the last part of the Canadian tour and into Europe for a double live album that was being planned for 1980. They didn't know it at the time, but out of this difficult period would emerge the live performances that would meet the exacting standards of the group and their resident sound wizards, Russel Pope and Pete Henderson, and become the basis of the live album. □

SUPERTRAMP
Paris

CHAPTER THIRTEEN

Group shot from *Breakfast In America* period.

Though the band was exhausted after a record-breaking concert tour that took them to well over 100 cities on two continents, it was a pretty heady time for everyone in the Supertramp organization.

They had received their first platinum album in the U.S. in the wake of three hit singles - "Logical Song," "Goodbye Stranger" and "Breakfast in America" - for the sale of over one million copies of *Breakfast In America*. The LP had spent 22 weeks in the top five of the American charts as well as receiving the NARM Cup for the most albums sold in the U.S. in 1979.

In Canada, Supertramp were honoured with an unprecedented two diamond awards for sales in excess of a million copies of both *Crime Of the Century* and *Breakfast In America*. There were gold and platinum awards presented throughout Europe, including a very special gold album for Rick and Roger honouring the outstanding sales of their first album released in 1970 entitled simply, *Supertramp*. (The platinum awards they received in Holland for *Breakfast In America* were actually each member's favourite breakfast enclosed in a plexiglass case.) In the months to come, the Breakfast LP would go on to sell over 16 million copies around the world.

Returning home to Los Angeles, there was a little unfinished business that the group had to look after before going their separate ways to get their personal lives together.

A number of the shows on the *Breakfast In America* tour had been recorded with an eye to finding the magic combination of tracks to be included on the band's planned live album.

"We had a number of motives for considering a live album at the time," explained Roger. "In America, where *Breakfast In America* was really the first album that took off for us, we wanted the American public to know that there were a few albums before that and so we felt that it would be a nice way of revamping a lot of the old songs and allowing our new public to get a listen to those. Also, there were a lot of songs that we weren't happy with when we recorded them in the studio and we knew that a lot of those songs were coming across better live. We wanted to have a record out of the live versions which we felt were better.

"Probably the main reason was to give us time to re-group and figure out where we wanted to go in the future because there was an incredible pressure on us to follow up on the incredible amount of momentum that we had built up with *Breakfast In America*. There was a lot of expectation built up for the next album which we knew wouldn't be ready until 1981 at the earliest. We had to fill the gap with something. For all those reasons it really felt like a good time to come out with a live album. There was also the feeling that we wouldn't be playing a lot of those songs ever again. It was also a good chance to sum up the seventies for Supertramp really."

John adds: "We always toyed with the idea of making a live album and we thought that 1979 would be a good year for it because it was the end of the 70s. Technically it was very difficult because we had to take the mobile studio with us everywhere. We started recording in Canada and carried on when we arrived in Europe.

"When we got home from the tour, Pete Henderson and Russel Pope made four or five rough mixes of songs from various places and didn't mark on the tapes any information as to where they were recorded. They just numbered them and we took all the cassettes home and gave our votes on which ones we liked the best. Coincidentally the majority of votes fell on the tapes that were made on the second night of our Paris concert at the Pavillon on November 29, 1980."

"Paris was such a fantastic place to be anyway but we played in a very weird building," comments Dougie. "It was torn down shortly after but when we were there, the Pavillon was a big barn of a place that used to be an abattoir. They had hung parachutes and put bleachers into it and we were told that they even had ballet in there. It was enjoyable playing there and being in Paris but I don't remember it as being a particularly outstanding night."

"We had a concept for an album which was originally going to be called Roadworks," continues John, "but we had the semi-French announcements so we settled on the title *Paris* and it kind of stuck. The problem was to decide on what to leave off. Russel and Pete did most of the leg work on it as far as mixing and we found that there was very little repairing that we had to do. There were a few things that maybe weren't right on particular tracks - some of my organ playing leaves a bit to be desired - so we had to redo a couple of things like a vocal here or there but there is not very much overdubbing on it. A lot of people, when they make a live album, just keep the drums and bass and redo everything else. We didn't have to do that."

"There really wasn't much debate on which concert we were going to use for the live album," says Roger. "We recorded most of the Canadian tour and we recorded about twelve or fourteen shows in Europe. The sound suffered in Canada because we were just getting used to having the mobile truck along and there were a lot of technical problems. Plus, the band was not performing at its best in Canada because we were having to deal with the newness of performing in the large outdoor venues. The band never really settled down in Canada.

"We had been really looking forward to Paris because there was a very special thing happening in France for us and I guess in a way we were anticipating the four nights we were going to play in Paris. It just so happened that those four really turned out well and the recording turned out well, so most of the tracks, in fact all of the tracks, were from one or another of the Paris nights."

There are a number of problems inherent in recording a band live as opposed to recording in a studio as Roger explained at the time.

"One of the first things you have to deal with is the leakage problem - all the other instruments feeding into the microphones. You'll have the drums coming through on the piano microphones and all the monitor speakers on stage which we tend to have quite loud. It's really an engineer's nightmare.

"From the mixing point of view, the problem that Russel Pope, our sound engineer, and Pete Henderson, our studio engineer, had was that the sound was *too* perfect. We had four microphones in the audience, recording them and the ambience of the arena. When they heard what they had captured on the individual instruments from the stage, it was near perfection. It was incredible. The sound was as good as any sound that we've managed to get anywhere. Then they pushed the faders up to see what would be added with the audience and the picture totally changed. It took a couple of months for them to find a way of approaching the whole thing because the key to the whole album was to be excitement. The first mixes they came up with were too perfect. They sounded like we were all in a bathroom. They eventually found the right approach in the end, which sounds like you are sitting in an auditorium listening to a band with all the excitement of the audience around you. That's the one that worked."

In most cases, when a band decides to do a live album, the selection of material is one of the most important aspects of the recording. This was the subject of much discussion and thought for Supertramp as well.

"It would have been nice if we'd come up with some new songs for the live album," muses Roger in retrospect. "There was a strong movement to try and do that. The pressure of getting the show ready for the tour and getting on the road was so great that we didn't have time to get some new songs in the act. The tour was so hectic that we never really had a chance to rehearse any while on the road. Thus, there's only really one new song on the album, "You Started Laughing," which is the B side of a single that we released quite a while ago.

"In my mind, there were a number of songs that came off better on the live album than on the studio album. "Soap Box Opera," to me, was massacred on *Crisis? What Crisis?* It didn't happen at all. "Fool's Overture" didn't come off for me on the *Even In the Quietest Moments* LP. A lot of the songs have much more energy on the live album. "Dreamer" for example. I think it's half a dozen of one and six of another as to which version you prefer. There are things with a studio version that are nicer, but the energy in live performance is greater. "Breakfast In America" and "Take the Long Way Home" for instance."

A notable omission from the live album was "Give A Little Bit."

"We tried to find a version that warranted being on the album but we were shocked when we listened back to the live tapes to find how bad all the versions were," says Roger. "There just wasn't one version that we felt that we wanted to put on the album. That was the only sad thing, because that would have been nice. It just missed on the *Even In the Quietest Moments* LP. It just didn't have the energy that I would have liked.

"When I listened to the live album for the first time, I was really pleasantly surprised. I don't listen to our albums much but I listened to it from beginning to end and I really felt that I was at a concert. I felt a lot of energy, and good energy, coming off it. I've put it on a few times since, just a few tracks, and it does give me energy. It makes me feel good and I'm happy with the way it turned out. If it didn't come out now, there would never have been a live album of a lot of these songs."

The *Paris* album that had been recorded with the Mobile 1 Remote studio was mixed at Chateau Recorders in North Hollywood and mastered at the A&M Recording Studios by Bernie Grundman after a superb production and engineering job by Russel Pope and Pete Henderson.

Once again, Mike Doud was the art director for the cover, which featured an original piece of art from illustrator Cindy Marsh. The interior picture - shot by Mark Hanauer - of the band going on stage in Paris for one of the concerts also catches an old friend of the band's. The Bear was bending over in the background to pick up a discarded towel as the group made their way up the ramp to the stage to the wild applause of the Paris audience. The Bear worked with Brimstone Productions in western Canada.

The short piece on the inside of the album jacket written by Supertramp's manager Dave Margereson perhaps, in a few words, sums up this particular phase of the Supertramp history better than anything else.

"This tour has been a hard one - 108 shows so far," wrote Margereson. "The crew has been incredible, as always. Humour and sense of purpose, those old Supertramp standbys, have prevailed despite the severe testing. Ah, Paris, a far cry from the first time we were here at the tiny Bataclan Theatre, where only eight people paid to get in, and Pascal our promoter has just had the courage to tell us that he bought six of them! Yes, the good old days - but, there's no more time, reminiscences are shattered by the roar of 8,000 voices, the lights are down, the blue curtain begins to move as Rick puts the harmonica to his lips - Bon Soir Paris!" □

The Crew at the warehouse.

Supertramp at Bob's home during the period of recording *Famous Last Words*, 1982.

CHAPTER FOURTEEN

After the lengthy Breakfast In America tour, the rumours were rife that not only would this be the last Supertramp tour, but, in fact, the end of Supertramp as a band. The various members of the band, especially Roger and Rick, had been discussing more and more their disenchantment with the touring grind and there were some subtle references being made about an eventual split between Roger and the rest of the group.

The live *Paris* LP was released in the fall of 1980. During that period, Canadian radio personality Doug Pringle, who had become quite close to Roger, talked to him as part of a radio special on the *Paris* LP developed for syndication in Canada. Pringle broached the subject of these rumours about a Supertramp split.

"Well, you know, after every world tour, the rumours are abundant within and without the band," commented Roger. "It's a tough thing to do and at the end of the tour you really wonder whether you ever want to do it again because it's just gruelling. I think at the end of this one we all came to the realization that, 'Okay, if we're going to do it again, we are going to do it in a much more fun way.' Up until this point, because of economics and necessity, we've had to really push it and cram the shows in on mammoth tours to make them pay for themselves let alone make money from them, because they were such expensive ventures. Hopefully, in the future, we can pace the tours more sensibly so that they're more enjoyable and the band will stay healthier because of that. That goes the same for recording too. Gone are the days when we can go into a studio for eight months and record an album like we did with *Breakfast In America*. None of us want to do that again so we're working on ways now in which we don't have to do that again.

"There is a lot of music lying around waiting. Now is the first time that we've really stopped in six years and a lot of water's gone under the bridge in that time. A lot of us got married, we've got children and we're needing time to kind of get into some stability in the form of home life and get grounded so that we can get a clear picture of where we want to go in the future. It's about eight months after the tour ended and there is a really positive feeling in the air. There's going to be some good things to get into in the future."

Since the tour, Roger had made a rather significant move out of Los Angeles to the interior of Northern California just outside of Nevada City where he bought a house, a lot of land and was in the process of building his own studio

Bob Siebenberg in his home studio shortly before a fire razed the house. March/80.

complex. At the time, there was a Utopian dream that Roger associated with this area.

"I'm going to call the land The Shire and hopefully, it's going to be a place where new forms of music, new forms of healing, new forms of energy and new forms of anything people can come up with really, that feel in tune with what the land is about, can find a place for experimentation and find a place where they can get support. If The Shire can be a place that can support new ways of thinking in whatever medium - in the visual arts, in music, in new forms of energy - that would be a nice ideal to chase.

"It's my way of giving back to the world what the world has given to me. The world has given me a lot in exchange for just singing a few songs. I feel a responsibility to try to repay it and try to give back some of the energy that I've been given. Hopefully, The Shire can be a place where different technologies and different philosophies can come and meet and create new ways of thinking and new ways of living for the benefit of mankind as a whole. My contribution I guess would be in new forms of music, as I really believe that Rock music is so primitive. We haven't even scratched the surface of what music can do for people. I'd like to experiment with music for healing and music for relaxing and music for getting people high, in the best sense of the word. To be honest, most music around today doesn't get me high. Anything's possible. It really depends on the people that are connected with it. If it's a place that people can live out their dreams and ideals and work on projects that normally they couldn't work on because the world doesn't want to know, then that would be great."

Though Roger felt very positive at that point about the relationship of the various members of Supertramp as a group, there was a hint that each member was beginning to broaden their own musical horizons outside of the band.

"I don't know how long this particular group of musicians will stay together as Supertramp. I know for certain that Rick and I will be working together for a long time to come and that really is the essence. That's the chemistry that makes Supertramp tick because we're two totally different individuals. That's the friction that makes for some great music. That's what made the Beatles great, having Lennon and McCartney, two different personalities, battling it out and getting the best from each other. They were in competition and in many ways I'm in competition with Rick. To have someone that you really respect and to better all of the time really makes for some great music.

"We stopped writing together after *Crime Of the Century* but to split up, to divide the writing team, somehow psychologically would have been bad for us internally, so we decided we wouldn't do that. That was the magic of the band so we decided to keep the Davies/Hodgson writing team intact.

"I think that in order to keep the artistic stimulation happening, we need to work with other musicians so we might bring in other musicians to record with us on a Supertramp album. For ten years, we've been building an incredibly strong foundation for all of us and to throw it away or to split up now would be crazy. We don't want to do that anyway. There's still life in the old beast and we'll take it until the energy stagnates; until the energy doesn't feel like it should go on any further.

"We've all got the freedom to get into individual things too. Dougie just bought a sailing boat and he'll probably sail around the world and have a great time, but he needs to do that in order to come back and put all his energy into the band. I need an outlet for a lot of music that doesn't belong to Supertramp that I have to do myself. I'll probably start on a solo album after the next Supertramp LP. Rick probably feels the same. He'd like to do a project himself. Bob is writing material now and he wants to get those songs out. John, I think, is going to take over the disco market. He's building a little studio with all his synthesizers and he's going to come up with some pretty unique things.

"I have a great relationship with John. He's not crazy about electric guitar and I'm not crazy about saxophone so we tease each other unmercifully. Funny enough, I'm not crazy about electric guitar either. I don't see myself as an electric guitarist. I see myself much more as an acoustic guitarist that was shoved into the electric guitar role because we couldn't find anyone else to do it. I was actually on bass in the beginning and we had auditioned about fifty guitarists who had all come along with their brand new gleaming Les Pauls and wailed away and hadn't touched us at all. In desperation, I was put on electric guitar and we looked for a bass player who turned out to be Dougie so here I am stuck with electric guitar. That's one of the things that we might do on the next Supertramp album. We might find an electric guitarist who is really fluid at it. We might even get in a percussionist to add a bit of percussion to our sound. The funny thing is, when it comes to drums, Rick is probably my favourite drummer in the world. He had to make a decision whether he was going to play drums or keyboards. Because of the limitation of drums in songwriting, he chose keyboards."

There was a tentative plan in the fall of 1980 to begin work on the next studio album that winter, to have it ready for release in the middle of 1981.

"There will probably be a short tour after that or maybe a long tour but it will have to be done in a much different way. For the next album I'd like to see us be more flexible. It'll really be the music that dictates that. I think that if a song is better with Rick drumming on it, then maybe that will be the way that we'll do it. I'd like to do some albums with just Rick and see what we can come up with. Anything's possible now that we have these studios. They're not completed yet, so we don't know. We're talking about it. It really comes down to the music and until that starts happening, none of us can say definitely what's going to happen.

"When we start creating music, it'll be crazy. We'll all start phoning each other up and saying, 'Hey come on over, I've got a great song. Come and do it!' I think it will be very creative. We're very excited at the fact that we don't have to go into someone else's idea of a studio again and pay $200 an hour or whatever it is, and watch the clock ticking away. In a way, we've earned the freedom to do it the way that we want to. So, hopefully, it will really add to the music.

"The Breakfast tour ended just before Christmas last year and shortly after, we actually got together to make some decisions on the cover of the live album but we hadn't actually got together because we wanted to get together. We had to go our different ways and get into other things in life that we had to take care of before the energy came back to want to get together as a fivesome again. Some people might think, 'Wow! Nine months of holiday!' It hasn't been a holiday. Work hasn't really stopped. The live album kept us hopping in spite of the fact that Russel and Pete have been mixing it, we still had to put energy into that. It's very difficult putting energy into old music, especially when you're dying to get on to some new music. Plus we've all been getting involved with these studios and other projects that have kept us full time."

Continuing his discussion of the relationships between the various members of Supertramp at that time, Roger talked about how it came to pass that he virtually handled most of the production chores for the albums on the band's behalf.

"Rick's more of an artist in the true sense of

Christine, Charles and John Helliwell.

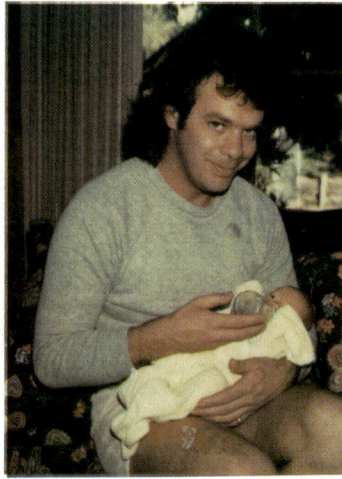

Bob C. Benberg with daughter Tori.

Supertramp considers their origin.

B.J. Wilson (right) drummer for Procol Harum at Bob's home studio during the recording of his solo LP, 1982.

the word - an artist/creator. When it comes down to anything technical, he's not very good. He knows what he likes and he knows what he wants to hear but to actually communicate that and to get in on to tape and through a mixing console, he's never really been interested in that so he's never bothered with it. I am interested in it so he has kind of thought, 'Great! Take it away!' So I've always filled that role.

"It is Rick and my songs that Supertramp perform and everyone in the band is very realistic about that situation. Bob is vying competitively to try and get one of his songs on the album and they're getting better and better. Maybe someday soon there will be a Bob Siebenberg song on one of the albums which would be great. I'd love that if it warrants it. The others really contribute in a different way. Dougie has always been the practical side of the band. Without Dougie, we wouldn't be here today. Without his energy to pull the artistic vagueness of Rick and myself together and apply it in the harsh world of the Rock business, we wouldn't be here. His contribution's really strong in that area. John has always been the front man. The performer. The lunatic. That has been his role. It's a whole different ball game now. The future's very exciting. Anything could happen. Anything will happen as long as growth is the motivation. The band will continue as long as it feels creative and it's still growing. That's why this live album has given us this extra time to think a lot about it and make the next studio album a cracker."

When the Breakfast tour came to an end and the final details for the release of the *Paris* LP had been taken care of, Dougie put his mind to a passion outside of the music business that had been part of his dreams for many years - sailing.

"After that tour we just bolted from each other," remembers Dougie. "I came back to Los Angeles and bought a yacht and then took off to some of the islands off the coast of California for a while. Then I went down to Mexico and came back before heading for the Caribbean. I have a place in Tortola in the British Virgin Islands that I share with Alan Gorrie, the bass player from the Average White Band. He had had the house down there and I tried to buy it from him but he didn't want to sell so I improved it and made it into a musician's rest home. It's a good place to be able to go down and write. It's a very quiet relaxed island. I'd been down there a couple of times before I bought this boat. I had chartered boats and sailed around the islands before and also I have some friends in the Bahamas who run a tourist diving school there. I spent quite a lot of my spare time down there with them just getting away from the music business. Not from the music so much but from the music business and all the stuff that goes with it. I miss the music and the band quite quickly but not all the excess.

"I've spent a lot of time over the last five years diving when I haven't been working. It sort of goes together with having a boat. I had the good fortune some years ago to meet a Canadian underwater cinematographer by the name of Paul Mortar. I spent some time with him and when he had some projects to do in the Bahamas, I would go down and visit with him. We became good friends. At the same time I did a few diving trips with Dusty Wade who used to be a diver with the Calypso."

For Dougie, buying the yacht that he named Trinity his permanent living quarters in Marina del Rey, was a dream come true.

"The idea of getting a yacht goes back to when I was about five years old. It's a lot more than I thought it would be. It's very fulfilling and a really good stabilizer for the music. It really gets me away from all of the stuff you have to deal with in the music business. In Marina del Rey, you've got your own little status thing with boats and boat people. It's a whole different world.

"I hadn't had experience with this size of boat. I had sailed smaller boats a lot and had seen this style of yacht before we went on tour. When I came back off the Breakfast tour, the idea was to buy a small boat and sail a lot. But on further consideration, I figured that I'd just be wasting my money that way because by the time you buy it, you'll never get your money back from it. I then decided just to go for it and really get into the experience of living on a boat. Within four weeks of coming home from the tour, I was on this yacht in Marina del Rey. I bought it in Newport and lived down there for a while before sailing it back up here."

After the tour, John went back to his home high in the Topanga Hills to spend some time with his wife Christine and son Charles and to start work on a small demo studio adjacent to his house. John recollects that period after the tour and a weird accident that sidelined him from any activity for a while.

"That tour really took a lot out of us and we really couldn't even look at the prospect of another tour. We gave our sound system and lights to the crew as a bonus and as a thank you for years of service to Supertramp. We retained two people, Ian Bisely and Norman Hall, who had the chance to go with the rest of the crew, who formed their own sound company. They decided to stay.

"We pretty well had the whole of 1980 off. Roger went to Northern California and everybody bought a new house or changed their living situation. I didn't go whole hog with the studio I was working on building. It was just small but good enough for doing demos of songs. I started a few songs but didn't really get too much together. Mostly it was used for practicing sax and just dabbling around on keyboards.

"In January of 1981, I was out bicycling like I usually do around some of the steep hills here. I was coming down the road, slipped on a slick rock, fell off and broke my leg which laid me up for quite a while. It was horrible. I broke the femur and had a pin put in it. I gradually got back to walking before I even attempted cycling again. It turned out that it was easier to cycle than it was to walk. I used to walk with a stick for a while then, just as a diversion, I started to run a bit when it was wet. I was scared off wet roads after the fall. Later I would go riding on the motorbike around the canyon and commute to Los Angeles on it. I started to get into dirt biking because my son Charles was into it. He was only about five or six when he got into it and he became a good rider so I had to get a dirt bike just to keep up with him."

"After the period of the Breakfast tour and the *Paris* album, things were starting to feel a little strange in the band," says Bob. "With Roger living so far away from the rest of us it seemed to change things. When we came back from the Breakfast tour, we all knew that our money was eventually going to catch up with us and everybody was going to have some money. The charm of Los Angeles had worn off on a few people and even I looked out of town for a place to live. I almost moved up to Los Gatos with Vicki and my two kids, Tory and Jesse but I didn't know if the band could take the strain of one of its members living so far away although I would have been prepared to travel, but it just makes things difficult. I thought, well while the band is still happening I would stay close by. There's plenty of time to live someplace else. But Roger was drawn so heavily to Northern California because that's where his guru guy lived. I think he fell out with that guy but liked it so much in that area that he decided to stay. I must admit it's a really nice place."

During this period, Bob moved into a house on the outskirts of Los Angeles in Woodland

John — in hospital, 1981.

Bob and Vicki in the kitchen of their home shortly before the fire. March/80.

Attic of Siebenberg house after fire, Oct. 20, 1980.

El Morro Beach off to surf, 1982.

A new look for Supertramp during the shooting of the video for My Kind of Lady.

Hills and began work on a studio that was located in one section of the house. Shortly after they moved in and the work had begun on the studio, disaster struck. A fire, that started in part of the electrical system of the unfinished studio, completely gutted the house and they were forced to go through the unpleasant task of collecting insurance and totally remodelling the house and the studio. When that work was done, Bob started work on recording his solo album that had been in the planning stages for a few years.

With all of this, there was also some time to fit in a bit of surfing, something that had been a part of Bob's life from his adolescent days in California before he moved to England.

"I've got a trailer down by Laguna Beach and I get down there most weekends and holidays. I've got my surfboard and suit down there and there's this guy who lives in a little trailer park that I have known since seventh grade. He's a lawyer now and I still go by his trailer and knock on his window at 7:30 in the morning. If the waves are good we go out surfing together. When it starts to get blown out or if the weather is crummy we just groove around on the beach. Then when it's sundown and the water starts getting glassy again, we're back in the water."

During this period, Rick and his wife Sue, spent most of their time in Los Angeles getting their house together, remodelling and overseeing the building of Rick's 24-track studio that he would call the Backyard Studio.

It was plain to see, given the fact that the various members of Supertramp were scattered to the four winds and busy putting some roots down in their individual family lives, that it was going to be no easy matter to get everyone back together in one place to start work on another album. But soon the inevitable had to be faced and the complex recording process involved in putting a Supertramp album together had its tentative beginnings in the spring of 1981.

"The period between *Breakfast In America* and the start of the new album was very fragmented," recollects Dougie. "Everyone changed their lifestyles quite a bit. Everyone grew further apart and we really didn't see much of each other. Sure, we saw each other occasionally but not on any grand scale for quite a long time. When we did start seeing each other again, it never really clicked the same as it did before."

Adds Bob: "At first, the situation of Roger living in Northern California and the rest of us living in Los Angeles didn't seem to be much of a problem except that Rick had a problem

SUPERTRAMP

"...famous last words..."

having to go up to Roger's place because Roger was pretty staunch about not coming down here. Certainly Dougie, John and I didn't really mind going to Roger's because you could get into a jeep, go out on the land, swim in the river and rehearse in the evening. But it was weird because Rick wasn't there so at the start it was four of us up there sometimes and four of us in Los Angeles at other times. The band format started to feel a little bit shaky. It finally came to the point where something had to be done about it. Rick and Roger finally agreed that they could compromise on it and Roger would come down to Los Angeles for two weeks and then Rick would go up to Nevada City for two weeks. Then in the end we finally agreed to rehearse mainly at Rick's place."

After the rehearsals and a little recording at Rick's studio, the band moved into Bill Schnee's studio in Los Angeles to start recording.

"The studio really wasn't ready to receive us because it was still being constructed," says Bob. "We tried to make a good job of it but they were just building it so it didn't really work out. The atmosphere wasn't very good either externally or internally. There was this struggle between Rick and Roger as to the direction of the album in terms of whether it should be another Pop album to follow up *Breakfast In America*, or from my point of view and Rick's, that we should go out and show people what Supertramp is really made of instead of coming out as a Pop band again. The feeling was, let's try to retain some of the earlier drama and meat and potatoes and show what Supertramp is really about. That kind of power struggle between Rick and Roger diluted the whole effort in the end. The mainstay song that we planned for the album was one of Rick's entitled "Brother Where You Bound" which was a ten-minute epic and a tremendous song but it didn't really make much sense on an album of Roger's songs which included lighter Pop tunes. In the end, they both kind of changed their formats and their picture of what they thought this album should be. It became a diluted version of what it started out to be. It was really neither here nor there.

"There was pressure on Rick and Roger because they had just come off this massive selling album as writers and now they were expected to try and do it again. We didn't try to do it the first time. We just went in there and those were the songs. That's what it became."

John gives another perspective of the period of recording for the album that would eventually become "... *famous last words* ..."

"As usual with this band, we were trying to get a democracy to work," observes John. "It's not the same as a dictatorship. Initially we really wanted to rehearse and prepare for the album so that we could shorten the recording time which we've always tried to do. We started off at Rick's place rehearsing and then moved to Bill Schnee's in Hollywood. That wasn't working out too well and by that time Roger's Unicorn studio in Nevada City was just about ready so we went up there. We came back to Los Angeles shortly after and went into The Captain and Tenille's Rumbo Recorders studio in North Hollywood and did some overdubbing there. Then the north/south war started. Not everybody wanted to go up there and Roger didn't want to come down to Los Angeles so we had to make compromises again. Personally, I enjoyed it up at Roger's place but Rick didn't like it much. It's a nice little country town and I could continue my bike riding and stuff. Anyway, we had problems in the studio and then at the end of 1981 right into 1982 we decided to mix up there. We got Pete Henderson back to do the LP and we just laboured on and on.

"Roger was obviously feeling the first pangs of wanting to withdraw so it was a more difficult process than it might have been. Roger seems to think it was so painful working on '... *famous last words* ...' It probably was for him but we finally got it done. I guess it depends on where your

At Roger's Unicorn Studio in Nevada City during recording of *Famous Last Words*. The Wilson sisters from Heart did some background vocals. (left to right) John, Pete Henderson, Russel Pope, Roger, Dougie, Nancy Wilson, Ann Wilson (seated).

mind is. If he's pissing off thinking that he'd like to go solo all the time, it obviously wouldn't be a pleasant experience. He's got some good material on the album. We were going to do Rick's "Brother Where You Bound" but it would have made the whole thing a bit too heavy so we decided to reserve that for the next one."

The recording of "...famous last words..." came to a close and it was more than clear that the next album would likely not involve the participation of Roger. At this point he had decided to leave Supertramp and pursue a solo career. As an observer, it was sometimes worth a giggle to watch the record industry machinery kick in to muzzle any sort of comment on this situation. At least until the record had cleared the cash registers and one last tour had been mounted with Roger as a member of the band.

"The name of the album itself, "... famous last words ...," and Mike Doud's Folonesque art work for the cover that depicted a tightrope walker caught in the spotlight, balanced precariously on a rope that stretched into infinity, warily eyeing a pair of scissors ready to cut the cord on which his mortality depends, seemed to have a message for even the most naive of Supertramp afficionados.

There would be no comment, officially or otherwise from the band on the matter and, as spokesman for the band, John was dispatched to the four corners of the globe to promote the album and fend off all compromising questions on the state of Supertramp as an ongoing entity.

The press release from the corridors of A&M Records promotion department, sent to the media around the world, was as dodgy. It ended with this non-statement.

"Fans of Supertramp might be dismayed by the title of their latest album and the scissors threatening to snap shut on its cover. They need only listen to be reassured: Supertramp is an inventive, supple and richly creative band as ever. Famous Last Words is anything but."

John had some comments on the period during the release of "... famous last words ..." and Roger's situation from his point of view.

"Roger likes to have people around him that are looking up to him. He's got this little group of people up there. Maybe he needs that. I wouldn't want all that attention from people but he's got his own organization of people. He's got his land and a few houses and he's involved in so much on his own. It was a painful experience for him to cut the album and it obviously led to his decision to want to split.

"I could see the way things were disjointed but I was behind the music that was on the LP so I went on a little world tour to promote it being the elected spokesman. I went all around Europe, South Africa and South America and talked about the LP as I did for *Paris*. It makes a lot of difference to go somewhere that you've never played before and promote it. It makes a big difference to album sales. People get interested if they've seen you on TV even if the group doesn't play there.

"It was kind of in the cards that Roger might be leaving even though he hadn't said it. His attitude and musical direction made it clear that something was going to happen. We hadn't made the decision to tell the public because nothing was really finalized so I didn't talk about it. I just talked about the LP and the probable tour. The only thing was the title. They said that there was a rumour around that it was the group's last LP because of the name. I didn't think at the time that it was the last; it isn't so I just had to dispel that.

"We thought of other titles for the album but they were a bit bland. We wanted a phrase that bore some relationship with what we were doing but was enigmatic at the same time. We always like to have enigmatic titles like *Crime Of the Century*. This was in the same vein. When anybody wanted to know an actual reason, I told them about making an LP. This last LP we thought was going to be real quick. We thought we were going to rehearse it and record it real quick and it ended up taking longer than any other so we had to eat our words again. For the past three or four LPs we've been saying, 'Let's be well prepared.' So the title sprung out of that as well. I can't remember who first thought of it. The graphic design came directly from the title. Trying to set up a situation of 'who knows what's going to happen' which turned out to be quite apt with the situation with the group...is the rope going to be cut or what? It's obviously going to go on as long as there's music there."

Upon the release of the album, the band went into the studio to do their first videos. Dressed in '50s apparel, beardless with slicked back hair, they produced a video for Rick's song, "My Kind Of Lady." On another video shoot, a story unfolded on film to the soundtrack of Roger's "It's Raining Again" in which the band played cameo roles.

"...famous last words..." was released in the fall of 1982. Shortly after, plans for another extended tour of North America and Europe were becoming very much a part of the endless number of meetings to decide on the band's future as they approached the tenth anniversary of this particular version of Supertramp. ☐

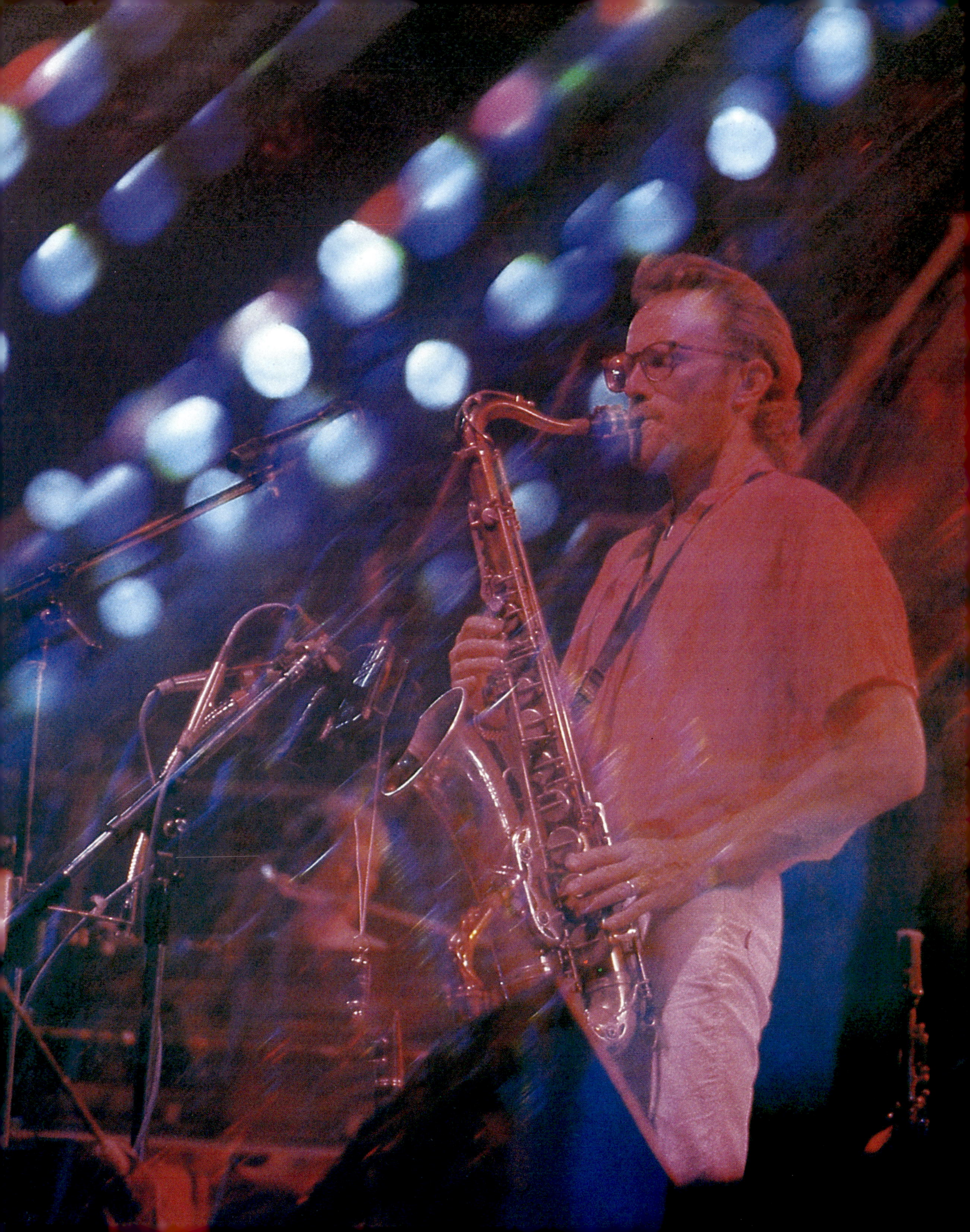

CHAPTER FIFTEEN

The period following the release of *...famous last words...* was a chaotic one within the group. It was obvious that Roger's decision to leave the band was irrevocable yet there were other considerations to ponder. There was talk of one last tour with Roger as a member of the band, a prospect that was acceptable or repellent depending on who you talked to and when.

Roger was anxious to get on with his solo career which had taken very definite steps toward fruition with the recording of an album entitled *Sleeping With the Enemy* done at his Unicorn Studios in Nevada City.

Rick was also anxious to get on with the creative and logistical problems of giving new character and life to Supertramp in its new formation.

Bob Siebenberg had started recording a solo album at his home studio in Woodland Hills, but in contrast to Roger's attitude, he was quite willing to pursue that side of his career within the context of Supertramp.

Shortly before the start of the tour (yes, a consensus was reached to the affirmative) both Bob and Roger were virtually spending every waking hour finishing their LPs. Beyond the consideration of just getting the music out on the street there was also the practical rationalization that, if the LPs came out during Supertramp's Europe/North American tour, it would provide a golden opportunity to do a little promotion on the side while they were on the road.

When it came time to rehearse for the tour, in Los Angeles, Bob and Roger were still finishing up. Bob had actually finished his LP by this time but the input he was getting from the record company and some close associates indicated that the album was missing the magic ingredient of a hit single. As the rehearsals rolled around in May, Bob was virtually burning the candle at both ends trying to be creative during the day and put in the time at night to go over the old songs with the rest of the band in preparation for their trip to Europe.

"The pressure was quite incredible," Bob said at the time as he took a breather beside his pool. "Normally I'd work with Derek, an old friend of mine who had worked on a number of music projects with me, during the day and we'd wrack our brains until the engineer arrived at which point we'd fine tune the sound. I'd record until about seven o'clock, grab a sandwich and be at Rick's by seven-thirty for the rehearsal. I usually wouldn't get home until about one o'clock in the morning. It was really getting to be just a little too much. I had originally delivered the album to A&M on March 1 for release in May but it got put on hold until after the tour."

The album had featured guest appearances by Rick, John and Dougie of Supertramp as well as Procol Harum drummer B.J. Wilson and Los Angeles session musician Scott Page. Bob handled the vocals on most of the tracks, some of which hinted at the Supertramp sound but all in all revealed some strong potential as a very personal musical statement. There was some suggestion that after the tour, Scott Gorham would be returning to California to write some songs with Bob.

In Nevada City, Roger had set up an organization that was indicative of the type of ambitious plans that he had for his solo career. Russell Pope, Supertramp's sound engineer had moved up to Nevada City to work with Roger on the album which was being completed slowly-but-surely to a rigid schedule marked on a calendar that hung like the Sword of Damocles on the back wall of the control room at Unicorn Studios. Assisting Roger and Russell on the production of the LP was Ken Allardyce, who with his wife Barb, had also moved to Northern California and was planning his own album under Roger's guidance. Tony Shepherd, Supertramp's light technician, with his girlfriend Clair, had also made the move to be with Roger.

A three-storey house adjoining the studio acted as the main offices for Roger's enterprises. There was a business manager, Dave Furano, who had previously worked with Bill Graham and Jerry Weintraub, two of the biggest promoter/managers in America. Shortly before the tour, they would install a few thousand dollars worth of computer equipment in the office to propel the Hodgson operation into the space age.

A new personality arrived in Nevada City during this period in the person of Doug Pringle, who with his lady Heidi, made the move from in Montreal to act as Roger's personal manager.

Pringle, an expatriate Englishman, who was a much-respected radio personality and broadcast consultant in Canada, had met Roger many times in the past four or five years and they had hit it off immediately. They had both come from similar backgrounds in their childhood, both being products of the British public school system and had found much in common in their overall attitudes to the music business and the world in general.

In Los Angeles, while a great deal of frantic energy was being put into the completion of Roger's solo project given the fact that rehearsals for the upcoming tour were around the corner, there was a certain amount of skepticism among the other band members and group management as to whether Roger could possibly finish the album in time before having to leave on the tour.

As May of 1983 rolled around, the LP had reached its mixing stage but it was time for everyone to leave Nevada City and move down to Los Angeles where the Supertramp rehearsals had begun. Having driven down from Northern California in their motor home, Roger and his wife Karuna used the vehicle as a mobile base of operations in L.A. Roger would get up in the morning for meetings with his business people, have breakfast, head off to the Supertramp rehearsals and continue working into the early morning hours on his album at the small mixing studio he had arranged for near Laurel Canyon. It was a tough schedule but as the tour began, the LP, which included a remake of the early Supertramp single "Land Ho," was completed along with the cover art work and a logistical plan for its launching.

But as Roger headed for Europe to join Supertramp for the opening dates of the tour, he was beginning to have some second thoughts about the direction and musical philosophy entrenched in the album that he had called *Sleeping With the Enemy*. His general perspective on his music was taking some rather radical turns during this period and in the end, he decided to scrap the project with the idea of going back into the studio after the tour to record a new LP that hopefully would be ready for release in the spring of 1984.

In a classic example of jumping the gun, *Circus Magazine* in the U.S., anticipating the LP's release, actually reviewed it, unheard, in one of their issues during this period.

While Roger was recording in Nevada City prior to the tour, Dougie was very much involved in pulling together a lot of details for the preparation of the Supertramp tour which would include the addition of two other musicians - Fred Mandel and Scott Page.

"It has only been since this tour was decided on that I feel that the members of Supertramp are all pulling together again," commented Dougie. "I'm sort of missing Rog but he's busy on his record while the rest of us are working away to pull this tour together. It feels good and really exciting to be getting back to it again. I felt extremely frustrated after the first year of our break following ... *famous last words* ... That first year was really good because we all really needed a break from each other. I was just fried when I came back from the last tour but by early 1981 I was ready to go again. I could have gone out on tour again at that point and I think that John felt the same way.

"I feel productivity around the corner because Roger is doing his record, and although it is not a Supertramp record, he's getting out the stuff that he had wanted to do for a while. Rick's been writing again and we're now getting a feeling for what it would be like to have some new blood in the band with the addition of Fred Mandel and Scott Page on this tour. It is the first step for us in making some changes. It's going to be really exciting to arrange things a little bit differently and broaden the sound. I think we got along well enough before but we've never been able to have the depth and total dimension that was possible in the sound. I'm really looking forward to it. We've also got a few surprises as far as the film presentations that have always been a part of our live show. We've made a few changes there too."

The two new additions for the 1983 tour were multi-instrumentalists who were no strangers to working with what are generally categorized as super groups.

Fred Mandel, originally from Toronto, worked during the early seventies with such locally-based acts as Grant Smith, Lighthouse and Domenic Troiano. He recorded with Dick Wagner, the musical director for Alice Cooper on his solo album, and from 1977 to 1980 worked with Alice Cooper's band, holding the position of musical director himself in 1978.

Dougie signing autograph for World Tour '83.

There was a short tour with Kiki Dee and some co-writing with Davey Johnstone on his LP *Flush the Fashion* in 1980. Mandel wrote a song entitled "Pain" for the soundtrack of the movie *Roadie* and in 1981 did some recording with Pink Floyd on *The Wall*. He played keyboards and synthesizers on a couple of Cheap Trick projects including their *One on One* LP and their musical contribution to the soundtrack of the animated film *Heavy Metal*. Back in Toronto, he produced songwriter Chris Hall's solo LP *Hypnotized* before getting a call from Queen to go out on tour with them through Japan and North America in 1982. When Fred received the call from Supertramp, he had been rehearsing with David Bowie for his tour. He liked the Supertramp situation better and decided to make the switch.

Fred had done some work on Queen member Brian May's solo LP with people like Eddie Van Halen and Phil Chinn. Following the Supertramp tour there was a possibility that he would be recording with Queen and accompanying them on a planned tour of South America before doing some solo projects of his own which would include some production work with other artists.

Scott Page comes from a musical background in Los Angeles. His father was a multi-instrumentalist with Lawrence Welk's band for thirteen years and after Scott had learned to play the trumpet at the age of six, he would make some appearances on the TV show, usually at Christmas, playing duets with his father. Since then his dad has moved on to play with Barry Manilow's band and Scott has significantly broadened his musical horizons.

In school, Scott studied architecture but realized his calling was elsewhere when he played in his first band, first called Merciful Soul and then Rural Still Life, with Jeff Porcaro and David Paich who would eventually go on to become top Los Angeles session musicians and form the band Toto.

Through college he mastered one instrument after another including flute, saxophone, guitar, oboe and English horn among others while working with a small orchestra headed up by Stan Worth.

His Supertramp connection came initially through Bob Siebenberg.

"Bob used to see me play at a club in the Valley called Jaysons where I used to work with a pick-up band three nights a week," recalls Scott. "I didn't really know Bob at the time but I would see him some weeks sitting at the end of the bar sipping a beer. We had a few chats but I

The stage is set – Europe '83.

Biggles, Mickey and Steve – The Trampettes, Europe '83.

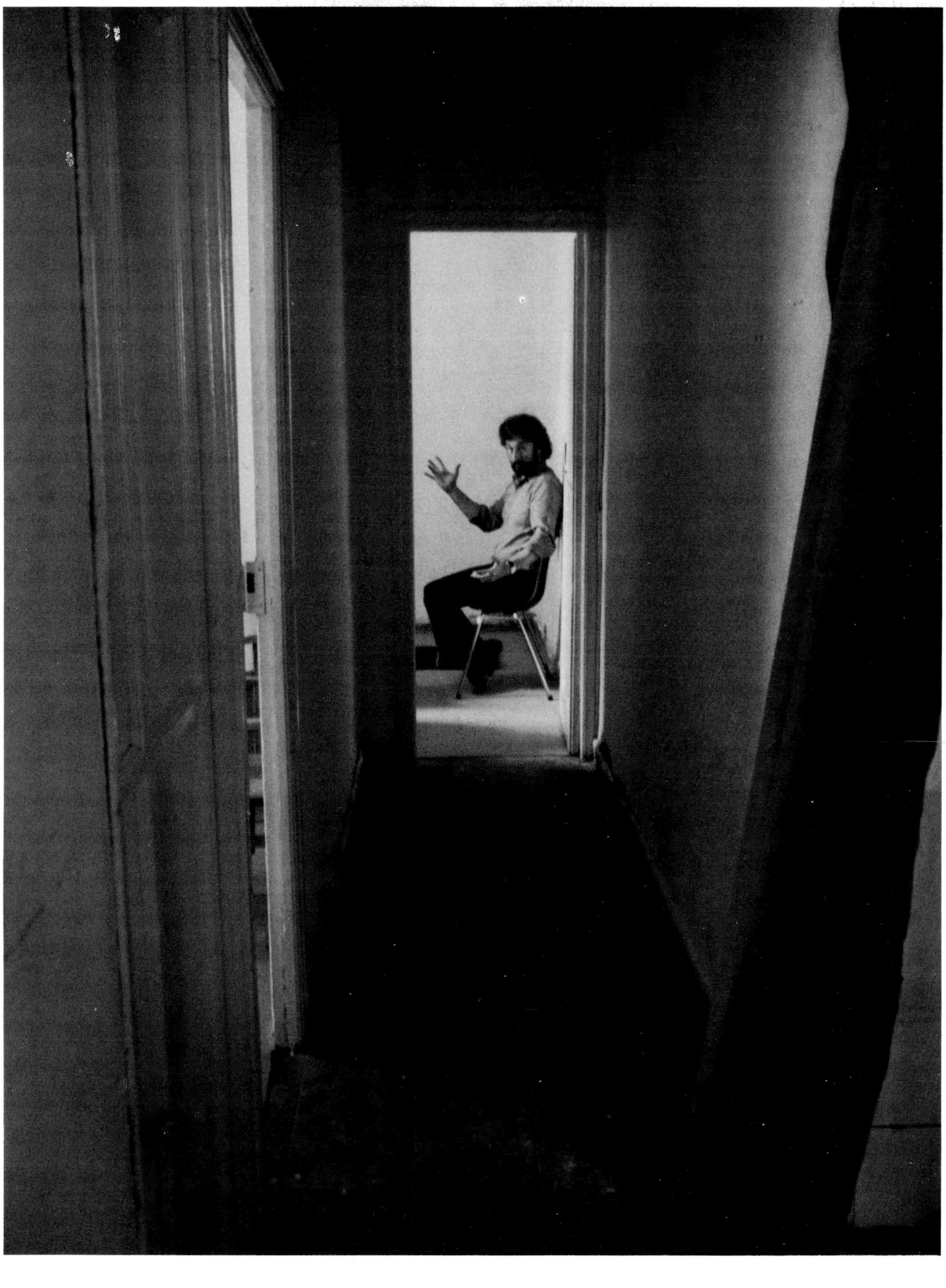

Pour atteindre la qualité Supertramp, des musiciens sans faille : Bob Benberg à la batterie, Roger Hodgson aux chants et aux claviers ; avec Richard Davies à la guitare – c'est lui le fondateur du groupe – et Fred Mendel, un guitariste de Queen. Quant au fameux saxophoniste John Helliwell, il est accompagné par Scott Paige

Supertramp receiving gold records in Toronto, August, 1983.

didn't find out until much later that he was with Supertramp. We had a number of mutual friends in the music business and he heard me once playing with Michael Smotherman. Shortly after that he asked me to come and play on the solo album he was working on at his studio. Just before the Supertramp tour, he asked me to come over and audition. I dropped around one day and got the gig."

Prior to the tour with Supertramp, Scott had worked with Seals and Croft for three years before playing in the house band on a couple of TV game shows incuding *Fun Factory* hosted by Bobby Van. He worked with Diana Ross for ten weeks before leaving to join the Supertramp tour.

Before the tour, there had been some trepidation in everyone concerned with the band, that because Supertramp had been out of the public eye for such a long time that people might have forgotten them. The initial reports of ticket sales from Europe indicated that they were moving pretty slowly. The band had one of the biggest surprises of their career in store.

The European leg of the tour turned out to be an overwhelming success and when the final count was in, the figures showed that it had been the second largest tour ever to be played in Europe in terms of attendance and gate receipts. Only the Rolling Stones had managed to mount a larger tour.

All across the continent, Supertramp played the largest outdoor venues available and filled them to capacity. In London, Lady Di, the Princess of Wales, declared during a press conference that Supertramp was her favourite band. In Paris, the group played in front of close to 82,000 people on the grounds of a large Chateau. Scott Page remembers that day very well.

"Given the magnitude and scale that things are done around Supertramp, it's amazing to see the people in the band take everything pretty lightly. Maybe it's just my viewpoint as the new guy. They're such nice people and you don't get any of that Rock Star syndrome from any of them.

"Nonetheless, when we arrived at the gig just outside of Paris, everybody's mouth dropped open as we got out of the cars and saw where we were going to play. It was the most magnificent place I've ever seen. There was a huge chateau at one end of these huge grounds that at this point was covered with people as far as the eye could see. In the back, there were tents set up for us with a large catering crew placing food on the long tables. It was just spectacular. The sound system we were using was more than twice as big as what we used on some of our American dates with relay towers further down the grounds so that people at the back could get the best sound possible.

"At one point, it started to pour but rather than putting a damper on everything the people really got into it. Some were even playing soccer in the mud. Spy, our tour manager, came in at one point on a motorcycle and the thing crashed screwing up his leg so he was taken off to hospital. Luckily it wasn't too serious. Then this guy got caught selling counterfeit tickets and a little police car (I think it was a Fiat) came in with its siren screaming. This cop jumped out looking like Inspector Clouseau with a bow-tie, grabs this guy and puts him in this little car and drives off with the siren on again. It was like a comedy movie. We were in hysterics.

"In the middle of the concert, because of the rain, the whole sound system cut out and it took a while for us to get it going again. But it was one of those days when no matter what goes wrong, the feeling from everybody was still good. It was an amazing day.

"At the end of the show, because of the large crowd and the bad road conditions, we decided to pull a hit and run. As soon as we came off stage we hopped into the cars and had a police motorcycle escort. This guy was crazy. He sped off down the road with his siren going and we were having trouble keeping up. At one point, he took a spill but he just picked the bike up and continued on, kicking at cars and yelling at people to get out of the way. As we looked back, they had formed the name Supertramp over the top of the chateau with lasers. It was a sight I'll never forget."

After the European tour, the band had a couple of weeks off in California before heading out on the North American leg of the tour.

Writer George Kanzler was at the New York-area concert at the Meadowlands Arena in New Jersey and reported:

"The prelude and the coda, along with the other orchestra devices, remain very much a part of the rock of Supertramp. Such devices are what have earned Supertramp the art-rock label.

"But, judging from their performance in East Rutherford, this British band plays a brand of pop that could just as easily be labelled cinematic rock - in wide-screen full color.

"Supertramp is presenting one of the most elaborately stage-lighted shows to play the arena circuit, a constantly shifting kaleidoscope of rainbow colors that bathe the wide, white stage

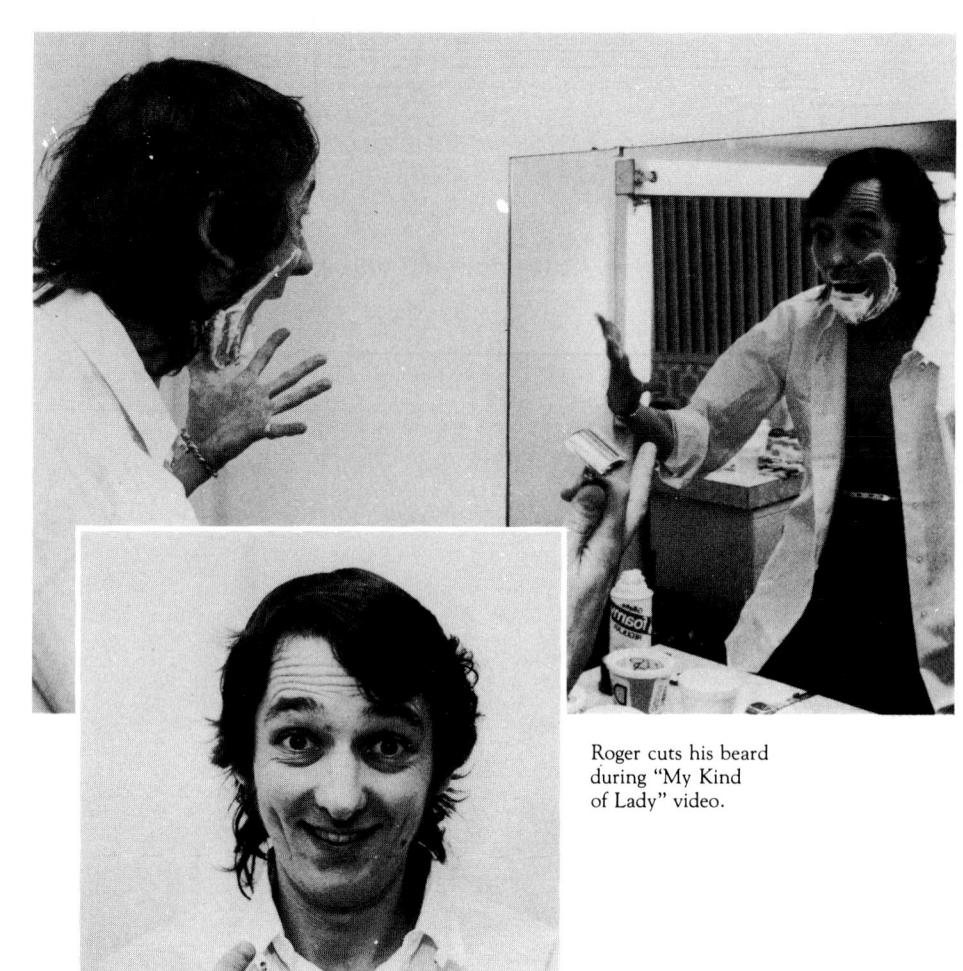

Roger cuts his beard during "My Kind of Lady" video.

Roger at his Shire Yuba River, Nevada City '82.

in multi-hues. With three pedestals across it, and half a dozen keyboard instruments, the stage is ideal for absorbing the full impact of the colorful light.

"However many pretensions may be there, in the films, overtures, rhapsodic passages and occasional attempts at lyric profundity, Supertramp manages to temper them with what the British might call a jolly affinity for the bright melody and the pop hook. The Logical Song, It's Raining Again, Give A Little Bit and many others have a catchy pop surface that shines like a lollipop over the dense instrumental textures.

"And although rock momentum is at a premium at a Supertramp concert, they compensate with a versatile approach to instrumental colors almost as rich and varied as their light show. Keyboards often dominate, but John Helliwell's saxophones often add a plaintive human note to the proceedings, and Roger Hodgson's acoustic guitar provided pretty strummed contrasts to the massed synthesizer-keyboard chords.

"Vocally the group also offers contrasts. Hodgson's reedy tenor contrasts as a lead voice with Rick Davies' deeper, raspy blues tone. And the other members of the band - with two additional musicians - sang some arching falsetto harmonies on choruses, a device that contrasted sharply with Davies lead singing on Goodbye Stranger.

"The sound mix and level was very good for the arena, and conveyed Supertramp's music with fidelity to its intricacies."

In Montreal, where Supertramp played an unprecedented three nights at the Montreal Forum, Peter Goddard, the long-time music critic for the *Toronto Star*, flew in to catch one of the shows and later in print considered the state of Supertramp after the departure of Roger Hodgson.

"It's a good hour to show time at the Forum and the ushers have their snappy red jackets off and their ties loosened. They're busy with their second favourite sport after gossiping about the Canadiens - watching girls on Atwater Street through the thick windows.

"But something's not right; it's the women. They're too young and bubbly and wholesome and middle class. Where, the ushers wonder, is the zap and flash and the Crescent Street flair?

"Obviously still on Crescent Street. This is the suburbs they're seeing. This is a Supertramp concert - one of three here before one in Ottawa and two at the CNE Stadium in Toronto - and it's a serious matter.

"No time for strutting. This is a concert for couples. This is a concert where you worry about value for a dollar, not about doing some nutsy freak-out.

"It's also the last time anyone will see this Supertramp line-up or hear a lot of the band's biggest hits. Next time around - if, that is, there is a next time around - there will be a different Supertramp.

"It all hinges on Roger Hodgson's decision to quit the band after more than 12 years. With him goes the band's pop inclinations, which made them so enormously successful their three nights at the CNE four years ago - the biggest draw by any band in all of North America.

"Hodgson's flair for a simple melody strung out over basic but telling chord changes was balanced by the introspective and brooding music and lyrics of the other chief songwriter, Rick Davies. Now the balance has been upset.

"'It'll be a darker, more sombre band. It'll be more inclined to rhythm 'n' blues. And we won't be doing his (Hodgson's) songs - things like Dreamer - when he's not with us anymore,' says reed player John Helliwell.

"The new Supertramp will be 'scaled down,' adds Dougie Thomson, the bassist. 'We'll have new music. It'll be interesting for us if we can play different kinds of shows, smaller ones.'

"We're sitting on an empty packing case behind the stage, Helliwell, bearded and laconic, has just lost a darts game: Thomson, the meat-and-potatoes guy, has just finished helping a photographer get a good vantage point. There's no pressure. The guards passing by don't even know who they are.

"But that brings up the band's big secret, something their next album and their career centres around. It's a 12-minute song by Davies 'about communism,' Helliwell explains. 'It's not exactly finished yet, but I can tell you that it's not pro communist. I mean, how can you be a rich rock star and write a song that supports communism?"

"Supertramp has been pop's best kept secret. Not their music, certainly. Their Breakfast In America album sold more than 1.5 million copies in Canada alone and their last single, It's Raining Again was a hit as well.

"But, as Rolling Stone magazine once said, the British quintet based in Los Angeles has been pop's 'silent success with a faceless image.' The point was, you could hum their songs but you'd never recognize them on the street.

"They like it that way. Almost 15 years since they first started playing English provincial pubs, they've become a band without a star system.

Christine Helliwell with son Charles in Europe, July '83.

They travel with their families, they don't party to all hours and they avoid the kind of restaurants where people go to be seen. Their kids sit backstage and pretend to play along with their dads.

"Before this tour began, word had it they were supposed to have been washed up. Finished. 'Everyone had written us off, all right,' Thomson says. 'And we were beginning to believe our own press. But after our tour had started in Europe and we saw how big the crowds were (82,000 people in Paris, for example), we knew it wasn't over, not now at least.'

"Helliwell says, 'You just can't get any bigger than we were in Europe. When (Dougie) talks about scaling down, we mean to the level we are now in North America. It's enormously expensive to do concerts on the scale we did in Europe. It costs millions just to get everything together and there's so much organization that, at best, we just managed to break even - if we broke even.'

"Two nights in Munich were filmed and, after the North America tour ends Sept. 26, Thomson is flying to Germany to edit a television show into shape. Plans are being made to shoot the pair of CNE concerts for pay-television for airing next spring or summer. 'We want to have a record of this band as it is now,' says Helliwell.

"Lushly orchestrated and lavishly lit, the Montreal concert was barely underway when it veered even more toward sentimentality. 'Do you know you were the first audience in North America to discover Supertramp?' Hodgson asks the crowd. The roar back is deafening. Self-congratulation is sweet indeed.

"'This is my last tour with Supertramp. I just want to say thank you all for the love and support you've shown over the years - et voici ma chanson pour vous.'"

Wilder Penfield III, the music critic for the *Toronto Sun*, had some other thoughts on the band's internal changes after a talk with Rick.

"The recent album called Famous Last Words was deemed a disaster for Supertramp when it failed to sell more than 4,000,000 copies worldwide. But the title at least has proved to be prophetic.

"The tightrope on which balanced one of the most fruitful songwriting partnerships of the 70s is being scissored at the end of the band's current tour.

"Roger Hodgson once again announced his planned departure last night, this time to a sold-

Fred Mandel.

Scott Page

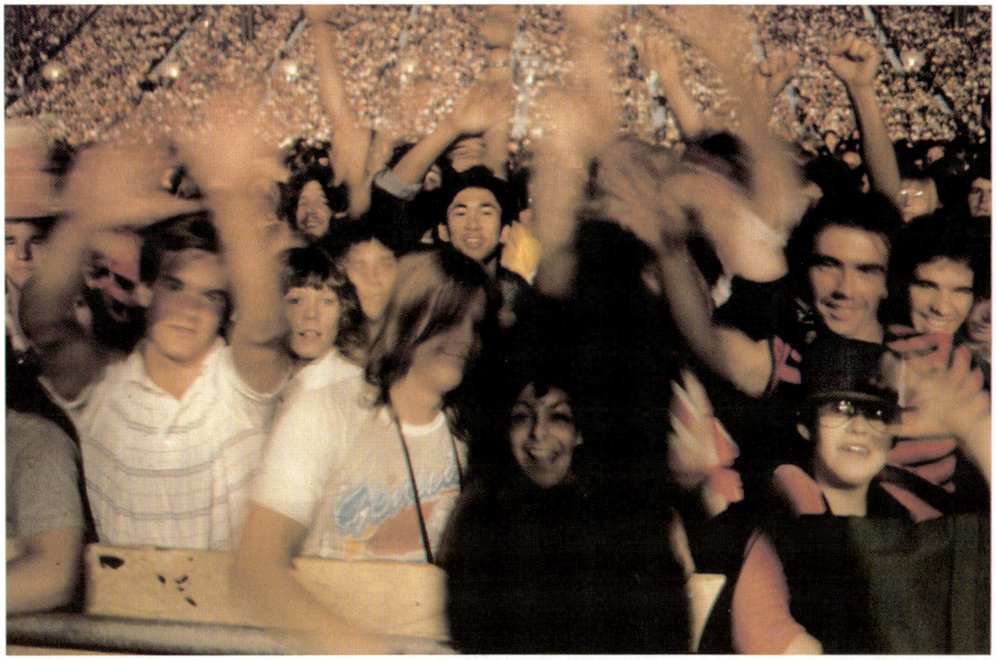

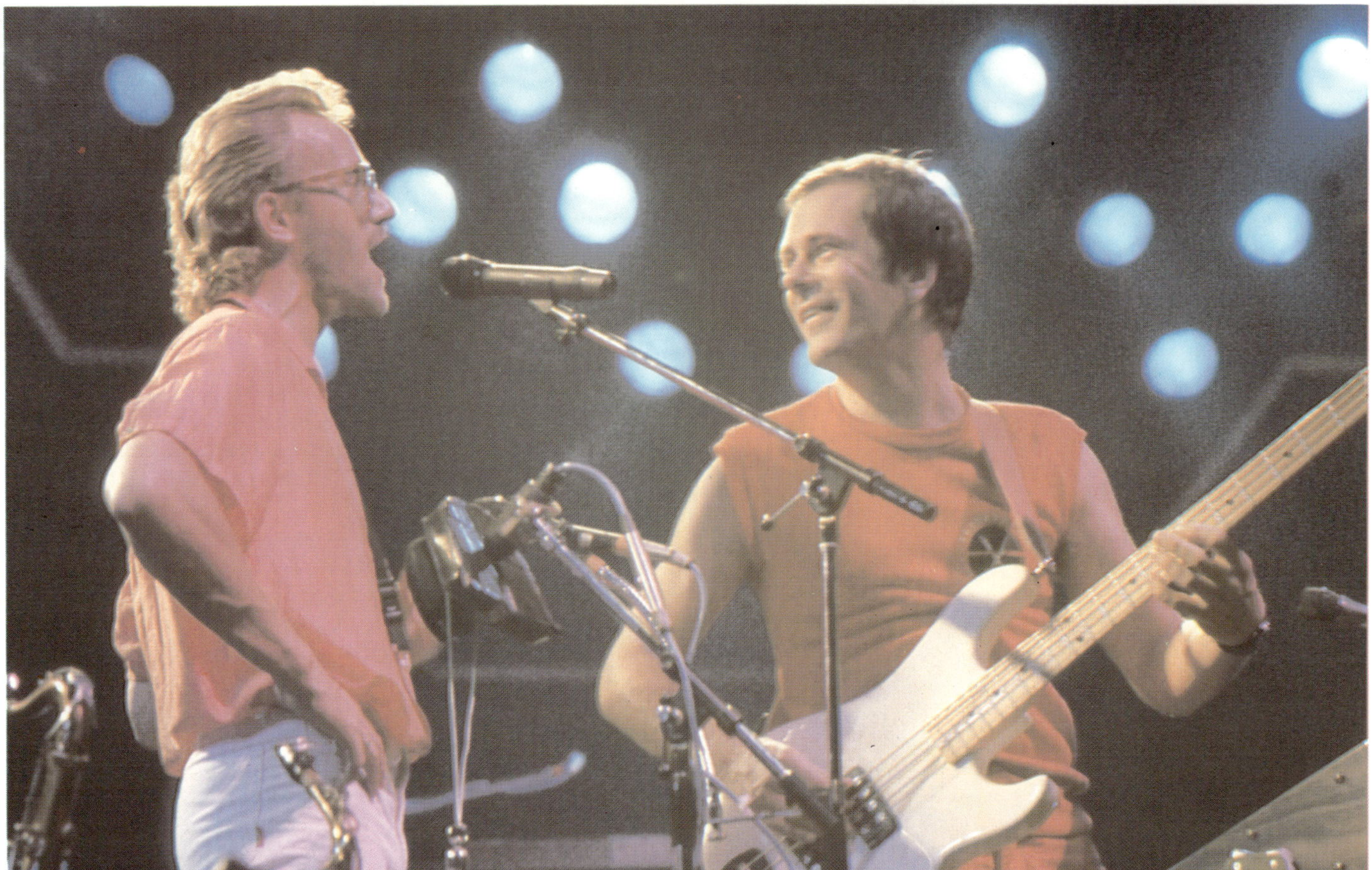

out Grandstand crowd of 25,000 (and, indirectly, to an unknown number of pay-TV subscribers for whom the concerts last night and tonight are being taped).

"It was one of Hodgson's first ever public utterances, but he has been advised to increase his profile before launching his solo career. The rest of the band members, who have tended in the past to toil anonymously in the shadow of group-stardom, have grumbled a bit but gone along. For Canadians, who are the band's longest-loyal fans, this is a particularly emotional part of the show. 'Sometimes change is a good thing, especially when it stimulates growth,' Hodgson said gently.

"Rick Davies, his 50/50 partner in singing and songwriting (though each sings his own songs), maintains his customary silence on stage. 'I space off into my playing,' he explained to me before the show.

"The rest of the band will carry on under his artistic leadership. There is speculation that the next album by Hodgson, who produced and arranged the band's albums as well as writing most of its hits, will sound more like Supertramp in future than Supertramp will.

"Davies tends either to underestimate or to downplay his own abilities. Yes, he has ambitious plans for the future of his band, but he is reluctant to provide details, and it takes several minutes to find out that there is - 'still in the production stage' - a piece called Brother Where You Bound? that may be the cornerstone of Supertramp Mark III. It's a long semi-humorous communist-paranoia thing he describes as 'an excuse to wail.'

"He has never cared much about being a star, nor much liked touring. And this tour is A Big Deal. The European stretch that preceded North America was as massive as anyone has attempted - 155 employees leap-frogging two custom stages from show to show.

"Providing some security is the continuing participation of Russell Pope, the 'sixth member' who provides the others with a dramatically crisp drum-centred sound. (Such an asset would be a liability for a lot of acts less prepared to be precise.)

"And this time out, the sextet has been expanded by two multi-instrumentalists: Toronto's Fred Mandel, who last came home officially on the Queen tour, and L.A.'s Scott Page, who has had experience on the road with Diana Ross and Seals & Croft, and wants to be the Jr. Walker of the 80s. Both add spirit to Supertramp's stately style, but remain dutiful servants of the Supertramp sound.

"The band's brilliantly lit tableaux continue to be worth watching, and occasionally coloured searchlights crisscrossed in the sky before bearing down to expose us all.

"In the midst of this visual opulence, Davies remained lower key than ever. It could be his mood. 'The decision that Roger and I weren't really contributing to each other was kind of out of my hands,' he told me with resignation. 'It's his life, he has to run it the way he sees it.'

"Fair enough. 'A group is like a very complicated marriage, and we've been married for 13 years, 10 with this particular combination of people.

"'But obviously after that amount of time you've got to get on each other's nerves.'

"My bet is that the change his ex-partner-to-be spoke of will stimulate growth in both of them."

As the tour came to a close in Los Angeles at the end of September (though there was some talk of added concerts in South America), it was clear that the future of Supertramp was squarely in the hands of Rick. As the group's writer, he was preparing to face the pressure of providing most of the creative input that would give the band a new life and structure. It had also been obvious throughout the tour that his wife Sue would be no small support in the next phase of his career. With the split from their management company that had occurred while the band was in Europe, Sue had virtually taken over most of the detail and organizational work that abound on a tour of this magnitude.

The crew tussles with the infernal video screen before a concert – Europe '83.

For Roger, the tour had given him a new outlook on his upcoming solo career and for the first time, he actually talked to the audience each night explaining the split between himself and the rest of the group. This was not particularly appreciated by the other members of Supertramp because on one hand they felt it was a bit of a downer and on the other hand it was an emotional moment that always brought a reaction from the crowd. "It's not something I lose sleep over," Rick admitted to Wilder Penfield III.

As the tour came to a close, Roger was already planning the concept for a new album project that he would start work on at his studio in Nevada City immediately following the tour. As well as forming a permanent band that would likely include Ken Allardyce on bass and Mike Shrieve on drums.

Roger worked on the recording of his solo LP at his studio in Nevada City through the latter months of 1983 and into 1984. In August, the LP, entitled *In the Eye Of the Storm*, was mixed at the Power Station in New York and released by A&M Records in late September. A gruelling promotional tour of North America and Europe followed in the wake of the first single from the LP, "Had A Dream", which, in turn, gave birth to a rather spectacular video that portrayed Roger, resplendent in loin cloth and war paint, agonizing over the ills of the world. Up on the screen was a reborn Roger Hodgson with a new energy and a fresh artistic commitment. It was, in short, a strong opening chapter to his career as a solo artist. In Canada, *In the Eye Of the Storm* became a platinum album within a month of its release.

Staying a part of Supertramp, Bob was set to return to his studio to complete his solo album possibly with some fresh input from Scott Gorham.

Dougie had always shown interest in getting more involved in the management side of the business and there was some indication he might join his brother Ken, Dave Margereson and Ken Macpherson in the Mismanagement organization that had previously handled Supertramp's career. Now Mismanagement was guiding the careers of Chris de Burgh, Make A Face, Marc Jordan, Ali Thomson and the Coup and had just established a music publishing company.

John, who was ready to put some time into his songwriting at his small studio in Topanga, has the last word here regarding the future for the group and its members.

"It's diversified now," comments John. "If people like Rick and Roger as songwriters, in a little while, they'll be able to buy an LP by Rick as a member of Supertramp and one by Roger. It'll spread out from there and there'll be more music. There's Bob's music and somewhere along the line there'll be some music from me."

But the "famous last word" goes to Rick, who during the course of the Canadian leg of the last tour, spoke to journalist Ritchie Yorke about what he felt the future held for Supertramp with Roger Hodgson embarking on a solo career.

"I have certain ideas in the works as a starting point," stated Rick. "We're trying to keep an open mind on the future. It is difficult to keep an open mind. But it will still be a band and we'll still be able to bounce ideas around and the other guys shouldn't be underestimated as far as their contributions to the creative end are concerned. It's important for me to have that sounding board. It makes it easier from an emotional standpoint to deal with everything; if you have down periods, you can share it with them. And you share the up periods.

"It would be unrealistic to just go off the road and into the studio the next day. So I think I'm gonna take about three weeks, put my feet up. Then I'm gonna get out there and start getting the guys around for a couple of days a week. So we'll slowly build up, and probably get a record together in 1984.

"I don't think that we're looking to be a massive immediate thing that we are now. I think we've done that. I think we're probably going to wet our feet a little in smaller markets the first time around. The band is going to be so different. I think it's going to be a little more intense in a way, which is probably going to lose a little bit of our mass appeal but I think everybody's aware of that.

"I'm very pleased with the two guys (Scott Page and Fred Mandel) that we have supplementing us now, but I don't want to lay any sort of heavy 'join-the-band' stuff on them and I don't think they'd particularly want that. But they do live in L.A. and my first choice would be them in helping to form the new stuff. I'm not adverse to looking at other writers and other creative input into Supertramp. I don't view Supertramp as a vehicle for my solo album - I *do* want to do that in the future, but I don't consider Supertramp to be my solo vehicle."

Rick also spoke about the split between himself and Roger. "On a personal level, Roger and I have never had too many problems. And once we've been separated in a creative sense, it'll be very easy to talk to Roger. It's even easier now. Obviously with the creativity thing, you

SUPERTRAMP

BROTHER WHERE YOU BOUND

Supertramp with VJ Christopher Ward on Canada's MuchMusic, May, 1985.

get into the whole soul of a person and that's why it becomes very difficult.

"It is a positive thing because you know it has become virtually impossible to actually create things. It sort of got to the point where he did his stuff and I did mine. Whereas in the old days, if he did something, I put a solo on top and obviously you became interested in that piece and the same for him-if he did the string arrangements on one of my pieces, he became much more involved.

"But the problem was he can't stand living in a big city and he moved out. I can't stand being in the country, so right there is a big problem ... he's 600 miles away from me. (laughs) It's as simple as that ... he likes red, I like blue. Whereas we lived off it in the past, it eventually caught up with us and now it's through."

Speaking to Roger shortly after the release of his solo album, he echoed some of Rick's sentiments about their split. "You know, it's funny. Now we're travelling our separate roads, I feel even closer to Rick in some ways. We often talk to each other on the phone and I have always felt that somewhere down the line, when we have both explored our own individual musical avenues, there's a possibility that the two of us might just get back together to work on a project."

In the spring of 1985, as Roger continued work on his second solo album in Nevada City between promotional jaunts to Europe, the Supertramp album, *Brother Where You Bound* was being completed in Los Angeles.

The 19-minute title track had been with Rick Davies for a number of years but it was just too heavy to fit into the musical plans of the previous incarnation of Supertramp that had leaned to the type of pop songs that marked the enormous success of the LP *Breakfast In America*. As the track was reminiscent of Pink Floyd's epic approach to music, the band looked for a guitarist who had a similar lyrical style as David Gilmour of Pink Floyd. They tried out a number of musicians without much luck and then one day, the record company suggested they approach Gilmour himself. They took the advice and Gilmour came in to play on the session.

The LP finally saw the light of day in May of 1985 and "Cannonball" was released as the first single from the album. It was a very apt word and title and could have been used to describe how the group's new project was launched. With the kind of promotional largesse not witnessed for many a year in the record biz, the band, manager Sue Davies and L.A. public

relations whiz Paul Bloch arranged to have about 50 reporters from around the world flown to Paris for a 22-hour trip aboard the legendary Orient Express to Venice where *Brother Where You Bound* and its accompanying 20-minute film were premiered at the very swank Excelsior Hotel.

One of the reporters along for the ride was Kevin Scanlon of the *Toronto Star*.

"If looks could kill, there would have been murder on this Orient Express," quipped Scanlon. "The staid, moneyed passengers who paid $600 a ticket for the trip of a lifetime from Paris to Venice watched in horror as the British rock band Supertramp and a scruffy entourage of hard-drinking reporters boarded the legendary train. If nothing else, the unusual and sometimes unsightly passengers dramatically lowered the tone of this classy railway act.

"The regulars were certainly appalled enough to scramble for their beds when the band and followers arrived noisily in the vintage, wood-panelled bar car, where a tuxedoed gray-haired man sat at a baby grand piano playing 'Feelings'.

"By 2 a.m., while the train rumbled through France in darkness, Davies was at the piano and John Helliwell played sax. A little blues, nothing serious, Davies said. Three hours later, the car was empty but for a yawning bartender and two thirsty Norwegian reporters who laughed and sang all the way to Venice.

"Next morning after breakfast, drummer Bob Siebenberg sat in his small cabin scouring the *International Herald Tribune* for news of his favourite team, the Los Angeles Dodgers, it was like watching television from across the street.

"The band members did interviews until lunch – la tourte depinards et de langoustines (leaf spinach and scampi in puff pastry) and le gigotin de lotte au fumet de cresson (steamed fish filets with watercress sauce) with a 1983 Pouilly-Fuisse – which was served during a long unscheduled stop at the Italian border. Customs agents spent almost an hour searching the train for drugs. Everyone agreed the high brows looked suspicious.

"Late in the afternoon with mist shrouding the rugged hills of northern Italy and rain dotting the windows, the band's new album was played for the press in the dining car. The champagne flowed and the Norwegians screamed for more beer.

"'I thought Cannonball was perfect for the train, that kinda travellin' music that really steps out,' drummer Siebenberg said of the group's new single. 'But there was a song called "No In-Between" which I find a bit bleak. You look outside and it's real gray and you're thunderin' along. Good atmosphere.'"

In Venice, the $500,000 film for *Brother Where You Bound*, directed by Rene Daalder, was given its first showing and shocked much of the gathered press corps with its graphic violence. Even Davies admitted at a press conference the following day that he found the violence "a hair too realistic." Heading back to the U.S. it would be interesting to see what American audiences thought of director Daalder's strong anti-war statement. On May 13, 1985, the band headed for Toronto where they premiered the *Brother Where You Bound* album and film live across Canada on the MuchMusic Video Network heading across the country on a media blitz.

In September of 1973, Roger wrote a letter to Sam in Geneva that in part read: "Isn't it incredible how time makes the past like a dream? Botolph's seems an eternity ago and the first album becomes more unbelievable every time I hear it. The History of Supertramp, Chapter Six (or is it Seven or Eight) - I hope someone gets around to writing it one day – is about to begin."

Sam answered in part: "Kicking bastards always make it sooner or later, especially when they know the product is good! Bless you both. Keep in touch."

Some emotions are timeless. ☐

ACKNOWLEDGEMENTS

In the completion of this book, there are many people to thank, not the least of which are Supertramp – Rick Davies, Roger Hodgson, John Helliwell, Bob Siebenberg and Dougie Thomson; along with Dave Margereson, Russel Pope, "Spy" Matthews, Ken Allardyce, Tony Shepherd, Ken Thomson and Ken McPhearson, who, at various times in the past have opened the door to the "inner sanctum."

To Charly Prevost, the catalyst for this book and an integral part of the Supertramp story himself, my heart-felt gratitude for your generosity and some memorable times over the last twelve years.

To Stanley August Miesegaes (aka Sam), thank you for your insights and personal memorabilia. From Los Angeles to New York to Geneva to Montreal to Toronto to New York to Geneva in five days. Federal Express has nothing on you.

A platinum acknowledgement to Jerry Moss and Herb Alpert and the worldwide A&M Records organization, not to mention Derek Green of A&M in Britain, for their contributions in making the Supertramp dream a reality. I would personally like to thank the A&M organization in Canada, present and past, including Gerry Lacoursiere, Joe Summers, J.P. Guilbert, James Monaco, Doug Chappell, Lorna Richards, Colin McDonald, Peter Beauchamp, Pat Ryan, Nick Carbone, Bob Roper and others who helped out along the way.

A tip of the hat to Pat Luce of A&M and Frank Barcelona and crew of Premier Talent for the breakfasts in America.

For hospitality above and beyond, hello to Linnea Graham-Prevost, Karuna Hodgson, Sue Davies, Vicki Siebenberg, Christine Helliwell, Lenice Bent, Cass Margereson, Vimala Rogers and Bucky Bratton.

Thank you to Jim Norris and Kathy Whitney of CM Books who got this project off the ground and to Janet Christie who handled the design of this-here tome.

Reed Hutchinson, Kandice Abbott, 'Sam' and Scott Page, a renaissance man if I ever saw one, deserve the F-Stop Fitzgerald Award for their pictures.

For their continued love and support, thanks to Edith and Philip Melhuish, Christine and Peter Broster, Doug Pringle and Heidi O'Carroll.

And in no particular order, this book was made easier by Sass Jordan, Dee Dee Petty, Ritchie Yorke, Wilder Penfield III, David Donald, Raphael Rudd, Cathy Hahn, David Farrell, Keith Sharp, Conny Kunz, The Bonaventure Hotel (Montreal), David Bendeth, The Sunset Marquis (Los Angeles), 7 Burton, Eda Kistler, Jim Doleman, Joan Adye, Moe and Jo-Anne at Toronto Business Machines, Huguette Legare, The Royal Bank, Richard Hahn and Chris Palladino at Gowling and Henderson, John Courish and Lesley Kennedy.